Rumpole and His Rivals

The Fairleigh Dickinson University Press

Series in Law, Culture, and the Humanities

Series Editor: Caroline Joan "Kay" S. Picart,
M.Phil. (Cantab), Ph.D., J.D.-M.A., Esquire

Appellate Assistant Public Defender, FL 10th Jud. Cir., former adjunct professor of law, FAMU, former professor of Philosophy, English & Humanities, FSU

The Fairleigh Dickinson University Press Series in Law, Culture, and the Humanities publishes scholarly works in which the field of Law intersects with, among others, Film, Criminology, Sociology, Communication, Critical/Cultural Studies, Literature, History, Philosophy, and the Humanities.

On the Web at http://www.fdu.edu/fdupress

Publications

Peter Robson, *Rumpole and His Rivals: Comic Legal Fiction* (2025)
Vincenzo Tomeo and Peter Robson (translator), *The Judge on the Screen: A Translation and Critical Edition* (2024)
Kevin S. Jobe, *Malevolent Legalities: Discriminatology and the Specters of Scalia* (2024)
Linda Myrsiades, *From Treason to Runaway Slaves: Legal Culture in New Republic Trials, 1783–1808* (2023)
Eamon P.H. Keane and Peter Robson, *The Ian Willock Collection on Law and Justice in the Twenty-First Century* (2023)
Peter Robson and Ferdinando Spina, *Vigilante Justice in Society and Popular Culture: A Global Perspective* (2022)
Joel Silverman, *The Legal Exhibitionist: Morris Ernst, Jewish Identity, and the Modern Celebrity Lawyer* (2022)
Matthew Sorrento and David Ryan, *David Fincher's* Zodiac*: Cinema of Investigation and (Mis)Interpretation* (2021)
T. Patrick Hill, *No Place for Ethics: Judicial Review, Legal Positivism, and the Supreme Court of the United States* (2021)
Caroline Joan "Kay" S. Picart, *Monsters, Law, Crime: Explorations in Gothic Criminology* (2020)
Elaine Wood, *Gender Justice and the Law: Theoretical Practices of Intersectional Identity* (2020)
Orit Kamir, *Betraying Dignity: The Toxic Seduction of Social Media, Shaming, and Radicalization* (2019)
Marouf A. Hasian, Jr., *Lawfare and the Ovaherero and Nama Pursuit of Restorative Justice, 1918–2018* (2019)
George Pate, *Enter the Undead Author: Intellectual Property, the Ideology of Authorship, and Performance Practices since the 1960s* (2019)

Rumpole and His Rivals

Comic Legal Fiction

Peter Robson

Fairleigh Dickinson

FAIRLEIGH DICKINSON UNIVERSITY PRESS

Vancouver • Madison • Teaneck • Wroxton

Published by Fairleigh Dickinson University Press
Copublished by Bloomsbury Publishing, Inc.
Bloomsbury Publishing Inc, 1385 Broadway, New York, NY 10018, USA
Bloomsbury Publishing Plc, 50 Bedford Square, London, WC1B 3DP, UK
Bloomsbury Publishing Ireland, 29 Earlsfort Terrace, Dublin 2, D02 AY28, Ireland
www.rowman.com

Fairleigh Dickinson University Press gratefully acknowledges the support received for scholarly publishing from the Friends of FDU Press.

British Library Cataloguing in Publication Information Available

Library of Congress Cataloging-in-Publication Data

Names: Robson, Peter, 1947- author.
Title: Rumpole and his rivals : comic legal fiction / Peter Robson.
Description: Vancouver ; Madison : Fairleigh Dickinson University Press, 2025. | Series: The Fairleigh Dickinson University press series in law, culture, and the humanities | Includes bibliographical references and index. | Summary: "Rumpole and His Rivals examines comic legal literature from 1924 to the present and its representation of law, lawyers, and the surprising role in which these books continue to inform the public of the nature and problems of legal issues" —Provided by publisher.
Identifiers: LCCN 2024046637 (print) | LCCN 2024046638 (ebook) | ISBN 9781683934141 (cloth) | ISBN 9781683934158 (epub)
Subjects: LCSH: Legal stories, English—History and criticism. | Humorous stories, English—History and criticism. | Law in literature. | Lawyers in popular culture. | LCGFT: Literary criticism.
Classification: LCC PR830.L43 R63 2025 (print) | LCC PR830.L43 (ebook) | DDC 823/.9093554—dc23/eng/20250101
LC record available at https://lccn.loc.gov/2024046637
LC ebook record available at https://lccn.loc.gov/2024046638

For safety related questions contact productsafety@bloomsbury.com.

Contents

Acknowledgements

I am, as ever, grateful to a whole range of people who have assisted in bringing this work to its final conclusion. As I explain in the introduction the light comedic novel first drew me in to legal study in the first place. Thanks to Slough Library for their book selection including AP Herbert and Henry Cecil along with TB Smith's *Short Commentary* on their shelves and to the Mitchell Library, Glasgow for their speed in producing back numbers of *Punch* magazine. In completing the text, I have received serious advice assistance from my colleagues and friends Professor Ian Lloyd and Dr Michael Randall. Constructive criticism has always been forthcoming from Eric Scott, Andrina Smith, Anthony Shimmin and Thérèse O'Donnell. Caroline Picart and Zach Nycum with Fairleigh Dickinson University Press have, as ever, provided excellent support in bringing this project to fruition.

Introduction

Comic Legal Literature in Context

APPROACHING COMIC LEGAL LITERATURE

There are good reasons for anyone to examine the area of light legal literature with serious intent. The portrayal of lawyers in any form of media can shine a light on the flaws as well as merits of the justice system. It may assist in our understanding of how the rule of law has been operating in society. My personal interest in this portrayal and its significance stemmed from my own earliest experiences with the work of Henry Cecil. I can recall deciding that the legal profession looked interesting from my viewing of the film *Brothers in Law*[1] when it was shown as I was starting adult life at Secondary School. From there I started to read the books by the judge and author Henry Cecil published in the early 1960s, which sparked my own decision to study law and qualify as a lawyer. Initially, I thought nothing more about this kind of literature until I started to consider the possibly dangerous impact of the work of John Grisham many years later. I had been struck by the way lawyers were portrayed in his book *The Client*[2] as parasites desperate to make money from the misfortunes of others. In this case, the victims were the sick and injured in hospital. So great was the reach of the Grisham books, with sales of over sixty million,[3] that I made the assumption that the image portrayed must carry some weight. My immediate concern was with the threat to the funding of legal aid for poor clients by politicians happy to take advantage of the damaged reputation of high earning "fat cat" lawyers shown in the media. This negative portrayal seemed light years away from the coterie of lawyers I knew in my professional legal and academic career. These lawyers were working extensively for the poor and dispossessed – squatters, homeless people, victims of domestic abuse and those reliant on social benefits. Their concern was to assist clients through legal aid or acting *pro bono*.

Along with similar portrayals in film and on television it seemed to me that the image of lawyers in Grisham's fiction was something which was worth investigating. Initially I did this simply to see whether my impression was correct. What I discovered was that in popular fiction there was a divide between the lone heroic lawyer fighting for justice and the rest of the legal profession which was indeed shown as venal and often corrupt. The underlying message, it seemed to me, was that the system worked because of the hero lawyer and that the rule of law was thereby safe. The system itself, and the interests it protected, was not under challenge. This was found in the books of not only John Grisham but in the works of Scott Turow and others like Michael Connolly, Richard North Patterson, and William Bernhardt.[4]

Whilst this was true in the American fictional portrayal of lawyers, it seemed that the same could not be said for the British fiction. The only work that looked at the legal profession with which I was familiar, was that of Henry Cecil from earlier decades. In an early assessment of the first novels of John Grisham I had dismissed the work of Henry Cecil as consisting of "slapstick routines and broad characters."[5] My research into the image of the justice system and its personnel then took in film and television where similar representations of the justice system were encountered.[6] This was a reflective status quo orientated cinema and television industry rather than a radical refractive one.[7]

Rereading Cecil's Roger Thursby trilogy it seemed to me that I had missed out on one of the important aspects of his work. What struck me reading afresh the Thursby trilogy was that within his tales of cads, bounders and the occasional villain were judgments and accounts of the law and its various failings. I determined to examine the complete body of work to see if this was just a feature of the books centred on the career of a young barrister or if it was a practice encountered elsewhere in Cecil's work. What I noticed was that whole chapters were devoted sometimes to this "editorialising." This was both informative and, with hindsight, unexpected. After all these other non-Thursby escapades were often comic romps with largely improbable plots and unlikely characters. Until Henry Cecil achieved success, however, with the film and theatrical version of the comedic *Brothers in Law*, some of the early books had centred around murder[8] but did not sell particularly well.[9] The majority, however, relied extensively on the final-page twist in the tale. They did, though, it seemed, provide a commentary on what was good and, occasionally, what was questionable in the English legal system across quite a wide range of issues. The comments were almost wholly those of the author. Only occasionally did I find the critiques in the mouth of an "Everyman" character like the ingénu barrister Roger Thursby.

Having examined the books in rather more detail, several clear and persistent themes were revealed. Judges and their foibles were recurring themes.

The fallibility of juries and the inaccuracy of witnesses were often the issues on which decisions turned. Some matters were noticeable by their absence. There were few women working outside the home. There were even fewer women working within the law in any capacity. The characters were, by and large, well-off professionals interspersed with a few eccentrics and a sprinkling of loveable, or at least non-vicious, "rogues."[10] This was the world which we came to recognise from the 1960s onward as "sitcom land." Nothing too terrible or traumatic occurred. Increasingly, within the pages of these books, Home Counties English society[11] was ordered and, but for a few issues worthy of comment, all was well with the world. Social comment was, though, also present. It is, of course, not unusual to find social comment and critique of institutions in visual comedy,[12] including unlikely places such as televised trials.[13]

HUMOUR AND THE LAW

Linking the visual and the written one can encounter many intersections of humour and the law. The most accessible is the joke. The "lawyer joke" has spread across the Atlantic from its spiritual home, the United States. There are several collections of such areas of humour focusing on jokes and cartoons.[14] They operate within the standard theories of humour. They can incorporate "superiority theory" as well as "release theory" and incongruity theory." Laura Little provides an excellent guide to the various different ways that such variants of jokes around the justice system have become a part of the cultural life of the United States. focusing on the cartoons in the *New Yorker* magazine.[15] Such humour is easily recognised in England too although there have traditionally been major differences in the way the legal profession and the judiciary are organised in the two jurisdictions. The coverage of humour in law which has proliferated in England in the past century has focused on stories rather than jokes as such. Levels of trust in lawyers in the United States and England are markedly different so that the jokes have less heft this side of the Atlantic.[16]

Humorous fiction about law itself, though, has fared rather poorly as an object of study. There is, nonetheless, an argument to be made that looking at humour may yield worthwhile insights. Rossi and Carbone have, for instance, noted that

> despite their inherent seriousness, the law and those who practice it, be it lawyers, judges, politicians, or bureaucrats, are amongst the most popular objects of comedy and humour.[17]

They point out that, although this may feel deeply counterintuitive, across cultures and historical eras, while the law is there to prevent and remedy injustice, it often ends up becoming the butt of comedy. They map out the many intersections of the law and laughter, from classical Greece to the present day. They look at well-known classical and modern works of literature and visual culture, from Aristophanes to Laurel and Hardy and from Nietzsche to Totò and Fernandel. They suggest that laughter and comedy bring law back to the complexity of the human soul and the unpredictability of life and law. This is, though, not an obvious location to find humour.

> Laws, judgments, wills, contracts, damages, the legitimate use of state force against those who do not respect its rules, fines, prison, or even capital punishment: none of this is funny.[18]

What they focus on in their text is the way that those confronted by the law are, in a variety of different ways, able to resist and subvert law's power. Much of their coverage examines how those in dire situations can use humour in this way.[19] They also cite a number of distinct instances from popular culture ranging from Laurel and Hardy[20] to the musical *Chicago*[21] where the rational world is challenged by the criminal.

One aspect, though, absent in their extensive overview of the field is to look at comedy from the viewpoint of those operating the mechanics of the system. That is what sets apart the authors I have selected to examine. They almost all utilise a form of mild satire. In her overview of the subject of humour, Little makes a distinction between satires and parodies.[22] She suggests that satire has "a sharper edge than parody."[23] It seems to me that how one categorises the humorous tales examined is an example of the reader seeing what the writer may never have had in mind. The relative fluidity of the categories of humour can be gauged from a quotation from the former Lord Chief Justice, Lord Hewart writing about AP Herbert's work.

> Recognising that aversion from the law and courts of law is naturally strong in the human mind, I do not doubt, however, that many thousands of distinctly respectable persons would chuckle, and chuckle again and again, over the neatness, the deftness, and the dexterity – the sense, the satire, and the scholarship – of these criticisms wrapped in the pleasant guise of parody. [24]

As the text below makes clear, is that all the writers examined seem to have been concerned with was education along with humour. Within the literature under examination in this monograph we find comedy from tales of legal practice encompassing parodies, spoofs, satires and mistakes. The writers opt to present a stylised account of how justice is meted out. Most take as their chief protagonist court pleaders – barristers – although we find solicitors and judges appearing too. They are not a million miles away from the lawyers we see in courtroom dramas and reality television. Within these narratives, then, there are versions of law and justice which the reader can identify with and recognise as authentic, whether accurate or not. It is this theme of instruction through humour which I wish to pursue.

The clearest example was the work of Henry Cecil. I would not wish to resort to some crude version of the biographical fallacy in which artistic creations are seen as merely versions of the life experiences of their writers.[25] Looking at his stories. it struck me that Cecil's worldview in his fiction might be, however, a plausibly authentic picture of the justice system. Was it based on, and did it reflect, his own experience as a practicing member of the Bar for some 25 years and a similar period as a judge in the County Court? His autobiography confirms this, as is noted below.[26] What seemed particularly striking was the style he adopted of addressing the audience directly unconnected to the development of the narrative or the characters in the works.

I sought to discover whether there were other British writers in the comic vein and whether any such writers provided any comparable direct commentaries on the justice system and its strengths and failings. It was the unlikeliness of the source which captured my attention. As I note below, there are plenty of non-fiction accounts of how the justice system operates. These provide what they advertise – a *true* account of law's life – to some extent, at least. The point about the comic material as a source is that the comments are unexpected and relatively insidious.

MODERN HUMOROUS LEGAL FICTION IN BRITAIN

I identified eight writers in total whose work was in the sub-genre of comic fiction rather than thrillers or legal procedurals – A. P. Herbert, Henry Cecil, John Mortimer, Hastings Draper, Julian Prescot, Tim Kevan, David Osborne and Peter Murphy.[27] Their work started in 1924 and has continued for the next century. They shared some characteristics. All but one were from the barrister branch of the English legal profession. Their work, though, varied considerably in style and extent. The writers also achieved different degrees of success. A. P. Herbert and John Mortimer have been the subjects of biographies and they and Henry Cecil have also written autobiographies. The details of the lives and careers of other writers are rather less well known. Only two of the writers, Tim Kevan and David Osborne are alive at time of writing. This has meant that attention has been, perforce, principally on the books themselves. Whilst I am not a particular adherent of Ivor Richards' focus solely on the text,[28] there is limited context available for the work of Draper,

Prescot and Murphy. In addition, apart from his somewhat uninformative and bland autobiography, we know little about the life of Cecil. As part of early research on his work I consulted the archive of the Cecil papers at McMaster University in Hamilton, Ontario. These provided little information about the works themselves. There was much correspondence from his agents in Britain and America as to how his sales were. There were also "thank you" letters from a range of individuals to whom Cecil sent complementary copies of his latest works. If Henry Cecil wrote extensively about his works, then he kept no record. Much of the archive consists of drafts of his various works. As is noted below this did not mean that Cecil did not expand on his views on the issues raised in his novels and short stories in both his non-fiction and other writings. These comments as noted below, were, however, somewhat sparse.[29]

In a sense, this absence of biographical material does not affect my principal interest. As indicated, I am looking at this corpus of work to determine what kind of legal and inter-related social issues are encountered in this unlikely locus. I am working within the area of cultural legal studies concerned with the role of the media in determining the public's perception of law and the justice system.

CULTURAL LEGAL STUDIES

Part of the focus of cultural legal studies centres on the way the public learns about the justice system. American Realist legal philosophers had suggested earlier that legal scholarship, to be more grounded in reality, would do well to shift from a focus on doctrinal developments and look to the composition and politics of the judiciary,[30] as well as the reality of jury decision making.[31] This approach has been complemented by a rich seam of recent scholarship stemming most eloquently from the initial observations of Anthony Chase,[32] Stewart Macaulay[33] and Lawrence Friedman.[34] In the context of popular culture, Chase, Macaulay and Friedman pointed legal scholars in this direction for a key to a more nuanced picture of the operation of the justice system. Friedman influentially suggested that legal culture transformed the norms of popular culture into legal form. He described legal culture as the ideas, attitudes, values and opinions about *law* held by people in a society. Popular culture referred to the norms and values held by ordinary people. Culture included books, films, television and plays. It was important to scrutinise how these cultural artefacts represented justice because of their ability to explain and shine a light on the justice system.[35] Social norms shifted over time and legal themes shifted with these changes, Friedman noted.[36] He cited, in the context of the United States, race and the shift from black invisibility to the periphery of the action and subsequently to a significant role as protagonists. The same applied to women's representation. This had not occurred, however, through any direct order of the government. Those involved in the media had merely reacted to what the audience wanted or were taken to want. The changes could be traced from the content and approach taken in the cultural material. As the old film channel *Talking Pictures* notes in its task of showing films, principally from earlier decades "The following programme may contain outdated cultural depictions that reflect societal attitudes at the time of production" or ". . . was made between . . . and . . . and contains some offensive and discriminatory language which reflects the prevailing attitudes of the time."[37]

THE EMERGENCE OF LAW AND POPULAR CULTURE SCHOLARSHIP

It is in the context of law and popular culture scholarship that I have looked at the changing themes and preoccupations of the comedic writers on the law in Britain. It is with film and, somewhat belatedly television, however, that most of the scholarship on popular culture has engaged rather than books. I did suggest at one point, somewhat tongue-in-cheek, when talking about the development of my own undergraduate course *Law, Film and Popular Culture*,[38] that one simple advantage that film possessed over the other areas of popular culture was the speed with which people can engage with the medium. In crude terms, students can gain at least a superficial acquaintance with a film after a mere two hours. Books cannot be processed in this time and television series such as *Rumpole*[39] and *Suits*[40] involve many hours of watching. There are, though, as has been noted elsewhere,[41] good reasons to engage with the most popular and accessible medium, television, as is noted below.

The attractions of modern fiction have proved to be of less allure to legal scholars. This despite the fact that writers like Robert Tressell,[42] John Steinbeck[43] and George Orwell[44] are often cited as being influential in the formation of the ideas of politicians, The areas where there has been serious and impressive scholarship have tended to be historical ones. Major figures of literature from Shakespeare,[45] Charles Dickens[46] and Thomas Hardy[47] to E.M. Forster [48] and Ibsen[49] have been the object of analysis. A glance through the principal journals concerned with law and literature reveals a fascinating range of topics. These have included extensive work on Shakespeare[50] and classical Greek authors,[51] What is noticeable is the absence of much interest in modern authors.[52] Whilst classical works may be mined for their humour[53] there appears to be none on modern comic writers.

DEVELOPMENTS IN SCHOLARSHIP ON LAW IN POPULAR CULTURE

At the start of academic interest in law and popular culture two simple alternative trends could be found. One method involved simply raiding film, television and fiction to find illustrations of legal concepts, principles and practice to enliven classical doctrinal law teaching.[54] Another approach looked to the role of "great" films or televison series in engendering an interest in law and justice. Since the principal storytelling stories from which the public drew their reality of what the law were television and film, this was where attention should be focused.[55] Film studies perspectives were also undertaken by those able to access this complex area.[56] As interest developed amongst scholars, theories were addressed in terms of what the actual nature and function of the study should be.[57] This then engendered an interest in the significance and impact of what these "law" films might be and empirical work emerged. This sought to address the elusive notion of the influence of this different strain of popular culture. Regrettably some outstanding pioneering work in this field went largely unnoticed due to language issues.[58] The theme, however, was taken up some thirty years later by scholars in relation to the influences on easily and cheaply accessible research subjects like students in relation to the media generally.[59]

A little later some scholars moved their attention from the initial emphasis on film and started to expand these questions into television.[60] This has included surveys of the field adopting principally a cultural studies approach and focusing on the variety of ways in which the justice system has been portrayed on the small screen.[61] This work has also included attempts to assess the influence of television on a range of actors.[62] More recently the academic interest has also included "alternative" approaches to justice such as vigilantism and the relationship between popular culture and "self-help" justice.[63] The expansion into theory and empirical studies and the broadening of focus away from film has enriched the field. There is, however, a new problem. The radical changes in the nature of how popular culture is consumed in the 21st century pose major problems for any attempts to assess the impact of popular culture on people's attitudes and actions. The future of such work might be called into question[64] without engaging in research in the style of that undertaken in the 1960s by Vincenzo Tomeo.[65]

This scholarship has focused, then, in the past, on the overall image of lawyers and the justice system. Whether or not the image of the lawyer has been tarnished by the cinema has been a preoccupation of the profession for over 80 years[66] and one of my own for some 30 years.[67] The assessments have varied from that of Michael Asimow's dark pessimism[68] and the jaundiced view of Nicky Rafter[69] to the more nuanced judgements of Greenfield, Osborn and myself.[70] There are other studies which look at specific aspects of justice systems through a cultural studies lens. The most comprehensive coverage comes in the series *Derecho y Cine* from Tirant Lo Blanch in Valencia.[71] There is also extensive material from Italian, French and German Scholars.[72] The core of the work reflected the interests of scholars and there was more specific work covering gender,[73] sexuality[74] and race.[75] When attention turned to television the focus was on how the justice system generally was shown.[76] More recently, as in law and film studies, the issues have included ethnicity, gender and diversity.[77]

There has been an interest in how the portrayals altered over the years reflecting changes in the politics of the day. This is found most graphically in the examination of television in the United States by Elayne Rapping[78] and Barbara Villez.[79] Rapping notes how the programmes on US television became less and less liberal in their outlook as the right came to dominate politically. Villez for her part suggests that there has been a shift in the focus of major American TV law shows. These started out focused on individuals, shifted to ensemble pieces and ended with female-centred series, In my own work I have suggested that these analyses are of limited accuracy in relation to the British TV.[80] Nonetheless, there have been shifts in the personnel of British TV lawyer shows which reflect such societal changes as women achieving success in the profession.[81] Despite this rich and burgeoning literature, however, coverage of legal fiction has been, as noted, limited. Comic fiction has been all but ignored.[82]

BRITISH LEGAL NON-FICTION

What has been done in the ensuing chapters is to isolate those themes which are encountered in the various works identified. The coverage seeks initially to systematise and provide a guide to the work some of which may be unfamiliar. The text finally goes beyond the descriptive in its examination of the material and looks at how it relates to the authors and their experience. As already indicated the extent of the extraneous material for the authors varies. There is also fairly limited additional perspective derived from the authors' background information available. Before looking at the comic fictional material, however, it is worth noting the contrast with the expanding body of nonfiction works from lawyers and those observing the legal scene. When we read nonfiction, non-doctrinal coverage of law and legal issues we are realistically expecting to be provided with more or less accurate information. Both the titles and the advertising matter for a range of books about law and lawyers promise the *truth* behind the once impenetrable façade of legal life. This is, after all, an area which, as many scholars have pointed out, a world with which few come into regular contact except through the media.[83] It has been possible for many years to read accounts from lawyers of their lives in the law from barristers and judges and to a much lesser extent, solicitors.[84] The material being discussed here then has been mainly produced by the advocates and practitioners themselves as well as accounts of their work by others.[85] These biographical and autobiographical works purport to show life from the lawyer's perspective.[86] There is an extensive body of such work from British authors[87] worthy of a separate historiographical study which is in hand. The books cited below give a flavour of what has been produced down the years.[88]

These books are not, to borrow the words of lawyer and crime writer Martin Edwards, "makey uppy."[89] In their various ways, and with different emphases over the years, they have provided a picture of legal practice and how those, principally involved in court practice, prepare, evaluate and carry out their respective roles. Things have shifted somewhat over the years and there is a more recently a much greater degree of frankness about the limitations of the system as already noted and seen in other publications.[90] How and why this has occurred is a fascinating topic in its own right and, as noted, worthy of further discussion. What is of interest here, however, at present, is to look at those other portrayals of the legal system which are rather more subtle as well as quite extensive. The focus here is on those works where exposition of the flaws and merits of the justice system are revealed within the world of fiction.[91] For reasons alluded to elsewhere,[92] there have been only a small cadre of writers making forays into the world of serious lawyer fiction in Britain,[93] although there are signs that this may be changing.[94] The contrast with America is stark.[95] Meantime there are over 50 works of comic fiction to explore. This is the world which this volume examines from A.P. Herbert to Peter Murphy.[96]

THE WORLD OF FICTION

No one seriously disputes that the serious fiction of the "committed novel" can have an impact. One text puts the matter succinctly

> The idea that novels can change history, fight slavery and oppression, bring about legal change and generally have a major role in political struggles is very old and deep-seated in the collective consciousness of the West.[97]

Authors and in particular, lawyer authors, have written fictional works featuring the legal profession and the justice system for many years with just such goals. The largely unappealing roster of lawyers from the pages of Dickens reflects his social criticism at its sharpest.[98] The opening montage of *Bleak House* would not cause lawyers, aware of the history of their profession, to swell with pride. Nor would the subsequent narrative. In the context of a family saga the portrayal of lawyers by John Galsworthy is also no paean to the legal profession in his work on the Forsyte family.[99] There is, though, as noted, a stream of work which looks at law and lawyers in a lighter vein. Examining this work involves accepting that in general social criticism can be found within comedy.[100] There is also limited but interesting discussion of this in relation to law on television with how its comic portrayal can become a strong vehicle for subtle social criticism.[101]

Anyone seeking some kind of "insider" view of the British legal system in operation has been well supplied over the past 100 years with a variety of material in all forms of media including film.[102] They have ranged on television, as well, from the deadly serious through dramedy to farce.[103] The written word is well represented from critical exposés of the system[104] to blatant self-promotion and spoofs.[105] It is on the works of comic or light legal fiction that this study focuses. There are, as noted, some eight authors with whose work this monograph engages – all, but one, of them are English barristers. Their work stretches from 1924 to the present day. These writers have used the comic elements of the justice system to provide entertainment and enlightenment as well as, it is suggested, instruction for their readers laced with some critical elements.

As indicated, part of the interest in looking at these cultural products is their ability to shine a light on the texture and undercurrents of legal culture and to supplement the "official" self-image of this culture available by examining Royal Commission Reports and texts focusing on the operation of the system and elements of law reform. As well as being located within cultural legal studies scholarship, it draws on the *zeitgeist* notion, expressed by cultural commentator Mark Lawson, as to the power of fiction to provide an insight into the national psyche at a particular time:

> Future historians considering why Sweden holds the improbable distinction of being the only western democracy to have both its prime minister and foreign minister assassinated in modern times – or why a racist gunman killed 77 people in Norway in 2011 – will find clues behind these events in crime novels written at least a decade earlier.[106]

In an age of serious social division and inequality it might be imagined that comic legal literature, like the workfree world created by PG Wodehouse might have disappeared from our bookshelves. Indeed, this was suggested by the American scholar on legal literature, Jon Breen. While bemoaning the absence of comic approaches to law in the United States,[107] also, more controversially, he suggested that the time for such approaches had passed with the demise of writer Henry Cecil in the mid-1970s.[108] Breen suggested that

> With all the changes in his country's society since his 1950s peak, it is possible not even a British Henry Cecil could flourish today.[109]

This is certainly not the case in terms of books as we shall see. Nor does it hold true for the comic lawyer on the British small screen.[110] Whether or not the future is bright for comic written work is a matter for speculation.[111] There is certainly scope for thriller/procedurals with a light comic touch if the experience of Scotland is anything to go by with the voluminous work of William McIntyre.[112]

BRITISH LEGAL HUMOUR

Jon Breen,[113] in his Introduction to a republishing of a book by Henry Cecil in 1991, notes a variety of factors that make the British legal scene a place more conducive to humour than the American equivalent. In terms of style, he suggests that "Cecil's distinctively British comedy" exists within a strong tradition of self-deprecating humour by members of learned professions and has its closest equivalent in PG Wodehouse.[114]

The comic "faux judgments" of the polymathic A.P. Herbert with his five volumes of "Misleading Cases" is a fine exemplar of modest and occasionally critical, self-mockery by a member of the legal profession. Herbert's work, though, is quite distinct from almost all the other authors examined here in its style and his relationship to legal practice. It appears in the form of a series of fictional "judgments" from the courts. Between 1924 and 1964, he published in book form no less than 131 of these "misleading cases" covering 806 pages.[115] They were, however, mainly written in a comic, spoofing and sometimes farcical vein. It is covered in the next chapter which also notes the contribution of another less productive, but highly influential practitioner of the "faux" judgment approach, the journalist J.B. Morton. Some of A.P. Herbert's pieces were dramatised on BBC TV as a series under the title of *A P Herbert's Misleading Cases* in 1967, 1968 and 1971. Many of the tapes have been wiped and only three were found by the author at the British Film Institute Library in the 1990s. YouTube has a number of episodes available but only the soundtrack.

The most prolific example of full-length novels and short stories on the less serious side of the lives of individual lawyers and encounters with the law is the writer Henry Cecil who has received limited coverage in the scholarship on law and literature.[116] Cecil is a largely overlooked British writer of legal comedy tales mainly from over half a century ago. His stories provide great potential for identifying persistent themes within legal popular culture. The work of Cecil is most eye catching for its extent and the fact it was produced for just short of 30 years. The sheer weight and breadth of his works explains the coverage in this monograph which might seem, at first blush, disproportionate. His 28 fictional works cover on average 190 pages and 5,715 pages in all. A serious vein though is also found here. In relation to his fictional work, Breen pointed out that "most of his novels address very serious social and legal questions and certainly all carry an educational impulse, though always with a light touch."[117] Initially it might seem that Cecil's Wodehousian register was a thing of its time. Perhaps this underestimates the power of the comedy genre to speak afresh to new generations. At the same time as Cecil was in his heyday, a young barrister, Roderic Jeffries, under the pseudonym of Hastings Draper, produced a more modest law-centred comic trilogy covering the life at the Bar of a recently qualified barrister between 1956 and 1961. A few years after Draper's trilogy, a Lancashire solicitor, John Budd took up his pen to produce a series of ten books centred on the practice of provincial solicitors. They were written between 1958 and 1967 under the pseudonym of Julian Prescot.

In the next decade, another barrister author who wrote comic tales with a serious undertow was John Mortimer. His comic legal fiction started out on television and developed from there. The comic legal stories published from 1978 to 1992 consisted of adaptations of the television scripts for the seven seasons of the television series *Rumpole*. Mortimer described the Rumpole episodes as "television plays."[118] Thereafter, he wrote a further three books and 26 short stories about his barrister creation.[119] All featured more tales of Horace Rumpole and one was the writing up of the Penge Bungalow Murders which the old defender referred to in a number of his adventures. All were published by the Penguin publishing house and continue to be available in bookshops. The almost thirty years of John Mortimer's Horace Rumpole fill over 3,000 pages. In addition to John Mortimer's stories, we have further exemplars of the comedic legal style in book form in the 21st century.

More recent exponents of the art of the smiling legal lawyer with something to say about society are barristers Tim Kevan[120] and David Osborne.[121] They explore the world of the ingénu barrister and the struggles of those in the early stages of their professional careers in the 21st century. Finally, the work of Peter Murphy takes a wry look at the judicial process from the rare viewpoint of the judge.[122] Tim Kevan's *BabyBarista* novels, just like Cecil, are signalled with legal puns. In addition, there are two works from by barrister David Osborne following the career of newly qualified fictional barrister Toby Potts.[123] The most recent works in this vein by barrister and retired judge, the late Peter Murphy, take a slightly different tack and follow the travails of *Charlie Walden*, Resident Judge of the fictional Bermondsey Crown Court.[124] Tim Kevan's two *BabyBarista* works weighs in with 570 pages. We have 566 pages from David Osborne's two *Toby Potts* novels and most recently Peter Murphy's four *Judge Walden* adventures encompassing 1,591 pages. It is little surprise that when we look at the observations and comments on the justice system that the writings of Cecil and to a lesser extent, Mortimer dominate, given their significantly greater output as well as didactic focus.

THE LIGHT LEGAL AUTHORS IN CONTEXT

In general terms it is possible to discern in all these comic writers' work a desire to explain and occasionally criticise the operation of the justice system. Although it could be said that they support the legal institutions in general to varying degrees, it is made clear that not everything is perfect as the subsequent chapters show in some detail. Although they are categorised in catalogues and search engines as legal humourists, it is clear that the writers are significantly involved in producing a critique of aspects of the justice system as well as entertaining the public. The perspective might seem at first blush rather less than radical, but, nonetheless, when one examines the full range of these fictional works there is enough material to suggest that the soubriquet of entertaining legal commentators is more appropriate than mere court jesters. Whatever judgment one finally makes, it is clear from the modern availability of the books,[125] the radio adaptations[126] and TV versions of the work[127] that they are very much "part of the cultural landscape . . . (and their) work goes on and on."[128] There are two principal modes employed for an analysis of this fiction. One notes the dominant themes within the stories. The other is the frequency of the author stepping out of the role of storyteller to "editorialise" – sometimes to state the "law" and at other times to comment on how things should be. The author breaks the fourth wall and addresses the audience. They are a constant and fascinating ongoing feature of all Henry Cecil's works. They are supplemented very occasionally by an "everyman" character like his ingénu barrister, Roger Thursby. Hastings Draper and Julian Prescot do the same thing on several occasions when a perspective emerges. Mortimer adopts a slightly different approach derived from the soliloquising of *Rumpole* on TV appearing as his thoughts expressed on the page in the fictional versions. They are "translated" from Leo McKern's voiceover to a statement of what he *would* have said but in fact did not as well as the occasional "editorials." We find the same kind of pattern in the more recent work of Tim Kevan, David Osborne and Peter Murphy. As for

A.P. Herbert there is little ambivalence as to his twin driving forces. Amuse and educate were his watchwords. As noted below, the emphasis in the vast majority of his "judgments" being the former.[129]

The themes which emerge from the texts of these writers form the basis of the following chapters. Rather than operate at a very general level it is, in my view, most useful to look in depth at a range of specific areas. The themes have been derived from the issues which occur most frequently throughout the works. Given the extent and coverage of his work, it is not surprising that Henry Cecil has most to say on most of the material. The chapters aim to place these comments in context and in due course relate them to some of the relevant prevailing issues of the day. Many of the negative comments, however, are depressingly timeless. All the writers address in their different ways persistent questions from the public about the deep suspicion that lawyers are happy to take money defending those they "know to be guilty." Henry Cecil and John Mortimer are found expressing horror at prison conditions between the 1950s and 1990s. Some issues are new and are specific to the 21st century and are encountered in the later writers but not before them such as the rationalisation of the court estate and the impact of digital technology. The attitudes and coverage of matters like gender, class and diversity have seen a major shift in the last century and this is reflected in the material analysed. Their work deserves, I would suggest, a closer scrutiny.

APPENDIX 1

Legal Non-Fiction

The authors of legal non-fiction include legal figures whose names are well-known as well as more obscure figures. Some two hundred years ago the tone of these accounts of the lawyers and their lives was notable for its frankness. For instance, the assessments of Henry Cockburn on the 18th-century Scottish judge, Lord Braxfield,[130] included such comments as "It is impossible to condemn Braxfield's conduct as a criminal judge too gravely, or too severely. It was a disgrace to the age."[131] It has been suggested that the remarks were coloured by Cockburn's strong Whig views.[132] Nonetheless, Braxfield is remembered even in the Scottish National Portrait gallery for his remark on the pliability of law in the service of the powerful "Let them bring me prisoners, and I will find them law."[133]

Lesser figures in the judicial hierarchy, in the past, also provided their comments on their contemporaries and their view of the legal issues of the age. John Alderson Foote, writing anonymously while still sitting as a judge,[134] described various personalities in terms of their style of advocacy when he was a young barrister in the 1880s and 1890s. In his account of the cases dealt with by the lawyers and judges visiting provincial towns on assize to administer justice he notes the diminution of much of the work due to the impact of fast efficient rail links.[135] He rates his past colleagues in civil tones and observes the decline of the fancy eloquence of the past with the decline in jury trials. He also notes such things as the relative popularity amongst the Bar of Madeira, Sherry and Port as opposed to Claret in the late Victorian era. It is a thoroughly pleasant set of reminiscences much like PG Wodehouse's "oldest member" – the clubhouse "bore" wont to recount tales of golfers and their problems with the game and their lives to anyone who was unwise enough to come within earshot.[136]

While Foote presented a picture of the West Country, another judge of the same rank described his own life and the professional travails of those on the Northern Circuit covering Carlisle, Lancaster, Appleby, Liverpool and Manchester.[137] Published in the year before his death, Arthur Ashton also provides a flavour of late Victorian and Edwardian legal practice and is reasonably polite about those colleagues whose work he discusses along with details of his travels round the world.[138] Post-career autobiographies, in the latter part of the 20th century, have been somewhat anodyne and relatively uncontroversial.[139] Biographies have tended towards the laudatory.[140]

Accounts of the lives of those still in practice have been rather more revealing. One from 1992, *No Holds Barred*, examined a jury trial, as seen through the eyes of the defence advocate taking the reader through the criminal process, from the moment the advocate first meets the accused, to acquittal or conviction and sentence. It claimed to strip away the mystique surrounding the law, lifting the veil on all the pomp and ceremony, and exposing a lot of the humbug that allegedly bedevilled a profession believed by many to be stuck in the nineteenth century.[141] These in-house accounts continue to be produced with great regularity[142] and are somewhat revealing of the stresses of life[143] and the changing background of lawyers.[144] They have also extended to those normally hidden from view in the legal scene like barristers' clerks.[145] Some works have focused on specific cases and one such contemporary author, former High Court judge, Sir Richard Henriques indicated his aim was "to give an insight into the inner workings of our criminal justice process at a time of fully justified public scrutiny"[146]

There is, indeed, a trend in the most recent works to take a highly critical and astringent view excoriating the justice system. These claim to expose us to some harsh truths and the suggestion that all is not well within the system. "Insider" critiques are not entirely new in themselves.[147] The 21st-century ones are, however, more insistent and plentiful than for some time. Sarah Langford entitles her 2018 account of the life of a defence barrister, *In Your Defence*.[148] Its content is clear from the subtitle is clear – *True Stories of Life and Law*. This is how it is in the courts. The author "describes eleven cases which reveal what goes on in our criminal and family courts: these are tales of domestic fall out, everyday burglary, sexual indiscretion, and children caught up in the law."[149] This is reality not imagined or confected tales to amuse. These are exposés of the hidden workings (and failings) of the justice system.

By the same token, a memoir with the legal-leaning title *Under the Wig*, published in May 2019, for example, is advertised as "a gripping memoir from one of our country's greatest jury advocates, offering a fascinating, no-holds-barred tour behind the scenes of some of the most famous criminal cases of modern times."[150] The publishers recognise the authenticity of the work and invite us to "Switch off the TV dramas and see real criminal law in action." The author, a practising barrister "lays bare the secrets of his profession, from the rivalry among barristers to the nervous moments before a verdict comes back, and how our right to a fair trial is now at risk."[151] This is "real law" just like "real crime" and its genre is "Biography and True Stories."

A further glimpse from 2019 into what really happens in the adjudication phase of the justice system is found in the work *The Secret Barrister*, which also promises "Stories of the Law and How It's Broken."[152] The author is on a mission of truth. "I'm a barrister. I work in the criminal justice system, and every day I see how fairness is not guaranteed. Too often the system fails those it is meant to protect. The innocent are wronged and the guilty allowed to walk free."[153] The follow up in 2021 is even clearer in its concern to expose the reality of the justice with its uncompromising title *Fake Law* and its location in the distorted post-truth world we have inherited from *inter alia*, Donald Trump and Boris Johnson. It is sub-titled *The Truth About Justice in an Age of Lies*.[154] The law is not a guarantee of liberty and justice for all. "This 'fake law' allows the powerful and the ignorant to corrupt justice without our knowledge."[155] Finally, the anonymous barrister trawls through his life providing "a helpful primer and a cringe-inducing account of one barrister's travails."[156] There are also works which principally discuss the shortcomings of the substantive law derived from the experiences of the authors.[157] It is also worth noting that there has been some coverage of atypical "outsider" experiences.[158] The subtitle of David Fendem's *Dirty Briefs* from 2022 leaves us in little doubt as to what kind of exposé we are likely to encounter – *the hilarious struggles and shocking tales of a bare-knuckle criminal barrister.*[159]

APPENDIX 2

British TV Comedy Legal Material

In the medium of television, in addition to the appearance of Horace Rumpole between 1975 and 1992, we have had five British TV series which take a more light-hearted look at lawyers and legal practice. In the 1990s there were 13 seasons in all of *May to December*,[160] *Law and Disorder*, [161] *Is It Legal?*[162] and *Chambers*.[163] These capitalised on the ability of actors with a track record on television being able to lead situation comedies where the legal setting was a vital but not necessary element of the production. In simple terms, these could have been set in almost any office setting from an accountant or architect to an unspecified industrial manufacturer. Their humour derives principally from culture clashes, age differences and class distinctions. The vulnerability of the law and legal system to mockery, though, adds further spice. *May to December*, for example, centred on the life of a widowed solicitor and his romance with a much younger client. It ran for 6 seasons – 39 episodes plus a Christmas Special – from 2 April 1989 to 27 May 1994 and is available on DVD and many parts of seasons 1, 2, 3, 4 and 5 are on YouTube. The episode titles are taken from popular songs such as *The Crying Game*, *Send in the Clowns* and *Let the Heartaches Begin* and reflect the practice of playful titles which we see in the earlier fiction of Henry Cecil discussed below. It shows legal practice as an untroubled pleasant pastime without the trauma and soul-searching of most other British TV legal dramas like *The Main Chance*,[164] *Kavanagh Q.C.*,[165] *New Street Law*[166] and *Silk*.[167]

Law and Disorder from 1994 dealt with the light-hearted cases[168] of a female English barrister played in her noted Margot Leadbetter/Audrey Fforbes-Hamilton[169] entitled middle class style by *Good Life* and *To the Manor Born* star Penelope Keith. It ran for one season of 6 episodes from 17 January to 21 February 1994. Again, the episodes have "jokey" titles in the Cecil style such as "A Night To Remember," "What Goes Up," "Safe as Houses" and is available on DVD.

Is It Legal? (ITV and Channel 4) (1995 to 1998) was set in the suburban offices of a firm of solicitors with comedy staff members. The minutiae of the personal lives of the dysfunctional staff of the office was the theme and legal matters were adverted to obliquely in between the failed romances and schemes of the three lawyers and three members of staff. It ran for three seasons from 1995 to 1998. Only one of the firm members appeared to be competent, albeit distracted. The comedy derived mainly from the characters' social ineptitude rather than the law and could have been set in any office setting in sitcom land. There is, in fact, only one scene where we reach a courtroom. The legal setting gave it a certain piquancy.

Into the 21st century, superficially rather more crucially located in the legal world was *Chambers*. It was set principally in barristers' Chambers (offices) with two lead character barristers, John Fuller-Carp and Ruth Quirke who were engaged in seeking to do each other down in a very broad and farcical manner. They were both self-regarding and venal and the punning Spoonerish name of the Fuller Carp gives an indication of his approach. Described in the British Comedy Guide as "incompetent, bigoted, greedy and pompous,"[170] Fuller-Carp is the nearest we have, perhaps, to a sober version of Cecil's incompetent solicitor Tewkesbury.[171] Both principal protagonists in *Chambers* were using the law for personal advancement with varying degrees of success. They were narcissistic but loveable anti-hero/heroines whose character flaws were in sharp contrast to the unworldly but kindly figure of the third barrister, Hilary Tripping. It ran on TV between 2000 and 2001 for three series.[172] It was written by barrister and writer, Clive Coleman, who was the BBC's Legal Correspondent from 2010 to 2020.

On a slightly different tack with a mix of gallows humour and realism in 2004 the series *Outlaws*[173] was shown for one season. This was a comedy drama centred around a legal aid solicitor's firm in Manchester where the principal protagonist relied on legal aid cases and superficially sought to exploit the system while, also, revealing its structural inadequacies. Although first rate, it was not recommissioned and its star, Phil Daniels took a role in the long-running successful BBC TV soap *East Ender*s. More recently, in 2019, the TV series, *Defending the Guilty* featured the trials and tribulations of a young pupil barrister, Will Packham, seeking to establish himself in a set of barristers' Chambers in competition with three other aspirants.[174] This was an adaptation of a book of the same name by barrister Alex McBride of his account of the lives of young aspirant barristers. The farcical reasonably upbeat "Thursby" tone is totally different, however, from the bleakness of the book.

There are also series, noted above, which avoid humour and strive to provide straightforward accounts of the operation of the court process. *Kavanagh Q.C.* (1995–2001), *New Street Law* (2000–2005); *Judge John Deed* (2001–2007), *Silk* (2011–2014) and *Law and Order: UK* (2009–2014) show the continued British appetite for home grown serious legal series.[175] To this can be added radio versions of *Chambers* as well as *Rumpole* in which John Mortimer's wish to "reinvent" Rumpole as a younger man[176] has been partially realised in the 2010 and 2012 mini-series.[177] As far as lighter approaches are concerned, then, Breen's prediction has proved less than accurate in both the medium of TV as well as books.

NOTES

1. Brothers in Law (1957) https://www.imdb.com/title/tt0050214/ (accessed 22 January 2024).
2. Grisham (1993).
3. Robson (1996) at 205.
4. Robson (1996) for a more extensive roster of lawyer authors – at 202–205.

5. Robson op cit at 203 – although I did not specify which of Cecil's books I had in mind – I suspect I was thinking of Colonel Brain and Mr Tewkesbury.

6. Greenfield, Osborn and Robson (2001) and (2010); Robson and Schulz (2016).

7. Black (1999).

8. No Bail for the Judge (1952); According to the Evidence (1954); Settled Out of Court (1959).

9. Cecil (1975) at 139 where Cecil records that in three weeks *Brothers in Law* outstripped the total sales of his six previous books.

10. See Chapter 2 Appendix.

11. The books were all set in London and its environs known as the "Home Counties" – Crouch (1975).

12. Bryant (1989); Galanter (1998) and (2005).

13. Machura and Livinova (2022) at 101.

14. Galanter (1998) and (2005); Little (2019).

15. Little op cit.

16. Levels of trust in lawyers in the United States have been recorded at 35% – Rasmussen (2022) compared with 87% for British lawyers – (Legal Services Consumer Panel Survey 2024).

17. Rossi and Carbone (2023) publicity material – see https://www.degruyter.com/document/doi/10.1515/9783111286778/html.

18. Rossi and Carbone op cit at 1.

19. Rossi and Carbone op cit at 100 ff.

20. Rossi and Carbone op cit at 47.

21. Rossi and Carbone op cit at 109 ff.

22. Little (2019) p. 7.

23. Ibid.

24. Introduction to the 6th edition of writer and barrister AP Herbert's comic collection, *Misleading Cases* (1935) quoted in Pound (1976) p. 127.

25. Thomas (2023).

26. Cecil (1975) and Chapter 2.

27. There is also a 9th other author – also a barrister – who wrote comically whom I mention in passing but whose work for reasons I explain below falls outwith the ambit of my inquiries. The barrister, Theobald Mathew wrote sketches in which he lampooned figures of the day in the inter-War years. The figures lampooned were anonymous and, at this distance it is not possible to identify the relevant persons. Nor did any of the tales contain any of the didactic elements which might have made them worthy of attention. I append an example in Appendix 1 to Chapter 1 to give a flavour of the Fables.

28. Richards (1924) and (1929).

29. See Chapter 2 below.

30. Llewellyn (1931); (1960).

31. Frank (1930); (1949).

32. Chase (1986).

33. Macaulay (1987).

34. Friedman (1989).
35. Friedman (1989) at 1579.
36. Ibid.
37. See https://talkingpicturestv.co.uk/.
38. The title included "film" to attract students into an area where for once they were on a rather more even playing field with the academic staff than in most classes.
39. https://www.imdb.com/title/tt0078680/
40. https://www.imdb.com/title/tt1632701/
41. Robson and Silbey (2012) Introduction.
42. Taylor (2020).
43. Johnson (2015) at 143.
44. Ibid.
45. Ward (1999); Quabeck (2013); Carpi and Ost (2018).
46. Gest (1905); Vaughan (1955); Quabeck (2021).
47. Davis (2002); Williams (2013).
48. Williams (2006).
49. Simonsen (2013).
50. Majeske (2009); Barker (2013).
51. Tiefenbrun (1999); Almog (2022).
52. *Pace* Papke (2001).
53. Bannon (2019).
54. Gunn (1994); Chase (2002); Elkins (2004).
55. Symposium: San Francisco (1996) per Sherwin at 892–4.
56. Moran, Sandon, Loizidou and Christie (2004); Sarat, Douglas and Umphrey (2005).
57. Osborn (2001); Elkins (2004); Kamir (2005); Silbey (2007); Machura (2016).
58. Tomeo (1973) – an English translation is now available per the author – Tomeo (2025).
59. Asimow et al (2005).
60. Freeman (2005) illustrated the limited scholarship hitherto on television compared with film.
61. Jarvis and Paul (eds) (1998); Asimow (ed) (2009); Robson and Silbey (eds) (2012).
62. Podlas (2009), (2012) and (2016).
63. Robson and Spina (2022).
64. Robson (2023).
65. Tomeo (1973) and (2024).
66. American Bar Association (1939).
67. Robson (1994); Robson and Spina (2022) Introduction.
68. Asimow (2000).
69. Rafter (2001).
70. Greenfield, Osborn and Robson (2001); Greenfield, Osborn and Robson (2010).
71. htttps://editorial.tirant.com (accessed 10 December 2023).
72. Greenfield, Osborn and Robson (2024).

73. Lucia (2005); Kamir (2000a), (2000b) and (2005a).

74. Moran (1998).

75. Greenfield, Osborn and Robson (2010) Chapter 5.

76. Robson and Silbey (eds) (2012); Robson and Schulz (eds) (2016).

77. Robson and Schulz (eds) (2018).

78. Rapping (2003).

79. Villez (2005) and (2010) [English translation].

80. Robson (2007a).

81. Robson (2015).

82. Robson (2014); Little (2019).

83. Stark (1987) p. 231; Macaulay (1987).

84. Smith (1996), 1997, 1998 & 2003); Terrell (2012).

85. Grant (2016); Robins (2018).

86. Analysis and accounts for the academic and professional market are excluded on the basis that they aimed at a very different scholarly and professional market – see for example Jackson (1940) et seq; Pannick (1987). There are some which attempt to appeal to the elusive "general" as well as academic/professional market – Pannick (1992). Also excluded are collections of miscellaneous extracts on law from larger fictional works – Gest (1913); Megarry (1955); Lothian (1991).

87. American authors also figure extensively although there has been rather more focus on seeking to replicate the success of John Grisham with fictional courtroom dramas and legal thrillers – Robson (1996) *pace* Murphy (2012a; 2012b; 2013; 2014a; 2014b; 2016; 2018a; 2018b; 2022) with his American and Ben Schroeder series.

88. See Appendix 1.

89. The response of Martin Edwards to intense questioning about the motivations of his lawyer hero, Harry Devlin at a Reader meets Author session at the Harrogate Crime Festival in 2010 was to remind readers that the stories and characters were fictional. Devlin appears in 8 novels between 1991 and 2008. Edwards has since focused on detective novels set in the Lake District.

90. Afzal (2020), Hanratty (2016 and 2020), Mansfield (2009 and 2023), Robertson (2018) and Wilson (2020).

91. McBride (2009) at first glance, defies this bifurcation between fiction and non-fiction due to its transmogrification into a TV comedy/drama series in 2018. It is described as a sitcom by Wikipedia which seems a trifle dismissive of its serious underlying themes. Its commissioned 2nd series fell victim to the Coronavirus epidemic which started in 2020. For this reason and from its style I have not included it in my overview but have included it in an analysis of British lawyer non-fiction books alluded to above.

92. Robson (2014); Robson (2018).

93. Caudwell (1984); (1984); (1986) and (2000) and Underwood (1954, 1981 and see Bibliography) have written legal thrillers/whodunnits with courtroom elements. See also the novelisations of the TV barrister series, *Kavanagh QC* (McGregor, [1995, 1996], Holden [1998] and Lowe [1997]) and also the work of Caro Fraser (Fraser 1994, 1995, 1998, 1999, 2002, 2004, 2007, 2013 and 2020) and Peter Murphy (2012a; 2012b; 2013; 2014a; 2014b; 2016; 2018a; 2018b; 2022) with his American

and Ben Schroeder series. There is also coverage of the distinctive Scottish legal system in the Best Defence thriller novels of solicitor William McIntyre – his hero Robbie Munro has appeared in 14 novels between 2012 and 2024 (2012a, 2012b, 2013a, 2013b, 2014, 2015, 2016, 2017, 2018, 2019, 2020, 2022, 2023, and 2024.

94. Milner (2021); Wilson (2023).

95. Robson (1996) plus a casual glance at the Internet seeking US Legal Thrillers produces a myriad of books – Grisham has written over 30 alone.

96. I have excluded from this coverage the works of Somerville and Ross (1899,1908 and 1915) on the grounds that, whilst technically some might classify Ireland as part of Britain in the late 19th century, its legal system has always been quite distinct. For a non-fiction account of this world see Healy (1939).

97. Belfiore and Bennett (2008) p. 155.

98. Gest (1905).

99. Galsworthy (1906) (1920) and (1921).

100. Greenfield, Osborn and Robson (2007); Ödmark (2020).

101. Machura and Litvinova (2021).

102. Greenfield, Osborn and Robson (2007).

103. See Appendix 2.

104. See Appendix 1.

105. Lincoln (1957).

106. Lawson (2012).

107. Cecil (Introduction to the 1991 US edition of *Daughters in Law* at the third page [pages of Introduction not numbered]).

108. Ibid.

109. Cecil (1991) Introduction at fifth unnumbered page, para 3.

110. See Appendix 2.

111. Robson (2023).

112. Robson (2024) citing the critical elements in the *Best Defence* series of McIntyre (2013–2024).

113. Breen (1984); Breen (1999).

114. Introduction to the 1991 US edition of *Daughters in Law* at the third page (pages of Introduction not numbered).

115. For a Guide to all 131 of these "cases" see Chapter 1 Appendix 2 – some can only be read in their original place of publication.

116. Robson (2014).

117. Cecil at 4th unnumbered page of Introduction to Daughters in Law (1991).

118. Mortimer (1994a).

119. The original commissioned "play" in which Rumpole appears has been published as *Rumpole and the Confession of Guilt* in Rumpole for the Defence (1981) [aka R v Rumpole]. It is also in volume 2 of the Rumpole Omnibus). Although the character is there, the mood is far from jolly.

120. Kevan (2009, 2010 and 2011).

121. Potts (2013); Osborne (2014).

122. Previously only Henry Cecil has sought to do this in his adapted plays and the six episodes of his 1960 television series Mr Justice Duncannon – there are no

surviving tapes but I have used the "shooting scripts" from the Frank Muir archive at Sussex University in my research to supplement my memory of watching Andrew Cruickshank's portrayal – Robson (2018). There is also some coverage in the third book in the Roger Thursby trilogy, *Sober as a Judg*e (1958) See also Mortimer's play *The Judge* (1967).

123. Potts (2013); Osborne (2014).

124. Murphy (2017); (2018); (2019) and (2024).

125. All the books mentioned are available in bookshops or online.

126. BBC Radio 4 Extra – most recent airing of *Brothers in Law* was in 2024.

127. Rumpole is available on *Talking Pictures* in 2024.

128. Per screenwriter of, *inter alia*, The Likely Lads, Porridge and Auf Wiedersehn, Pet, Ian La Frenais in conversation with Mark Lawson (BBC March 2013) https://www.bbc.co.uk/programmes/b01rd378 – last broadcast 2 March 2021.

129. Chapter 1 Appendix 2.

130. 1722–1799 – Lord Justice Clerk (no 2 Scottish judge in seniority).

131. Cockburn (1856) at p. 82.

132. Op cit at p. 81.

133. Comment attached to his painting by John Beugo – https://www.nationalgalleries.org/art-and-artists/25358 (last accessed April 7 2023).

134. Recorder for Exeter 1899–1922 – the first step on the judicial ladder to appointment to the bench handling less complex issues.

135. Foote (1911) at p. 5.

136. Wodehouse (1922) (1926)(1950) and (1959) – 27 stories.

137. Ashton (1924) – 1855–1925.

138. E.g. loc cit at p 214 ff on Shee and Pickford.

139. *Inter alia* Cecil (1976); Wheatley (1987) – albeit with a Celtic tale included; Brand (1996).

140. Jackson (1959); Hyde (1964); Hostettler and Brady (2010); Fraser (2017).

141. Osborne (1992) – per the publicity material.

142. Although the British works seem plentiful at first glance, there is a veritable tsunami of works by American judges and attorneys – see coverage by the online book store Alibris at https://www.alibris.co.uk/search/books/subject/Biography-Autobiography-Lawyers-Judges?qsort=&page=21&matches=1744 (accessed 14 October 2021) – this lists almost 500 current titles available. All but a dozen are by US based attorneys and judges.

143. Boal (2021).

144. Bell (2015); Dyson (2019).

145. Ward and Parsliffe (2020); see also Flood (1983) for an earlier view, albeit from an "outsider"; for a fictional version of this world see Moss (2019). There is also a radio spinoff from Silk focusing on the work of the barristers' clerks – *Silk: The Clerks' Room (2014)* – audio available at https://www.audible.co.uk/pd/Silk-The-Clerks-Room-Series-1-and-2-Audiobook/B09S4N5NXH?source_code=M2M14DFT1BkSH082015011R&&ipRedirectOverride=true&overrideBaseCountry=true&gclid=CjwKCAjw6IiiBhAOEiwALNqncZI7GpDTwkmsSj6tgX2TVqfnv3w0NhbaA7bBdWVtjId9Z77nSpMAgxoCeTcQAvD_BwE&gclsrc=aw.ds (last accessed April 21 2023).

146. Henriques (2021) – excerpt from https://www.thebookseller.com/news/hodder-publish-legal-memoir-top-judge-sir-richard-henriques-1175151 (accessed 13 October 2021).

147. Harvey (1958) – its restrained tone can be inferred from the review in the Cambridge Law Journal which notes that the principal "devils" are judges and the common law but that the critiques of the judges are "cloaked with decent anonymity" Cambridge Law Journal Vol 16 Issue 2 at 258.

148. Langford (2018).

149. Advertising material on the website of the publisher – https://www.penguin.co.uk/books/111/1114624/in-your-defence/9781784163082.html (accessed 13 October 2021).

150. Clegg (2019).

151. Advertising material on the website of the publisher https://www.quercusbooks.co.uk/titles/william-clegg/under-the-wig/9781529401233/ (accessed 14 October 2021).

152. The Secret Barrister (2019).

153. Advertising material https://www.panmacmillan.com/authors/the-secret-barrister/the-secret-barrister/9781509841141 (accessed 13 October 2021).

154. The Secret Barrister (2021).

155. Advertising material https://www.panmacmillan.com/authors/the-secret-barrister/fake-law/9781529009941 (accessed April 21 2023).

156. The Secret Barrister (2023) – publicity material (from Daily Telegraph puff).

157. See Afzal (2020), Hanratty (2016 and 2020), Kennedy (2004) , Mansfield (2009), Robertson (2018) and Wilson (2020) would fall within this category. Precisely which group any of these works falls into is moot since the focus of this book is not actually on these accounts and critiques.

158. Buckhaven (1986); Comyn (1993).

159. Fendem (2022).

160. *May to December* (BBC 1) (https:// imdb.com/title/tt0096651/).

161. *Law and Disorder* (ITV) (https:// imdb.com/title/tt0108834).

162. *Is It Legal?* (ITV and Channel 4) (https://www.imdb.com/title/tt0112019).

163. *Chambers* (BBC) (https://www.imdb.tt0249285).

164. The Main Chance (1969–1975) https://www.imdb.com/title/tt0159179/.

165. Kavanagh QC (1995–2001) https://www.imdb.com/title/tt0108826/.

166. New Street Law (2006–2007) https://www.imdb.com/title/tt0770620/.

167. Silk (2011–2014) https://www.imdb.com/title/tt1717455/.

168. The issues covered were a prize bull being scared to death by a hot air balloon (1); a woman photographed as a baby seeking royalties (2); a sleepwalker accused of criminal activities (3); a football fan receiving the wrong tattoo (4); a man accused of eating his sailing companion (5); a cash dispenser failing to release money (6).

169. Spellings include Forbes Hamilton, Forbes-Hamilton and Fforbes Hamilton.

170. Arnold, Steve (2005) https://www.comedy.co.uk/tv/chambers/ (accessed 28 May 2021).

171. See Chapter 2.

172. There was an earlier radio version between 1996 and 1999. 4 episodes of the radio version are available in the BBC Radio Cassette series. All 3 radio series can be

found on YouTube under John Bird and Sarah Lancashire. For a précis of the radio series see www.britishcomedy.org.uk/comedy/chambers.html. Not to be confused with the Uma Thurman horror series of the same name from the United States.

173. *Outlaws* (2004) BBC (https://www.imdb.com/title/tt0426341).

174. *Defending the Guilty* (2019) BBC (https://www.imdb.com/title/tt8363040/).

175. Robson (2007 a) and (2007 b).

176. Interview with the author 2005.

177. Having started on the brink of retirement in series 1 Episode 1 in 1978, Rumpole survived an impressive further 14 years. Leo McKern, the actor started out at 58 himself in the TV series and was 72 when he last played Rumpole.

Chapter 1

The Interwar Years

The Faux Legal Judgment

INTRODUCTION

Although not the sole comic writer in this era, the interwar years were dominated, in terms of legal humour by the figure of the writer and lawyer A. P. Herbert and, to a lesser extent, J. B. Morton. It might be argued that there are good reasons for excluding the category of comic legal judgements from this study of comic legal writers. The very nature of the form they chose to adopt means that their comments and perspective have a much narrower focus and are expressed by the single voice of a "judge" – or occasionally a panel of judges. Nonetheless, due to their adaptation into visual form as a television series and sketches they can be said to be part of the reservoir of popular culture on which this study focuses. They also merit consideration since, in Herbert's view, his fictional cases were aimed to reform and hopefully amend the law as well as provide amusement.[1]

Alan Patrick Herbert was born 24 September 1890 in Ashstead, Surrey. His father was a Civil Servant working in Whitehall. His mother died of T. B. when Herbert was only eight. After active service in the armed forces during the First World War he was called to the Bar in 1919 although he never practised.[2] He supported himself through his writing from early on including a lauded novel based on his experiences in the ill-fated Allied expedition to Gallipoli.[3] Although he was called to the Bar (Inner Temple), he never practised but relied for his income on writing and as a member of the staff at the humorous weekly magazine Punch from early 1924. As a staff member he received a "good salary" of £50 a week (£128,000 per year in 2023).[4] He spent much of his career writing musicals and other works for the stage along with novels, poems, essays and articles. In his autobiography this occupies 60 pages and the enthusiasm is evident, even from the chapter title – "Creative

Joy."[5] He was very much a child of the Edwardian era. The world when he left University was a very different one from when he wrote many of his judgments. History professor AJP Taylor summed up the liberal environment aptly:

> In August 1914 a sensible, law-abiding Englishman could pass through life and hardly notice the existence of the state, beyond the post office and the policeman. He could live where we liked and as he liked. He could travel abroad to leave his country forever without a passport or any sort of official permission. He could exchange his money for any other currency without restriction or limit. He could buy goods from any country in the world on the same terms he bought goods at home. For that matter, a foreigner could spend his life in this country without permit without informing the police. . . . The state intervened to prevent the citizens from eating adulterated food or contracting certain infectious diseases, imposed safety rules in factories and prevented women, and adult males in some industries, from working excessive hours. . . . Broadly speaking the state acted only to help those who could not help themselves. It left the adult citizen alone.[6]

LEGAL CONTRIBUTION

By contrast with the world of the theatre, A. P. Herbert's potential legal career receives no mention in his autobiography, and he devotes a mere seven pages to "The Law."[7] It was suggested by his biographer that Herbert "(N)o doubt (*he*) would have been a good advocate"[8] although his habit of jerking his head had earned him the nickname of "Peck" at school. [9] A combination of this, a facial tic, blinking and a stammer may have been one of the reasons he never practised. The writer of the profile of Herbert in 1952 noted the potential for an Albert Haddock[10] type of misunderstanding

> Herbert has a facial tic, especially when, as usual, he is worried. His eyes blink of themselves. On a park bench or in a railway train he is often startled, in the middle of agonized reflection about the insecurity of everything in the world, by the rising up of some furious young woman to call a policeman or pull the communication cord. And when he tries to explain himself, he is seized with a stammer which still further alarms the lady. The situation, as he expected from the beginning, then becomes hopeless. The lady has hysterics, and Herbert can only laff (sic) at the whole disaster.[11]

As to his legal "work," he noted in 1970 that it had given him "pleasure to concoct and plan and polish my Misleading Cases. . . " for forty six years and that "it was a wonder how they have multiplied and endured."[12] He did not consider the law to be an ass[13] or he would not have been called to the Bar nor given so much time and toil to the sincerest form of flattery, namely imitation.[14] Most of the contributions consist of judgements by either individual judges or banks of judges. Occasionally the "Misleading Case" takes the form of a debate between counsel and the Bench.[15] His admiration for the way the common law had developed through principles and practice being applied by judges, however, did not blind him to the fact that some of these required replacing. While he talked of his fictional cases being "frolics in jurisprudence" they were sometimes "essays in reform and were shyly intended not only to amuse but amend."[16] He singled out several cases for particular mention in this context. His *Board of Inland Revenue v Haddock* – Why is the House of Lords[17] receives pride of place. Here he posed the question – if there is a Court of Appeal, why is there a need for an appeal from this court? Whilst there is no reason why there should be only a single appeal level, nonetheless, it did result, some 33 years later, in the "leapfrogging procedure "introduced by sections 12 and 13 of the Administration of Justice Act of 1969, which allowed appeals from the lower courts direct to the highest appeal court in certain circumstances.

His first contribution, a satire on the mythical figure of the "reasonable man" was another favourite.[18] This mocks the paragon of virtue which the common law has used as a measure of reasonable behaviour. He was amused that a "case" from the 1930s *Board of Inland v Haddock; Haddock v Board of Inland Revenue*[19] involving payment of a cheque to the Inland Revenue written on a cow was reported as fact in a newspaper in the United States in 1967 – albeit reported as a 19th-century occurrence.[20] This notion of people mistaking these satires, parodies and pieces of whimsy for reality was also found in the 1960s when the aforementioned fictional Albert Haddock was convicted of breach of the peace due to accidentally looking at the legs of young women when travelling on the tube. Not his finest hour as a comedy writer and rejected by Punch, this did nonetheless appear in the Evening Standard. It was subsequently reported as fact in various foreign newspapers.[21] Finally, the 1927 case of *R v Haddock: Is it a free country*[22] involving Haddock jumping off Hammersmith Bridge into the River Thames attracted serious condemnation in an American text. Here the concern was that the fining of Haddock for his actions was in contravention of the principle that crimes cannot be declared as such *after* the action – *nullum crimen sine lege* (aka *nulla poena sine lege*). It was also provided with the made-up legal citation concocted by Herbert which should have given the game away.[23]

Herbert was flattered by this attention which he took as compliments as they seemed to show that "my judges' conclusions are at least plausibly expressed."[24] This had always been his "ambitious aim." It was, he said, "easy enough to make spasmodic fun of the law, with the Latin expressions, for example: sustained parody, correct in logic and language, is another thing."[25] He compared himself favourably, in this regard to JB Morton's Mr Justice Cocklecarrot who "will never, I fear, be quoted on the bench of the Supreme Court of the United States."[26] At least two judges in the Maryland Court of Appeals were, indeed, attracted by the approach of an American "Albert Haddock." In the 2003 case of *Messing v Bank of America*,[27] one Jeff Messing had refused to provide a thumbprint in addition to his driving licence and credit card as identification. One of the judges suggested "(t)he circumstances which gave rise to the case before us are, in terms of its genesis, reminiscent of those described in the case of *Board of Inland Revenue v. Haddock*.[28] Although the reluctant bank customer was unsuccessful at first instance as well as on appeal, he did convince two of the five judges including the son of a sharecropper, Chief Justice Robert M Bell. His colleague, Eldridge J opined that "The most reasonable thing in this case was the petitioner's "irritation with the Bank of America's Thumbprint Signature Program."[29] The amount of the cheque was $976.

Other writers have looked at various of Herbert's cases and commented on the thinking within them. As Professor W. L. Prosser put it in the 1950s:

> They concern questions of the day arising out of facts which never have occurred before on land or sea, and they are not lacking in legal difficulty.[30]

The cases struck a chord with Professor Prosser. He wondered whether when defamatory words are recorded on a phonograph record, which is played in public, was the defendant to be charged with libel or slander?[31] The matter is of importance due to the damages being potentially greater for the written rather than the verbal form of defamation. Others are much more whimsical involving, on occasion, pieces of antique legislation. For instance, when a golfer lapsed into profanity after his 15th unsuccessful attempt to get out of a hazard and was prosecuted under the Profane Oaths Act, was he to be assessed at the five-shillings rate applicable to "of the Degree of Gentlemen" or the cheaper rate of two shillings for those "under the Degree of Gentleman." In other words, is a golfer ever a gentleman? The Act was not repealed until 1967 but by the time Herbert wrote had fallen into desuetude. Others were no more than facetious jibes as where Herbert asked when a politician, after the usual campaign promises, is elected to office and draws his salary and fails to make the promised changes – is he guilty of obtaining money under false pretences? [32]

Some of the issues raised have an eerie prescience although, when written, were of limited policy interest. Mr Justice Codd's last case, which dealt with the necessity of crying "Stop!" before shooting a burglar which was an issue more recently in Britain.[33] One article in "a scholarly publication devoted to all aspects of admiralty and maritime law,"[34] provides an account of his judgment" from Punch of 2 July 1930.[35] The inspiration for AP Herbert's spoof *Rumpelheimer* case was suggested by Professor Sweeney thus:

> Legend has it that the first mid-air collision of aircraft occurred on the London-Paris (or Paris-Londres) Commercial Service, begun in 1919. As was the custom, pilots followed railroad tracks at a sufficiently low level so as not to lose their way. A London-Paris pilot kept to the left of the tracks going southeasterly, while a Paris-Londres pilot kept to the right of the tracks going northwesterly.[36]

In the "case" Herbert portrayed, the collision took place on a road which was temporarily under water and the question arose as to whether one passed on the left (roads in Britain) or the right (at sea).

POLITICAL WORK

Even before he stood for Parliament, Herbert had sought to point up the anomalous position of the House of Commons in relation to the licensing laws. He drew attention to the situation in Punch whereby the House of Commons were not covered by the licensing law which the rest of the country had to observe.[37] He had earlier raised a complaint with the magistrates at Bow Street Police Court that he had been served alcohol in the House of Commons which did not have a licence to serve alcohol. This was rejected by the magistrate on the grounds of lack of jurisdiction over the House of Commons, which determined its own affairs. The decision was upheld on appeal.[38] One commentator suggested this stemmed from Herbert's Anglo-Irish background:

> He is a man who believes, on logical grounds, that humanity should be allowed any possible escape from its misery, any feasible alleviation of despair, such as a drink. He set out, therefore, in 1934, to prevent the whole 1,500 Members of Parliament, Lords and Commons, from taking any drink at all.
>
> His argument was:
>
> The Drink laws of England are foolish.
>
> The Drink laws of Parliament, where anyone can get a drink at any time, do not exist.
>
> If Parliament is brought under the law it will look like a fool.
>
> Therefore, the way to make Parliament reform the laws of England is to make it look like a fool.[39]

Herbert's own account suggests that this was a bit of fun and that through his "rash act the liberties of the faithful commons were proclaimed and freed from doubt by the High Court of Justice, and established for ever."[40]

In the same year as this litigation, seemingly, almost by accident according to his own account, he was elected as a Member of Parliament for Oxford University in 1935.[41] Here he brought forward the Parliamentary Bill which resulted in the passing of the Matrimonial Causes Act 1937 into statute. This allowed the grounds for divorce to go beyond adultery and include desertion for over three years as well as cruelty, incurable insanity, incest or sodomy.

He also advocated reform of the gambling laws and the repeal of the entertainments tax, among other causes. He was knighted in 1945 in Winston Churchill's Honours list. *The Times* wrote that Herbert had "his individual niche in the parliamentary temple as the doughty vindicator of the private member's rights, including not least the right to legislate."[42]

It has been suggested by one writer that "Herbert once wrote a check on a brandy bottle, stamped it and sent it to be cashed at his bank."[43] There is no mention of such a cheque in either his biography or autobiography. His biographer, Pound does record that a cheque for £1 was written on a napkin in 1927[44] and using his own notepaper in 1961 and a 24-line poem.[45] Cheques are "promissory notes" at law. They are no more than promises to pay so such means are acceptable in the same ways as I.O.Us. The problem would, of course, be in persuading third parties to regard them as viable "currency."

Again, Herbert delighted in taking a play on words from everyday speech and subjecting it to pseudo-forensic analysis. So, we have a decision of the Division of Probate, Admiralty and Divorce that part of its jurisdiction must terminate, because marriage is a lottery, in which the "element of skill is negligible and the element of chance predominates" so that the Court cannot assist the victims of these unlawful betting arrangements.[46] Some stem from neat twists of events in everyday life such as the arrest of Albert Haddock at his daughter's wedding just because he felt he had the right to say a few words in answer to "Who giveth this woman?" "As a matter of fact I do . . . but I'm also giving the wedding dress, and three, at least of those horrible brides-maids' dresses. . . . What's more, I'm giving the party afterwards. . . ." Justice prevails for Albert as he comes before a judge who has 5 daughters himself.[47]

BEACHCOMBER, J. B. MORTON, PRIVATE EYE, AND MR JUSTICE COCKLECAROTT

Superficially adopting the same vehicle, the "faux" legal judgment is the work of J. B. Morton. A recurring source of legal satirical humour can be found in the figure of Mr Justice Cocklecarrot and the cases which came before him.

He appears from the 1920s up until the present day. He first appeared in the Daily Express *By the Way* column written most notably by J. B. Morton from 1924.[48] The style, however, was surreal and whimsical beyond the relative authenticity of the A. P. Herbert parodies. There was surely never any danger of anyone mistaking these writings as actual cases as we saw with Albert Haddock's encounters with the law. For instance, one column reads

> Mr Justice Cocklecarrot began the hearing of a very curious case yesterday. A Mrs Tasker is accused of continually ringing the doorbell of a Mrs Renton, and then, when the door is opened, pushing a dozen red-bearded dwarfs into the hall and leaving them there.

An expert witness is called . . .

Mr Bastin Hermitage (for the defence): Now, Dr Spunton, is there, to your knowledge, any disease which would account for Mrs Tasker's strange habits?
Dr Spunton: There is. It is called rufo-nanitis. The spymptoms-
Mr Hermitage: Symptoms.
Dr Spunton: Yes, spymptoms, but I always put a 'p' before a 'y'.
Cocklecarrot: With what object, might we ask?
Dr Spunton: I can't help it, m'lud.
Cocklecarrot: Do you say pyesterday?
Dr Spunton: Pyes, unfortunatelpy. It's hereditarpy. Mpy familpy all do it.
Cocklecarrot: But why 'p'?
Dr Spunton: No, py, m'lud.

Later

> The court had to be cleared owing to the roars of ribald laughter which greeted the appearance in the witness-box of the twelve red-bearded dwarfs all in a heap. Their names were read out amid growing uproar. The names appeared to be: Sophus Barkayo-Tong, Amaninter Axling, Farjole Merrybody, Guttergorm Guttergormpton, Badly Oronparser, Churm Rincewind, Cleveland Zackhouse, Molonay Tubilderborst, Edeledel Edel, Scorpion de Rooftrouser, Listenis Youghaupt, Frums Gillygottle.

Cocklecarrot: Are these genuine names?
A Dwarf: No, m'worship.
Cocklecarrot: Then what's your name?
Dwarf: Bogus, m'ludship.
Cocklecarrot: No, your real name.

Dwarf: My real name is Bogus, your excellency.
(At this point the court had to be cleared) [49]

Several of the cases can be found in the various collections of Morton's work.[50] It is clear from reading the stories that are currently easily accessible that AP Herbert was entirely right. None of these cases whether in the 1974 Collection[51] or the cases in the 1991 Bumper Collection[52] could conceivably be mistaken for genuine cases. Nor would anyone go through them looking for aperçus on the justice system or its personnel as was done with Herbert's *Misleading Cases.*[53]

The columns, however, were adapted for both television in the 1960s[54] and radio in the 1980s.[55] With their penchant for outlandish characters and names they provide a link via the work of their adapter, Spike Milligan, through to the comedy of *Q5 - 8*[56], *Monty Python's Flying Circus*,[57] *Not the Nine O'Clock News*,[58] *The League of Gentlemen* [59] and *Inside No 9*.[60] In fact, one of the most memorable moments in the Monty Python series involves the second appearance of the Spanish Inquisition in the context of a court cross examination of a judge charged with breach of the peace.[61]

There continue to be references to Mr Justice Cocklecarott as a touchstone for the absurd-seeming and antediluvian elements in the justice system in the media. [62] Mr Justice Cocklecarott has been identified as an exemplar of the "out of touch" judge by the British magazine of exposés and satire, the magazine *Private Eye*. For instance, in the obituary of irascible judge Sir Michael Davies it is stated that the judge "was satirised as a latterday Mr Justice Cocklecarrot in Private Eye."[63] The BBC suggested "Senior judges have long been stereotyped as upper class, public-school educated, white male twits, easily blundering into causing offence and mercilessly parodied in Private Eye's Mr Justice Cocklecarrot." [64]

The name of Mr Justice Cocklecarrot also appears in the potted Law Reports of the Jolly Contrarian on the Internet. These appear to be potted versions of noted actual cases like *Carlill v Carbolic Smoke Ball Company, Rylands v Fletcher* and *Salomon v Salomon* plus the odd one from AP Herbert. They are slightly in the style of that excellent satirical guide to British history, *1066 and All That*. [65]

Also worthy of brief mention in the inter-War period is a series of short comments in a humorous vein by barrister Theobald Mathew under the soubriquet of "forensic fables." There were 110 of these fables published between 1926 and 1932. They range from 200 to 450 words, and each is illustrated by a cartoon by Mathew himself. He was a popular pupil master for aspiring barristers. Among these were the future socialist British Prime Minister Clement Attlee, his Chancellor of the Exchequer, Sir Stafford Cripps and Quintin Hogg – later Lord Chancellor Hailsham. These fables were described some 60 years ago by Lord Birkett as timeless.[66] The intervening years seem to have exposed this assessment as being rather hopeful. Whilst humour is a highly personal thing, what Mathew might be said to have done is to have "captured the atmosphere of that wonderful world of the interwar legal system."[67] What amused then seems, rather like golf club and Lawyers' Faculty dinner speeches, to have altered.[68] The edited 1959 collection has an extensive Index of each Fable. It is, however, clear that, apart from some casual sexism, anti-Semitism and racism in a few of the Fables, there are no consistent themes or ideas.[69] Principally the humour seems to stem from observations of various legal luminaries of the time rather than any deep socio-political themes. Given the anonymity of these characters the Fables offer little of substance to readers eighty years on other than to a literary archaeologist.

CONCLUSION

The comic legal literature which dominated the interwar era did not have any clear unifying themes. As indicated, there were occasional forays into serious issues. The general impression is that there is lurking in these pages a wry smile at the idiosyncrasies of the justice system and its practitioners. Many are also aimed at politicians of the day and their shortcomings. The majority are aiming for laughter rather than deep reflection. The modest number of "serious" judgments from the pen of the major interwar figure A. P. Herbert provide us with critiques of only a handful of issues.[70] I have sought to provide a guide to the full range of the coverage of the Misleading Cases to substantiate this assertion, which can be found at the end of this chapter.[71]

In a slightly different vein, the continued existence of Beachcomber's weekly column in a major British daily newspaper[72] demonstrates that the desire to find enjoyment in surreal humour is still in operation and that from time to time the law and justice system, with their attachment to pomp, flummery and verbal obscurity, are seen as appropriate targets.[73]

APPENDIX 1

Forensic Fable 89

THE JUDICIAL PERSONAGE WHO DISAPPROVED OF CINEMAS AND SENSATIONAL LITERATURE

A judicial personage of the right experience held decided views on the subject of cinemas and sensational literature. He felt they were the main causes of the demoralisation of the working classes, the state of unrest in India, and the general decadence of the present generation. Whenever a suitable opportunity presented itself, the judicial personage let fly at both of these weapons of the evil one. If informed by the police officer in charge of the case that the oaf or flapper in the dock had been a constant attendant at the flicks or a regular reader of detective tales the judicial personage preached an impressive sermon and gave the offender not less than nine months. And when responding at a public dinner for the bench, the guests of the evening, or what not, the judicial personage did not fail to say a few forcible words on each of these topics.

Though, greatly to his disappointment, his sermon seemed to fall upon deaf ears, the judicial personage manfully continued to sow the good seed.

Once a week (on Saturday afternoons) the judicial personage allowed himself a little relaxation. He lunched at the Megatherium, took a two and fourpenny seat at whatever cinema the hall-porter recommended, and returned to his club to tea. During the latter refection, he read the last Edgar Wallace.

Moral – *Quite Right Too.*

APPENDIX 2

Key		More Misleading Cases 1930 – MMC	General Cargo 1939 – GC	Uncommon law 1935 –UL	More Uncommon Law 1952 – MUL	Wigs at Work 1966 – WW	
CASE NO.	*CASE NAME*	*SHORT TITLE*	*LOCATED*	*DATE*	*TOPIC*	*STYLE*	*COMMENTS*
	Fardell v Potts	The Reasonable Man	Punch p. 38 UL 1	9 July 1924	The improbable attributes of the fictional "reasonable man" in the context of a river boat accident	Satire on a core aspect of the male centred legal system many years ahead of its time	The view that there exists a class of beings, illogical, impulsive, careless, irresponsible, extravagant, prejudiced etc etc.
	Trott v Tulip	The Highbrow 1	Punch p. 218 UL 42	20 August 1924	Book review in which the word "highbrow" was used	Bit of mild fun	Is it libellous to be called "highbrow"
	Trott v Tulip	The Highbrow 2	Punch p. 232 UL 42	27 August 1924	Book review in which the word "highbrow" was used	Bit of mild fun	Is it libellous to be called "highbrow"
	Tinrib, Rumble and others v The King and Queen	Fish Royal aka The Whale	Punch p.429 UL 7	15 October 1924	Who is responsible for a dead beached whale	Satire	buckpassing in bureaucracy between departments of government

(*Continued*)

Key	More Misleading Cases 1930 – MMC	General Cargo 1939 – GC	Uncommon law 1935 –UL	More Uncommon Law 1952 – MUL	Wigs at Work 1966 – WW	
The Sagacious Dog	Soak Riddle	Punch p. 542	12 November 1924	Man dies when a dog is presumed to have hurled himself at the new fangled radio –	Satire on the new BBC	BBC had started 2 years earlier
X and Co v The – Society	In Open Court	Punch p 650	10 December 1924	Lots of daft questions with judge upbraiding the witness	Spoof on the way counsel and judges conduct themselves	Much more like a JB Morton case
The Bishop of Bowl et al v Haddock	A Cross Action	Punch p. 67 UL 82	18 February 1925	Defamation in crossword puzzles	Bit of fun	Clues spell out the names of prominent people – who took offence
R v Figg, Figg and Crole	Romance	Punch p. 66	22 July 1925	Conspiracy and fraud by pretending wife had been murdered	Quite tasteless	Fame and fortune followed *Chicago* style
R v Haddock	Is it a free country?	Punch p. 68 UL 24	19 January 1927	Jumping off a bridge for a bet	Libertarian *reductio ad absurdum*	"It cannot be too clearly understood that this is not a free country. . .,. People must not do things for fun. You're not here for fun."
R v Lord Oodle	False Pretences	Punch p 94	26 January 1927	M.P. Charged for taking his salary and being "for the people" whilst not "one of the people"	Sort of satire – although target not clear	Off colour swipe at inverted class snobbery

Chicken v Ham	The Lawyers' Dream	Punch p. 150 UL 71	9 February 1927	The different approaches of the law to libel and slander to a record – need for damage in slander	Serious	On the costs of litigation and the problem of conflicting judgments – comment on finality of House of Lords' decision at 72
R v Haddock	Is Magna Carta Law? aka Where is Magna Carta?	Punch p. 180 UL 53	16 February 1927	Using Magna Carta as a test for a parking offence	Bit of fun	Shows that appeals to Magna Carta are in fact misplaced
In re McAllister et al	Which is the Liberal Party? aka Legacy to the Liberal Party	Punch p. 256 UL 59	9 March 1927	Centres on history of conflict within the Liberal Party from 1924 General Election from 158 to 40 seats	Political Satire	Interesting piece of history about one phase in the decline of the Liberal Party
Pratt v Pratt & Mugg aka Pritt v Pritt	A Swan Song	Punch p. 340 UL 36	30 March 1927	Spoof speech by retiring Counsel on the artificial nature of pre-1937 divorce laws	Serious issue	Herbert's first sally into the inadequacy of the divorce laws
R v Garvin et al aka R v Williams et al	The Sabbath-Breakers aka Pleasant Sunday Mornings	Punch p. 542 UL 13	18 May 1927	Sunday observance laws	Mild Satire	From the viewpoint of the impact on those selling Sunday newspapers

(Continued)

Key	*More Misleading Cases 1930 – MMC*	*General Cargo 1939 – GC*	*Uncommon law 1935 –UL*	*More Uncommon Law 1952 – MUL*	*Wigs at Work 1966 – WW*	
Suet v Haddock	Status of Authors	Punch p. 608 UL 66	1 June 1927	Covers an author who wrote reviews in the style of a drama critic. Was taken to court by one unhappy manufacturer of a patent medicine	Satire	Anticipates “influencers” – joke comparing manufacturers of goods (good) with authors (bad)
R v The Commissioner of Metropolitan Police et al	Exploits of Boot aka Are Constables Quite Nice or The Spy System	Punch p. 627 UL 77	8 June 1927	Attack on shop restrictions	Very broad satire	Starts with an attack on the stupidity of juries
R v The Licensing Justices of Muddletown	The Red Cow case	Punch p. 662 UL 30	15 June 1927	Licensing change causing reduction of business	Mild satire	Out of touch judge
Marrowfat v Marrowfat	Is Marriage Lawful?	Punch p. 40 UL 95	13 July 1927	Spoof defence to a divorce petition	Satire	Marriage is a lottery – courts do not deal with gambling disputes involving no skill just chance.
Engheim et al v The King	Free Speech – Why?	Punch p. 68 UL 89	20 July 1927	Right of assembly in Trafalgar Square	Satire	Assertion that there are no civil liberties- all actions can be caught by the law
R v Haddock	Can a Worm Turn? aka A Worm Turns	Punch p. 90	27 July 1927	Income tax return error	Spoof on complexity of tax forms	Bug bear of Herbert

R v Haddock	Is a golfer a gentleman?	Punch p. 150 UL 18	10 August 1927	Playing golf on a Sunday and level of penalty	Old laws are funny	Scale of fines depending on rank
R v Smith	Poodle racing: or the Big Humbug	Punch p. 325	21 September 1927	Gambling on unusual dog racing of poodles	Mildly serious satire	Gambling yet again an issue
Haddock v Thwale	What is a Motor Car?	Punch p. 538 UL 124 MMC 19	13 November 1927	Damages action for personal injury	Serious point about standards of care required of motorists – big concern of AP Herbert	Motor accident with mention of Rylands v Fletcher – pre – 30 mph speed limit under Road Traffic Act of 1934 – RTA 1930 had abolished previous limit of 20 mph
R v Leather	Is fox-hunting fun? aka What is Fox hunting?	Punch p 580 UL 195 MMC 109	20 November 1929	Liability for Entertainment Tax	Spoof on foxhunting as a sport compared to the theatre	Tax on takings not profits a bugbear of APH since introduced in 1916 – see R v Cochran below
Haddock v The King; Haddock v Constable Boot; Haddock v The Southern Railway	The Let and Hindrance aka Back to the Constitution	Punch p. 597 UL 110 MMC 10	27 November 1929	On the status of passports	Light spoof	Fun about the wording on passports addressed to foreign governments rather than anyone in Britain
R v Skelton and Dew	What are Stockbrokers? aka What is a bet?	Punch p 622 UL 189 MMC 102	4 December 1929	Street betting offence	Spoof on the nature of Stock Exchange transactions	Broker and jobber charged with betting as they were making contracts in the street
Bacon v Egg; Kidney v Egg	The Law of Criticism	Punch p 6 UL 224 MMC 151	1 January 1930	Damages for libel	Serious critique of libel laws	Limits to the right of critics – in this case an intemperate attack on a play

(*Continued*)

Key		*More Misleading Cases 1930 – MMC*	*General Cargo 1939 – GC*	*Uncommon law 1935 –UL*	*More Uncommon Law 1952 – MUL*	*Wigs at Work 1966 – WW*	
	R v The Headmaster of Eton	Lord Campbell's Act aka What are the Classics? aka Is Homer obscene?	Punch p. 37 UL 164 MMC 65	8 January 1930	Obscene Publications Act deprave and corrupt test used in relation to classics	Light-hearted spoof	The deaths and other awful things in Classical literature
	Carrot & Co. v The Guano Association	The Expert Witness	UL 100	c. 1930 as it appears in MMC published that year	On the complexity of expert evidence	Quite a lengthy spoof	All powder puff entertaining nonsense but with a barb about how long cases are drawn out to benefit counsel.
	The Recalcitrant Jury and the Mad KCs	Judge goes ballistic at Jury (PR)	Punch p. 205	19 February 1930	Judge and Jury disagree about a divorce case	Bit of fun about judicial behaviour	Jury imprisoned for calling into question judge's comments on their decision
	R v Baldwin et al	The Ward-Room's Wife aka The Sailor's Wife	Punch p. 244 UL 177 MMC 81	26 February 1930	Action for recovery of money from Government who fail to keep a promise	Serious – marital disparity now regarded as indefensible	Failure to provide married naval officers with parity to other members of HM Forces
	In re John Walker	Prohibition and Barbarism aka What is Prohibition?	UL 183 MMC 88	c. 1930 - as it appears in MMC published that year	Extradition for murder	Off-colour defence of alcohol trade	Revenue Officer killed by shots fired during Prohibition raid on smuggler

R v Bloggs	What is Education?	Punch p. 356 UL 133 MMC 26	26 March 1930	Conviction for failure to educate children	Satire – quite tongue in cheek	Cost of education at a time of national crisis and pointlessness of much education – the advantages of practical skills and the disadvantages of being able to read, write or do arithmetic – no gambling, cheating at accounts, no forgery nor free verse.
R v Puddle	Blackmail	Punch p. 383 UL 159 MMC 59	2 April 1930	Blackmail	Silly fun – part of a stream of attacks on Tax Collection	Taxes as demanding money with menaces – taxman convicted and sentenced to penal servitude for life and solitary confinement for 10 years.
R v Low	What are politicians?	Punch p. 333 UL 207 MMC125	7 May 1930	Ridicule by cartoon	Light-hearted survey of the failings of politicos	Making fun of various prominent 30s politicians
R v "The Colonel" et al	The Fortune-Tellers	Punch p. 566 UL 138 MMC 33	21 May 1930	Allegation of fortune telling by giving racing tips	Bit of fun	On the unworldliness of judges
Cowfat v Wheedle	What are snails? aka What is a snail?	Punch p. 594 UL 171 MMC 73	28 May 1930	Trespass and damage to a neighbour	Piece of fluff – could have had a serious side	Throwing snails into a neighbour's garden

(Continued)

Key		*More Misleading Cases 1930 – MMC*	*General Cargo 1939 – GC*	*Uncommon law 1935 –UL*	*More Uncommon Law 1952 – MUL*	*Wigs at Work 1966 – WW*	
	Board of Inland Revenue v Haddock; R v Haddock	The Negotiable Cow aka What is a cheque?	Punch p. 652 UL 201 MMC 117	11 June 1930	What form must a cheque be in? Here cheque written on a cow	Spoof on the plastic nature of cheques as mere promises to pay via a bank	Vague attack on the nature of income tax – another APH hobby horse
	Sparrow v Pipp	The Lords Rebel, aka Rebellion in the Lords	Punch p. 704 UL 153 MMC 51	25 June 1930	Political libel action	Serious point and relatively judicial	Libel/slander laws and need for actual damage to be shown in slander PLUS House of Lords not being bound by precedent – changed *sua sponte* in 1966
	Rumpelheimer v Haddock	Port to Port	Punch p. 6 UL 237 MMC 174	2 July 1930	Right of way on flooded road	Bit of fun	Flooded road where a boat and car collide
	Huxley and others v Phipps, Potts Slammer and Co	Sad Case of Mr Justice Wool	Punch p. 34 MMC 96	9 July 1930	Libel action where judge decides not the jury	Fun with a judge suffering from a cold	Prohibited book list published
	Tyke v Tyke	The Magic Hour	Punch p.62 UL 144 MMC 41	16 July 1930	Suit for restitution of conjugal rights – man getting out of marriage he regretted – not valid as post 3 p.m.	Funny things old laws – but serious basis	Exposé of the rule that marriage had to be before a certain hour – since changed by Act of Parliament - Marriage (Extension Hours) Act of 1934 – since 2012 no time limits

R v Smith, Brown, Jones Robinson and others	Sauce for the Gander	Punch p.89 MMC 135	23 July 1930	Rights of pedestrians to use the highway	Josh about the problems of crossing roads with lots of cars	Road safety was one of Herbert's more communal concerns
Haddock et al v Board of Revenue aka Haddock v. Commissioners for Income Tax	Wear and Tear	Punch p. 118 UL 231 MMC 167	30 July 1930	Tax expenses claim	Bit of fluff	Another one of APH repeat issues – the unkindness of the tax system
UDC of Burbleton v Haddock	The Freedom of the Shores	Punch p. 149 UL 216 MMC 142	6 August 1930	Swimming in defiance of local byelaws	Quite a serious rescuing of the dissenting judgment in Blundell v Catterall	Reference to an actual 1821 case on the rights to the foreshore
R v George, MacDonald, Maxton and others	Corrupt Practices	Punch p. 118 UL 275	4 February 1931	Corruption	Political Spoof featuring the big names of the day	Politicians failing to keep their promises to provide work etc.
Dahlia Ltd v Yvonne	Act of God untitled in Punch	Punch p. 370 UL 314	7 October 1931	Centred on a case	Nice spoof	House of Lords so unpredictable as to amount to an Act of God
R v Chancellor of the Exchequer	Tax for the Memory (PR)	Punch p. 88	25 January 1933	Entertainment tax due for being elected as House of Commons a place of entertainment	Light satire	Frequent appearance of this topic
R v The Minister of Drains	The Employment Tax aka The Man Tax	Punch p 174 UL 309	15 February 1933	Unclear if there is such a thing as the employment tax	Making fun of law and legal terminology	A bit subtle

(*Continued*)

Key	More Misleading Cases 1930 – MMC	General Cargo 1939 – GC	Uncommon law 1935 –UL	More Uncommon Law 1952 – MUL	Wigs at Work 1966 – WW	
Willow v Capital Pictures Corporation	What is a Judge?	Punch p. 203 UL 279	22 February 1933	Judicial security of tenure	Mild spoof	A judge loses the plot in trying a case following the reduction in wages in 1931. If wages can be reduced, then this ends the security of tenure of judges.
Tripp v The Milko Corporation	The Echoing Horn	Punch p. 286 UL 297	15 March 1933	Rights of Way	Light but on a mildly serious actual problem	Thorpe v Brumfritt cited on rights of way – the use of horns at night by cars – 1934 legislation noted prohibiting use after 11.30 pm
Bold v The Attorney General	What is the Crown?	Punch p. 316 UL 291	22 March 1933	Crown immunity	Quite serious	On the notion that the Crown can do no wrong.
Haddock v Mogul Hotels Ltd.	The Last Glass aka The law of banquets	Punch p. 346 UL 269	29 March 1933	Licensing Laws	Playful style but includes racist language	Attack on the licensing laws and restrictions of hotels
British Phosphates and Beef Extract Ltd v The United Guano Simplex Association	Why is a Jury?	Punch p.372 UL 346	5 April 1933	on the law being too complicated for juries.	Satire	Years ahead of its time in prescience
Cowan's Case: The Speaker of the House of Commons v The Metropolitan Magistrate of Westminster	Sauce for the Goose	Punch p. 400	12 April 1933	Sale of liquor in the House of Commons	Mild satire	The case which led to Herbert actually taking a case against the House of Commons

Macintosh et al v Haddock, Haddock etc	Incorporation of Haddock	Punch p 432 UL 326	19 April 1933	When does copyright end if the book is written by a company – which never dies.	Realistic satire	The actual answer is that it is no different from any author – the relevant years after the death of the human being who wrote it
The Postmaster – General v Slot Slate in Punch	The Bookmaker's Telephone	Punch p. 456 UL 333	26 April 1933	Post Office suing a bookie for costs of telephone calls	Realistic	cites Pearce v Brooks on ex *turpi causa non oritur actio* principle
Haddock v Jones	The law of libel reformed aka Triumph of Haddock	Punch p. 488 UL 303	3 May 1933	Libel law	Quite serious piece	Canvasses the end of the House of Lords being bound by its own decisions – which was ended in 1966 by declaration
In re Macdonald – Bathbourne Clinic v Bathbourne Hospital	Enter the Lady Chancellor aka Why is the Woolsack?	Punch p. 511 UL 352	10 May 1933	about the old traditions including the woolsack and the political appointment of the Lord Chancellor	A bit of fun	Serious underlying political gender issue addressed quite obliquely
R v Boot, Mallock and Tate aka Are Constables Quite Nice aka Exploits of Boot	Triumph of Boot	Punch p. 544	17 May 1933	Agent provocateur policeman and a burglary	Prescient point made in very broad style	Includes insensitive remarks on provoking a murder to head off a serial murderer
Cowan's Case Pt 2 The Speaker of the House of Commons v The Metropolitan Magistrate of Westminster		Punch p. 570	24 May 1933	Sale of liquor in the House of Commons	More fun	See above – Cowan's Case Pt 1

(Continued)

Key	*More Misleading Cases 1930 – MMC*	*General Cargo 1939 – GC*	*Uncommon law 1935 –UL*	*More Uncommon Law 1952 – MUL*	*Wigs at Work 1966 – WW*	
Tristram v The Moon Life Assurance Company	Why is the Coroner?	Punch p. 600 UL 261	31 May 1933	Coroners and their suitability and qualification	Quite serious and lacking much by way of humour	Lots on intemperate remarks on the abilities of doctors.
R v Cochran	The Education Tax	Punch p. 626 UL 243	7 June 1933	Taxation	Bit of fun but not very funny	Old hobby horse of the Entertainment Tax applied to theatres
R v Jackson	Are suicides insane?	Punch p. 656 UL 285	14 June 1933	Suicide	Quite tasteless	about the conflict between the jury and the coroner's jury and whether one person was insane when they failed in an attempted suicide
Haddock v. London County Council	Legal profession swimming and boating in the Thames (PR)	Punch p. 682	21 June 1933	About the Thames Embankment preventing access to the Courts and Inns of Court	Bit of heavy-handed fun	Obscure
R v Haddock	The Human Hen	Punch p. 708 UL 339	28 June 1933	on lack of speed limit on cars – pedestrian Haddock using a horn on the pavement.	Spoof with serious undertones	30 mph limit introduced 2 years later – concern of APH as MP.
Haddock v London County Council aka Haddock's case		Punch p. 6	5 July 1933	Haddock up for contempt of House of Commons for getting drink in Parliament in disguise	Mild satire – a bit of overkill	Further milking of Cowan's case – drink in Parliament
Fowl v Myer	The Doctrine of Enticement 1	Punch p. 39 UL 365	12 July 1933	presided over by the Lady Chancellor – feminist rejection of the concept of enticement based on the wife being a chattel.	Neo-realist and cites R v Jackson 1891	Serious underlying issue about an action from the past

Fowl v Myer	The Doctrine of Enticement 2	Punch p. 68 UL 365	19 July 1933	presided over by the Lady Chancellor- feminist rejection of the concept of enticement based on the wife being a chattel.	Neo-realist and cites R v Jackson 1891	Serious underlying issue about an action from the past
Pipp v Pipp and Forrest	Decree Nisi	Punch p 118 UL 379	2 August 1933	attack on the whole concept of the six-month wait	Light spoof using judge unfamiliar with the six-month rule to mock its rationale	Contrast with Scotland and serious underlying issue
Board of Inland Revenue v Haddock	The Judges' Reply	Punch p. 152 UL 374	9 August 1933	revenue case in which the judges have an interest as their salaries will be returned to normal if the economy picks up.	Interesting rather than particularly humorous	Very much of its time
Aley v Fish aka Oley v Posh	Slander of Men aka Justice for Men	Punch p. 204 UL 320	23 August 1933	About "banter" and the application of the Act to benefit women but with no male equivalent	Serious point about the Slander of Women Act 1891	Another early version of House of Lords changing its views on self-binding precedent
R v Smith	Felony and Misdemeanour	Punch p. 402 UL 384	11 October 1933	panegyric on the false dichotomy between felonies and misdemeanours	Long and serious	Covert appeal to the vigilante lurking in us all
R v Bitter aka R v Barrel	The Agent Provocateur	Punch p. 428 UL 390	18 October 1933	Sweepstake issue	Serious in tone	Based on a real case but quite of its time
R v Pratt & Merry R v Pratt and Fairy in Punch	The Tax on Virtue	Punch p. 488 UL 397	1 November 1933	couple obtaining a divorce and then living together for tax purposes.	Serious issue	At a time when living together was reserved for artists and such - 50 years until standard

(*Continued*)

Key		*More Misleading Cases 1930 – MMC*	*General Cargo 1939 – GC*	*Uncommon law 1935 –UL*	*More Uncommon Law 1952 – MUL*	*Wigs at Work 1966 – WW*	
	R v Bitter	What is "Publishing"?	UL 402		about the Betting and Lotteries Act 1924	Mild satire	Pretty time specific
	R v Haddock	Crime in the Commons	Punch p. 542 UL 414	15 November 1933	Consumption of alcohol in the House of Commons	Spoof with serious undertone and some prescience	Based on Herbert's action against the House of Commons
	HM Customs and Excise v Bathbourne Literary Society	Is Laughter Illegal?	Punch p. 622 UL 408	6 December 1933	on entertainment duty and an educational lecture with fun bits	Mild satire	Return of the entertainment tax hobby horse
	Haddock v Mr Justice Foot	What is A Jury	MMC 159	c. 1933	Judge loses the plot with a jury who take exception to his remarks	Interesting points about judicial power and on the law being too complicated for juries.	Nice "reductio ad absurdum" of the notion of unaccountable power
	Pale v Pale and Hume aka Adam v Adam & Tott	The King's Proctor Showing Cause		c. 1933	Much much longer essay on the state of the divorce laws	serious and effective	Uses same case as Holy Deadlock and refers to Scottish situation
		Not a Crime	UL 425				
	R v Venables et al	The "Dead" Pronunciation	Punch p. 129 UL 360	31 January 1934	on pronouncing Latin brocards	Trivial seeming spoof	Draws attention to the cut off world of lawyers
	R v Haddock	Wearing armorial bearings	Punch p.409	11 April 1934	On the lack of a licence to put on a stamp	Mildly amusing	No clear target
	R v Haddock	Betting by Pigeon (PR) – no actual extra title	Punch p. 10	2 January 1935	On Irish Hospital sweepstakes and betting using a pigeon	Spoof on a mildly serious issue	Constant concern of APH

Hogby v Hogby	The Price of Justice	Punch p. 90 MUL 1	27 July 1938	husband pays court costs of actions brought by wife where husband defended action on grounds of cruelty - heard in London - would have lost job if allowed to go undefended	Serious and not amusing	includes gratuitous reference to Sudetan Germans and Czecho-Slovakians being concern of Government rather than own citizens
Integrated Press v The Postmaster -General	What is a newspaper?	Punch p. 160 MUL 14	10 August 1938	change of nature of newspaper by incorporating pictures from Swim Girl - finds against it being a newspaper and being posted cheaper	Mild satire	Of its time but predictor of Page 3 glamour pinups in tabloid presses possibly
R v Benevolent Greyhounds Ltd, Coates and others	What is a Dog-Race?	GC 111	c. 1939	Obsession with betting and its regulation	Mildly serious	Rerun of previous theme from 1927
R v Haddock and the Friendly Feeding Place	The Sandwich Case aka The Indiarubber Sandwich	Punch p. 64 GC 44	18 January 1939	Licencing dispute	Mild satire A nice play on changing standards	Remarkably prescient for the same issue arose in Covid 2020-2021 when drinks could be bought with a meal and what this meant
Mullins et al v Bouverie	The Case of the Hundred Members	Punch p. 94 GC 154	25 January 1939	Eviction of MPs on a "sit in"	Serious about in re Herbert case	Reflection of position as MP 1935 – 1951
Greenwich Women's Rowing Club v Haddock	What is a rowing boat?	Punch p. 446 MUL 21	6 November 1940	revamp of steam v sail point	Mild fun	A good example of Herbert capturing the essence of how judgments read

(Continued)

Key	*More Misleading Cases 1930 – MMC*	*General Cargo 1939 – GC*	*Uncommon law 1935 –UL*	*More Uncommon Law 1952 – MUL*	*Wigs at Work 1966 – WW*	
Haddock v Silkworm	Books into Bombs	Punch p. 542 MUL 27	30 June 1943	book included in window display for salvage drive along with other items - pulped and re-used or given to service personnel	Quite a serious point	Line between serious and spoofery nicely maintained
Haddock v Mole	The Case of the Orange Globes	Punch p. 142 MUL 32	16 February 1944	on crossing the road where no lamps at the designated crossing - data on high number of road deaths	Quite serious – theme features in Henry Cecil below	Again, one of the issues with which Herbert was seriously concerned – pedestrian safety
Haddock v Tomkins & Isaac	What is a reactionary	Punch p. 250 MUL 37	22 March 1944	test of "hatred, ridicule or contempt" noted and how a word can acquire a derogatory meaning	Serious	progressive ideas outlined which mirror Herbert's own constant worries – divorce, drink, betting, libel, Sunday entertainments, income tax, entertainment tax
Fester v The King; Fester v Philpott, Rory & Co; Fester v Platt	The "Law of the Land"	Punch p. 336 MUL 42	18 April 1945	about the meaning of "serious misconduct" in the workplace	Serious	about the arbitrary nature of wartime regulations
The Incorporation of Burbleton v Stanislavski	How Free is a Freeman?	Punch p. 12 MUL 47	4 July 1945	Whether being a freeman is covered by parking and driving laws	Spoof but not very amusing	refers to Honorary Freedom of Boroughs Act of1885 – which exists
The King v Broadwick	The Dodged Deposit	Punch p. 292 MUL 52	3 October 1945	about Parliamentary Deposit	Spoof but not wildly funny	Not clear if it is true

Haddock v Oundle; Haddock v Smith; Haddock v The General Press: Haddock v Buzzings and the Bilious Weekly; Haddock v Cooper	The Whale Case	Punch p. 234 MUL 58	19 March 1947	defamation action by writer assumed dead after falling into Arctic waters	Spoof on news	Sprightly comments on writers seeking publicity and having imagination
In re. Haddock	The Political Will (PR)	Punch p. 332	16 April 1947	Will bequest challenged on grounds of being contrary to public policy	Political diatribe against redistributive taxation policies	Money left to expose fallacies of a government alleged to be against profit
R v Bopple	'Avoid Litigation'	Punch p. 410 MUL 63	12 May 1948	murder case and the contrast between living poor after a life of work and prison conditions	Slightly tasteless	Very time specific – when death penalty temporarily suspended
House of Commons (Kitchen Committee) v Haddock	The Egg of Exchange	MUL 68	16 February 1949	cheque drawn on an egg	Gallows humour	Fun about austerity during the tough economic times of the 1940s
In re Earl of Munsey:Stewer v Cobley	The Missing Day Case	MUL 74	7 December 1949	The international date line and its impact	Harmless fun and some references to the attractiveness of the plaintiff's mother as a factor in the court case	Classic example of APH going off on a frolic on an inconsequential topic
Mortimer v The British Broadcasting Corporation et al	Sunday on the Air	Punch p. 646 MUL 84	14 June 1950	Lord's Day observance case regarding the BBC TV programme	Mild satire	footnote to a speech by AP Herbert on 1 April 1941

(Continued)

Key		*More Misleading Cases 1930 – MMC*	*General Cargo 1939 – GC*	*Uncommon law 1935 –UL*	*More Uncommon Law 1952 – MUL*	*Wigs at Work 1966 – WW*	
	R v Dark and Haddock	'Cheap Literature'	MUL 205	4 January 1951	on the rights of various libraries to receive copies of all publications.	Quite serious tone	Would that it were complied with
	Canter et al v Howard	The Canter Poll aka The Haddock Poll	MUL 88	6 June 1951	about an Opinion Poll	Bit of serious fun	About the scientific nature of these polls
	R v Haddock & Vine	Bookmakers All aka The Bookmaker's Case	Punch p. 722 MUL 92	13 June 1951	A publisher acts as a bookie betting against his authors producing their work sometime or their sales. Turns out to be a scam with authors waiving their royalties but not having to pay tax on their betting wins	Satire on taxation	A Herbert bête noire
	Thomas v Lowden; Lowden v Thomas aka Thomas v Lowden; Lowden v Thomas	The Law of the Bar	Punch p. 750 MUL 97	20 June 1951	defamation action against a policeman who remarked that it was late since it was after 10:30 p.m.	Bit of fun	No obvious point
	The Merchants' Case	Does Magna Carta Matter?	Punch p. 782 MUL 101	27 June 1951	rehash of an earlier piece on Magna Carta	Not very funny	Quite obscure
	R v Gentle, Good and Haddock	'Paying to Rule'	Punch p. 102 MUL 106	25 July 1951	on the collection of the entertainment tax	Serious in tone	Another Herbert bête noire

R v Rungle	Codd's Last Case	MUL 133	7 September 1951	centred on killing of a burglar by a householder – acquitted	Quite tasteless then and now – but gets "star billing" on the cover of More Uncommon Law	Judge's last uninhibited address to the jury on a subject which is hard to find laughs or smiles
Temper v Hume & Haddock	Slander at Sea - 1	Punch p. 386 MUL 123	3 October 1951	use of flag signals to defame someone	A bit of fluff	Not his finest hour – or classic Herbert to some maybe
Temper v Hume & Haddock	Slander at Sea – 2	Punch p. 414 MUL 123	10 October 1951	use of flag signals to defame someone	More fluff	Still not his finest hour
R v Haddock; Haddock v R	The Lords Rebel	Punch p. 446 MUL 111	17 October 1951	Exchange control issue	Dull satire on currency control	Very time specific
Albert & Gloria Haddock v The King	Whose Passport is Yours?	Punch p. 470 MUL 116	24 October 1951	moan about Passports	Mild satire lacking in humour	Anticipates pre-Brexit xenophobic nonsense
R v Reinstein	The Wizardry Case	Punch p. 498 MUL 8	31 October 1951	Fortune telling covered by vagrancy Act 1824 – contrast with modern technology, weather forecasting and water divining	Fair satire	Interesting and timely reference to witchcraft

(Continued)

Key	*More Misleading Cases 1930 – MMC*	*General Cargo 1939 – GC*	*Uncommon law 1935 –UL*	*More Uncommon Law 1952 – MUL*	*Wigs at Work 1966 – WW*	
Victoria Building Society v The Queen	Sex of a Corporation	Punch p. 457	9 April 1952	Josh about male and female treatment in retirement	Spoof	Serious theme which has had major consequences
In re the goods of Trample deceased:Trample v Commissioners of Inland Revenue	"I Thee Endow. . ."	MUL 143		widow not taking probate on her husband's estate and the inland revenue seeking most of the money.	Quite an obscure spoof	Nice Judge highly influenced by the attractiveness of the plaintiff. Marriage contract takes precedence over the will.
Trout, MP v Celestial Publicity Co & Broot	End of a Nonsense 1	Punch p. 502 MUL 165	22 October 1952	loudhailer and sky writing used in an election. Errors indicated candidate a drunk. Is it slander where no damage is required?	rather long and heavy handed spoof	Review of previous pieces on libel and slander. Indirect critique of the variation of appeal judges.
R v Hockey	How Much Can You Kill a Burglar?	MUL 160		Shooting fleeing burglar – discussion of reasonable force quoting Kenny on Criminal Law	Not a very good choice of comedy subject matter even then	Hanging and the errors and misjudgements very much an issue at this time in the 1950s
R v Wilpot	Members' Pay	MUL 187	31 May 1954	about the conflict between the rise in MPs pay and the statute of 1707	Mild satirical josh	repealed in 1957.
Board of Inland Revenue v Haddock	No Taxation Without Representation	WW	14 July 1954	Taxation again	Mildly amusing	Taxation theme not forgotten
R v Haddock	"Who Giveth This Woman"	MUL 175	20 July 1955	on the diminished role of fathers in relation to weddings.	Quite droll.	Nice example of APH case with interchanges between judge and witness

Inland Revenue v Haddock	The Bottle Case	MUL 181		payment of taxes by putting money in a bottle – caused by strikes.	Quite unpleasant rant against ideas of welfare and Trade Unions	Famous for being memorable but a poor shallow effort intellectually
The Queen v The SS Emperor Dulles	Money in the Channel	Punch p. 209 MUL 251	21 August 1957	payment of toll for passing through the straits of Dover	Not clear where the smiles might be on this one or the politics	Not even nationalist nonsense
Haddock v British Atlantic Aircraft Corporation		Punch p. 293	11 September 1957	Civil aviation tax attacked on the basis of Magna Carta	Mild satire	APH on the evils of taxation once again
R v Feathers, Furblow and Philanthropic Pools Ltd	The Law of the Pin aka The Pools Case	MUL 192	December 1959	about the lack of skill doing the football pools.	Humour not clear in this dull spoof	Possibly class envy although Herbert was appointed to the Pools panel himself
Board of Inland Revenue v Hoe	Born to be Taxed	MUL 199		about a successful businessman retiring and living off his money and avoiding tax thereby and working *gratis*	Playful satire on the serious theme of taxation which Herbert always resented	About anti-Tax avoidance measures in the Finance Act of 1960
Haddock v The Arts Council of Great Britain	What is Literature? aka What is the Arts Council Up to or Good Old Scire Facias	MUL 213		about the absence of literature formally from the remit of the Arts Council as not being fine arts.	Quite a serious discussion	Herbert claims he raised the issue with Tory Chancellor, Reggie Maudling who said it was a non-issue
Ex Parte Haddock	'Stamp out Stampery'	MUL 220		about passports and the limited space for stamps in them.	Fluff	A space filler – again to some, presumablyclassic APH

(*Continued*)

Key		*More Misleading Cases 1930 – MMC*	*General Cargo 1939 – GC*	*Uncommon law 1935 –UL*	*More Uncommon Law 1952 – MUL*	*Wigs at Work 1966 – WW*	
	The Queen v Mortimer	The Laws of Sunday	Punch p. 646 MUL 226	11 May 1960	a charity football match and the Lord's Day Observance Society	Dull and puzzling references to the relevant Acts – 1677 and 1780	Maybe of its time. Strange to refer to the Sunday Observance Act of 1781 - Act was 1780
	R v Clatter	The Queen in the City	MUL 231		passing a death sentence without jurisdiction as Queen in environs - and it is her job - accused freed	Satire? Who knows?	More than a bit tasteless
	R v Rake, Smoot and Shepley	Who deceives Whom?	Punch p. 237 MUL 155	17 August 1960	about what is meant by "I promise to pay the bearer £1 end of ". False and genuine notes equally worthless it's no longer backed by gold.	Fun with words	Space filler
	The Queen v Quirk	'Fair' Comment?	Punch p. 675 MUL 150	9 November 1960	criminal libel of a theatre critic and the need to look at the whole play	Thoughtful satire on the nature of criticism	Not very amusing.
	R v Walton ex parte Rusk	A Tent in the Road	MUL 247		contrast with the cars and caravans on the street	Very mild satire	Bit "So what?"
	R v Strool	The Split Sentence	Punch p. 677 MUL 236	3 May 1961	On bigamy	Tasteless joshing about psychological issues.	Not a good choice of topic for his style of humour

R v Haddock	The Law of Sitting Sir Galahad Spurned	Punch p. 942	21 June 1961	Women's rights and policing in conflict in the person of Haddock	Very weak sort of spoof	Potentially interesting issue not accorded proper weight
Common Time		Punch p. 832 MUL 255	30 May 1962	Common Market being one hour ahead	Long and tedious - maybe it is a spoof of long rambling judgments	Puzzling
Brigitte Bardot MP?		Punch p. 855 MUL 264	6 June 1962	election following joining Common Market of Italian and French person	Very mild satire on the notion of nationality	All foreigners are funny? EEC must be dangerous
Haddock v The Chancellor of the Exchequer	Common Tea	MUL 269		Taxation issues in the EEC	Satire of the dull kind	EEC is a tricky place – all about being in the EEC which Britain was not in until 1973
Bardot Regained		Punch p. 943 MUL 275		return of foreign MP issue	Very mild spoof – not a rib tickler	We love foreigners really
Haddock v The Generous Bank Ltd, Computer 1578/32/W1, The Magical Electronic Contrivances Ltd. and the Central Electricity Board	Reign of Error	Punch p. 239 MUL 279	13 February 1963	on computer errors and computers with free will and ability to answer questions. Rylands v Fletcher mentioned.	Spoof	Quite prescient for the time
R v Raddle: R v Slout	Summer Time Abroad	Punch p. 487	3 April 1963	Impact of clocks changing on burglary and licensing	Bit of fun	No real serious issue and only mild humour

(*Continued*)

Key	*More Misleading Cases 1930 – MMC*	*General Cargo 1939 – GC*	*Uncommon law 1935 –UL*	*More Uncommon Law 1952 – MUL*	*Wigs at Work 1966 – WW*	
The Queen v Haddock	One Cherry, One Bite	Punch p. 426	18 September 1963	Charges of kidnapping, abduction, blackmail etc	Satire about the costs of justice of trials	Pretty obscure and not too funny
Rate Racket Revealed	What are Rates? (PR)	Punch p. 606	23 October 1963	No-one understands what the rates are	Play on words commonly used but not really understood	Weak
R v Art Prints and Phascinating Photographs	The Case of the Incorruptible Cops	Punch p. 378	11 March 1964	Obscene photographs	Serious examination of who can be corrupted by obscenity	Interesting issue
The Queen v Gangling, Muffet, O'Shanaghan and many others	Dolphin Sands Piracy in the Thames	Punch p. 683 WW	10 November 1965	On pirate radio stations	Satire on Government ham-fistedness in dealing with Pirate radio stations	An issue at the time with Radio Caroline the first home of national treasure Tony Blackburn
Re. Haddock and mini-skirts	Leering Haddock (PR)	Evening Standard See UL Introduction at 3 where APH discusses the "case" and its reporting abroad	1967	Breach of the peace caused by Haddock sitting opposite women in min-skirts	Serious issue dealt with in the APH way but rejected by Punch	Re-run of theme from earlier – this time about leering men on the Tube Hard to access

NOTES

1. Herbert (1970) at 140.

2. Herbert op cit at 144 – other sources give the date as 1918 which seems improbable given his war service – the autobiographical details in his book *Number Nine* for example – Herbert 1951.

3. *The Secret Battle* (1919) (London, Methuen).

4. Pound (1976) at p. 82 – at a time when income tax was a modest 22%.

5. Herbert (1970) at 78–137.

6. Taylor (1970) p. 25.

7. Herbert (1970) pp. 138–145.

8. Pound (1976) at 65.

9. Pound op cit at 21.

10. An annoying (or endearing to some) kind of "everyman" character who was involved in much of the comic "litigation" in Herbert's "judgments."

11. Time magazine http://content.time.com/time/subscriber/article/0,33009,822222-3,00.html 2 Aug 2024 accessed.

12. Herbert (1970) at 138.

13. Dickens (1838) per Mr Bumble the Beadle in the Workhouse on the notion that a man could control the actions of his wife – "...if the law supposes that then the law be a ass; a idiot. If that's the eye of the law, the law is a bachelor."

14. Herbert (1966) Introduction [Wigs at Work].

15. Examples include *Dahlia, Ltd v Yvonne* (Act of God) Uncommon Law 314 (Punch 7 October 1931); *Macintosh et al v Haddock et al* (Incorporation of Haddock) Uncommon Law 326 (Punch 19 April 1933) and *Haddock v the Generous Bank Ltd et al* (Reign of Error) More Uncommon Law 279 (Punch 13 February 1963).

16. Herbert (1970) at 140.

17. Punch [Herbert 1935 case 39].

18. Punch 9 July 1924, Fardell v Potts [Herbert 1935 at 201].

19. Herbert 1935 Case 32 [The Negotiable Cow aka What is a cheque?].

20. Memphis – Press Scimitar – paper published between 1926 and 1983 - https://en.wikipedia.org/wiki/Memphis_Press-Scimitar (accessed 10/1/22).

21. Herbert (1970) at 143.

22. Herbert (1935) case 5 – see Appendix 2.

23. Ibid.

24. Herbert (1970) at 144.

25. Ibid.

26. Ibid.

27. 373 Md. 672.

28. Loc cit at 678.

29. Loc cit at 704.

30. University of Chicago Law Review (1954) Vol 21 p. 509.

31. Loc cit. at p. 510.

32. R v George, Macdonald, Maxton et al (Uncommon Law 275) Punch 4 February 1931.

33. Robson (2022) at p. 65.

34. https://law.rwu.edu/academics/marine-affairs-institute/journal-maritime-law-and-commerce (accessed 26/1/22).

35. Sweeney (2000).

36. Loc cit at 551.

37. Punch 15 November 1933 p 542 (R v Haddock (Uncommon Law Case 66) at p. 414.

38. R. v. Graham-Campbell; Ex parte Herbert, [1935] 1 K.B. 594.

39. Time magazine http://content.time.com/time/subscriber/article/0,33009,822222-3,00.html 2 Aug 2024 accessed.

40. Herbert (1950) at p. 21.

41. Herbert (1937) at 3.

42. *The Times* 14 August 1945 at 5.

43. Time magazine http://content.time.com/time/subscriber/article/0,33009,822222-3,00.html 3/10/22 accessed.

44. Pound (1976) p. 87.

45. Loc cit at 265.

46. Marrowfat v Marrowfat UL 95 (Is marriage lawful?).

47. R v Haddock MUL 175 (Who Giveth This Woman?).

48. In 1924 John Cameron Audrieu Bingham Michael Morton took over authorship of the column "By The Way" in the *Daily Express*. He inherited the pseudonym "Beachcomber" from his predecessors on the job and, in fact, the column had existed since 1917. Morton wrote the column for over 50 years, six times a week, until 1965 when the column became a weekly feature, and continued to the last column in November 1975. http://www.edwards.eclipse.co.uk/beachcom.htm (accessed 6/1/22). The Beachcomber column was revived in the 1990s and is still found today in the Daily Express. Mr Justice Cocklecarrot and his companions from the old Beachcomber pieces have been replaced by a host of equally surreal characters.

49. http://www.edwards.eclipse.co.uk/JBM-rbd.htm (accessed 6/1/22) – this is a different case from that reported in Ingrams (1991) at p. 133.

50. Ingrams (1974) and (1991).

51. Ingrams (1974) The Case of the Twelve Red-Bearded Dwarves (p. 139) involving a woman accused of ringing a doorbell and when it was answered pushing in said dwarves; The Case of the Rocking Horse (p. 144) concerning material for the tails of rocking horses and involving the 12 red-bearded dwarves appearing; The Case of the Polo Pony (p. 146) an action to restrain a neighbour keeping a polo pony in a disused railway truck overlooking a conservatory; The Case of Juliette Milton (p. 153) letters about the twelve dwarfs; Hotel Superbe v The Filthistan Trio (p. 174) damages action; The Case of the False Beard (p. 243) involving a false beard becoming detached after getting caught in a swing-door; see also Mr Justice Cocklecarrot Home Life (p. 203) on a cat falling down a man-hole.

52. Ingrams (1991) The Case of the Twelve Red-Bearded Dwarves (p. 133) involving a woman accused of ringing a doorbell and when it was answered pushing in said dwarves; The Case of Juliette Milton (p. 171) dealing with alleged sexual harassment by one of the dwarves on a fellow lodger; Hotel Superbe v The Filthistan Trio (p. 201) damages action against Persian trio playing see-saw in the hotel lounge; The Case of the False Beard (p. 296) involving a false beard becoming detached after getting

caught in a swing-door; see also Mr Justice Cocklecarrot Home Life (p. 246) on a cat falling down a man-hole.

53. See Appendix 2.

54. The World Of Beachcomber *UK, BBC, Sketch, Colour, 1968* https://web.archive.org/web/20060615034825/http://www.bbc.co.uk/comedy/guide/articles/w/worldofbeachcomb_1299002088.shtml (accessed 6/1/22).

55. BBC Radio 4 with Richard Ingrams, John Wells, Patricia Routledge and John Sessions in the first of several series starting 18 March 1989.

56. McCall (1991); http://www.screenonline.org.uk/tv/id/725039/index.html (accessed 12/1/22).

57. http://www.screenonline.org.uk/tv/id/1377417/index.html (accessed 12/1/22).

58. *Aleebee* Season 4 programme 1 February 1 1982 (available on Amazon).

59. https://m.imdb.com.leagueofgentlemen (1999–2017).

60. https://m.imdb.com.insideno9 (2014–).

61. The Spanish Inquisition, Series 2 Episode 2, first broadcast 22 September 1971 for the text https://www.ibras.dk/montypython/episode15.htm (accessed 10/1/22).

62. Core Blimey! Bring on the Red-Bearded Dwarves Daily Mail online 08 February 2008 – a rant about someone prosecuted for throwing an apple core from her car - https://www.dailymail.co.uk/debate/article-512959/Core-Blimey-Bring-Red-Bearded-Dwarves.html (accessed 6/1/22) – the charges were dropped; Mr Justice Cocklecarott and the Elf 'n' Safety Smurfs who had to escort 12 jurors across the road; Daily Mail 7 May 2012 – where a judge instructed a jury to cross at the traffic lights. This was seized on by far right commentator Richard Littlejohn as an example of health and safety gone mad" – a recurring libertarian theme in the Daily Mail. https://www.dailymail.co.uk/debate/article-2140946/Mr-Justice-Cocklecarrot-Elf-n-Safety-Smurfs-escort-12-jurors-road.html (accessed 6/1/22).

63. https://www.theguardian.com/news/2006/oct/10/guardianobituaries.law (accessed 6/1/22).

64. http://news.bbc.co.uk/1/hi/uk/3706939.stm 12 May 2004 (accessed 6/1/22).

65. https://jollycontrarian.com/index.php?title=Jolly_Contrarian%E2%80%99s_Law_Reports – 65 cases at the time of writing – last updated in 2022 (accessed 1/4/24).

66. Mathew (1959) at p. vi.

67. Loc cit at p. v.

68. See Appendix 1 for an example of one of Mathew's Forensic Fables.

69. Mathew (1959) Forensic Fables – The Elderly Junior and the Lady Pupil (at p. 26); The Sarcastic Counsel and Mr MacIntosh, the Money Lender (at p. 68); The Kindly Judge and the Lady Barrister (at p. 100).

70. E.g., Pratt v Pratt & Mugg (divorce laws); Chicken v Ham (costs of litigation); Haddock v Thwale (motor accidents); Sparrow v Pipp (precedent).

71. See Appendix 2 for full personal précis.

72. The Daily Express (163k) is one of 5 major national tabloid newspapers in Britain – The Sun (1.2m), Daily Mail (745k) Daily Mirror (258k), Daily Star (146k) – daily circulations.

73. Daily Express Saturday 15/4/23 – spoof of the Stormy Daniels $130,000 payoff by former TV show host Donald Trump.

Chapter 2

Henry Cecil

INTRODUCTION

Henry Cecil was a lawyer who took to writing comic legal stories shortly after the Second World War. He was involved as a barrister in the interwar years and went on to practice until he took up a position on the Bench between 1949 and 1968. Roderic Jeffries, practised as a barrister between 1953 and 1955. He did, however, use his experience of qualifying and practising as a barrister to produce a trilogy of comic legal novels. John Budd was a Blackpool solicitor who wrote 10 novels dealing with legal practice in a humorous way too. Both are discussed in Chapter 3. The dominant figure in this field, during the 30 years after the Second World War, was, however, Henry Cecil with a string of novels and short stories.

BACKGROUND

Henry Cecil Leon was a full-time practising lawyer throughout his whole professional life working in the English courts from his calling in 1924 until his retirement in 1968. This was interrupted by his service in the Army between 1939 and 1945 where he was awarded the Military Cross at the Battle of Alamein in 1942.[1] He became a County Court judge in 1949. He also had what he described as his "second string"[2] as an author and wrote not only works of fiction but also non-fiction, all under the pen name "Henry Cecil." Those currently publicising his work online indicate how his work emerged

> He wrote during the three-week-long family holidays which were usually spent in comfortable hotels in Britain. He would sit in a deck chair in a sunny garden,

exercise book on lap and pen in hand, writing from 10 am to 1 pm, then again from 2.30 to 4 pm each day. His writing career is attributed to his Second World War experiences. Sailing around the Cape on a "dry" troop ship on the way to Cairo, the colonel asked his adjutant (Cecil) to tell stories to keep the officers' minds off alcohol. The stories were so popular that they became a regular feature, and formed the basis of his first collection, "Full Circle," published in 1948. Thereafter, the legal year, his impressions at court, or at other official functions, as well as dinners at the Savoy Grill or at his club, the Garrick, all provided material for his considerable brain power.[3]

THE GOALS OF HENRY CECIL

Henry Cecil's work was conceived by him as a way of continuing his love of writing and to fill up the time as he was feeling "utterly miserable" after his first wife, Lettice died in her mid-40s.[4] He was keenly aware of the deficiencies of the legal system which he described. In the more than a quarter century, during which he wrote his 28 works of fiction and 7 nonfiction works he was conscious of the ability of fiction to educate as well as entertain. Although he has been promoted principally as a man who wrote "comedies of criminal life (which were) ingenious, sprightly and immensely amusing"[5] this was not really how he saw himself. He used his literary skills to provide a forum for modest discussions of legal issues. His style was to halt the narrative arc of the story in question and address the audience with authority on a particular issue. It is from these asides to the audience that the views and perspectives of Cecil are principally drawn. It is only on a few occasions that we find Cecil utilising an "everyman" character to embody a "common sense" perspective.

CECIL'S NONFICTION

Henry Cecil also expressed his views in a range of nonfiction works which are worth briefly mentioning as they shed some light on his attachment to the *status quo* in general. His first foray into nonfiction was a guide to the Bar in 1958, *Brief to Counsel*.[6] This was a book which dealt with what a barrister should know about his professional task as opposed to legal doctrine. It ranged over the qualities required of a successful advocate as well as career prospects and brought in how barristers' training operated. The "hit and miss" element of this process in the 1950s which Cecil deals with became a subtheme in his first fictional commercial success *Brothers in Law*[7] – a "laugh filled legal diversion" according to the dust jacket. *Brief to Counsel* explains rather more prosaically the complex relationships between pupils, masters, clerks and solicitors. The perennial lay question "What do you do when you know your client is guilty?" is also addressed,[8] as well as issues like women at the Bar[9] and barristers' behaviour. [10] An examination of broader issues in the justice system followed in *Not Such an Ass* in 1961. As the title indicates this is a defence of areas where lawyers and their practices were criticised in the work of writers like Harvey[11] and later DN Pritt.[12] Cecil provides an explanation of such things as costs in civil cases, delays in the law and imprisonment for debt. Cecil is no radical. He takes as axiomatic the need, for instance, for lawyers to be well paid to ensure there can be justice. The *status quo* is seldom in jeopardy when Cecil examines an issue like judge-made law, although he recognises the need for a cheap way of dealing with "test" cases.[13]

He went on to write a history of judicial corruption over the ages entitled *Tipping the Scales* on how judicial integrity in England had been "painfully achieved."[14] He also presented the prestigious Hamlyn lectures in 1970 following in the footsteps of such legal heavyweights as Lord Denning and Lord Kilbrandon.[15] His topic, *The English Judge*, involved an empirical study of the background of the judiciary undertaken by Cecil as well as an examination of their image. Given the critiques of the profession found in the 1960s by Abel-Smith and Stevens[16] and Michael Zander,[17] and the author's years as a judge, the defensive tone and assurance that the system was working pretty well is not perhaps surprising.[18]

He also wrote on the subject of the great Stock Exchange Fraud of 1814. This centred on news in February 1814 that the French had been defeated and that Napoleon was dead. Government Bond prices briefly spiked before falling back to their previous levels. A six-man syndicate made a killing. The membership included the naval hero Lord Cochrane. He and his fellow members were charged and found guilty of fraud. Stripped of his knighthood and expelled from the House of Commons, Cochrane also spent a year in jail. He was pardoned in 1832 and his knighthood returned. Compensation was in due course paid to his descendants following a Report of a Commons Select Committee. In his 1965 offering *A Matter of Speculation*, Cecil concluded that the evidence against Lord Cochrane was entirely justified and that only his naval record and the persistence of his protestations of innocence had created doubt.[19] There was additional evidence available to later writers examining Cochrane's career but their opinions differ. Richard Dale regards the evidence extraneous to the trial as making clear that Cochrane manipulated and misrepresented evidence and sides with Cecil's "guilty."[20] The other, David Cordingly, proclaims his belief in Cochrane's innocence reaching his verdict after consulting the views of a distinguished judge on the evidence presented at the trial.[21]

Henry Cecil provided a couple of introductions to English law aimed at those who were considering a career in the profession entitled *Know About English Law* in 1965 and a revised version in 1974 renamed *Learn About English Law*. These contain a guide to how we need law and where it comes from. It is aimed, presumably, at a youthful audience. It explains in simple language the personnel of the law and the court system focusing on criminal justice as well as debt. Of interest is one of the 14 illustrations by Edward Ardizzone of various court stages includes a female barrister in full flood.[22] It is the only indications in either volume of women having a role in the justice system.

His final forays into non-fiction work included another re-examination of the case of a man hanged for the murder of a woman in Manchester by means of a hammer attack. The defence relied on the fact that another man, David Ware, had confessed to the murder. This confession was later retracted, and the accused Walter Rowland was hanged in 1947. In 1951, David Ware was charged with attempted murder after attacking a woman – with a hammer. He was deemed criminally insane. In *The Trial of Walter Rowland* Cecil, nonetheless, concludes that there was no miscarriage of justice. His autobiography, *Just Within the Law,* was published in January 1975 and some 17 months later, on 23 May 1976, Cecil died. As is noted below, this is a surprisingly truncated account of what was a fascinating life for a barrister from a modest background. In the account of the themes which intrigued Judge Leon below, the autobiography provides rather limited insights into his sociopolitical views. These are encountered in some of his work for newspapers which also provide an interesting support for the notion that his fiction did indeed have a strong informational thrust.

THE WAXING AND WANING OF POPULARITY

There were several phases in the publishing career of Henry Cecil. In the first phase his books achieved only modest sales in hardback – *Full Circle* (1949), *The Painswick Line* (1951), *No Bail for the Judge* (1952), *Ways and Means* (1952), *Natural Causes* (1953) and *According to the Evidence* (1954). This period included his work being published in paperback by Pan who were a cheaper "downmarket" rival to the dominant Penguin brand. Thus, we find here both *No Bail for the Judge* and surprisingly *Full Circle* with much more lurid covers than is found in the jovial 1960s Penguin artwork from *Daily Mail* cartoonist Kenneth Mahood.

The next phase saw his work progress from the printed word to the theatre, cinema, radio and television. The success of the 1957 film version and then the 1961 TV series of *Brothers in Law* with Richard Briers – subsequently to become a "national treasure"[23] – as the hapless young barrister Roger Thursby led to a much greater level of commercial success for his next books. There were also radio spinoffs of *Brothers in Law* for three series and 39 episodes.[24] The Roger Thursby trilogy's success, completed by *Friends at Court* (1956) and *Sober as a Judge* (1958), led to a further three of the early novels being re-published in paperback by Penguin and significant sales.[25] *According to the Evidence* (1954), *Much in Evidence* (1957), *Settled Out of Court* (1959) and *Alibi for a Judge* (1960) fall into this category with them coming out in paperback between 1962 and 1964.[26] Henry Cecil continued to produce works throughout the 1960s and 1970s until his death, all with Michael Joseph. They appeared in paperback with Penguin until 1968 when there was a shift to Sphere.

The next surge of publishing interest did not come until 1991 when three of the novels were published by International Polygonics of New York as part of their Legal Diversion series. These Crime Classics covered reprints of such authors as Ellery Queen and PG Wodehouse. Finally, in 2000 the whole of the fictional works of Henry Cecil were reprinted in a new edition by the London-based publisher, House of Stratus. They specialise in reprinting works that are no longer available but were once in vogue. Their list includes writers popular in the inter-War period through to the 1960s such as Leslie Charteris, Dornford Yates and HC McNeile (Sapper).[27]

Although Cecil may have a relatively low profile for readers in the 21st century with his work absent from bookshops and libraries, this chapter examines the full range of his work spanning as it did almost thirty years from 1948 to 1977 and covering a period of major social change. This chapter looks at both the substance as well as the style of his work and in the concluding chapter I seek to relate it to the stream of comic legal fiction in which he operated and which, to some extent, he seemed to have inspired. David Kynaston draws a telling portrait of the world when Cecil commenced his writing as being one with major differences from the world when his final novels were published in the mid-1970s.

> Britain in 1945. No supermarkets. No motorways, no teabags, no sliced bread, no frozen food, no flavoured crisps, no lager, no microwaves, dishwashers, no Formica, no vinyl, no CDs, no computers, no mobiles, no duvets, no pill, no trainers, no Hoodies, no Starbucks. Four Indian restaurants. Shops on every corner, pubs on every corner, cinemas in every High Street, red telephone boxes, Lyons corner house, trams, trolleybuses, Steam trains, Woodbines, Craven A, Senior Service, smoke, smoke, Vape X inhalant. No launderettes, no automatic washing machines, wash day every Monday, clothes boiled in a tub, scrubbed on the draining board, rinsed in the sink, put through a mango, hung out to dry. Central heating rare, Coke boilers, water cases, the coal fire, the hearth, the

> home, children's colds common. Abortion illegal, homosexual relationships illegal, suicide illegal, capital punishment legal. White faces everywhere. Back to backs, narrow cobbled streets, Victorian terraces, no high-rises.[28]

Originally dismissed rather cavalierly by myself as producing works involving only "slapstick routines and broad characters,"[29] closer reading, as ever, reveals rather more. There are many indications throughout Cecil's work, both fiction and non-fiction, that Cecil always retained a strong pedagogic strain. Whilst the book covers of his original works and the various reprints may indicate a "legal PG Wodehouse" between the covers, the central themes of some of Cecil's work cover such serious matters as vigilantism and murder. In addition, Cecil frequently takes the opportunity to editorialise on the ills or good points of the English justice system. Whilst I would not want to suggest that a comprehensive and rounded legal education can be obtained from the novels of Henry Cecil, it is not going too far to say that an "insider" version of some of the major controversies, stresses and strains of legal practice of this era in England can be divined from such reading. These include the problematic nature of legal education, the fallibility of the jury system, the prejudices of judges and the impact of gender in legal circles. Some crucial issues like race, class inequality and sexual preference are, however, almost entirely missing. Looking at the themes which recur with other writers in this genre of light legal fiction allows a richer perspective. A start in the process of assessing the extent to which the long-running perspective from Cecil provides a partial and limited view of the justice system can be achieved by examining his work thematically in some depth.

THE WORLD VIEW OF HENRY CECIL

Ethics and the Lawyer

Henry Cecil starts off in his 1948 short story collection with a fairly "relaxed" view on ethical standards by having a number of his protagonists involved in making choices which are far from ethical. These include his central character using his expertise to become a "fixer" of alibis for criminals and proceeds to use his "skills" to engineer a murder to serve his own romantic interests.[30] Another sees a magistrate losing his position and ending up as a vagrant as a result of his kindly action.[31] Yet another, on the theme of dreams, reveals the self-serving nature of the career path of a successful Q.C. resulting in him *not* turning over a new leaf and becoming a better person.[32] Cecil is prepared to accept that the ethical standards at the Bar are not always of the highest. Such occasions are very much the exception as he makes clear in the middle of a tale about blackmail:

> The temptation to which (barristers) succumb very occasionally is to behave improperly in the course of an action. Such improprieties are nearly always due to misplaced enthusiasm on behalf of a client. Either judgment becomes warped or there is a lack of appreciation of what is demanded of an advocate or there is a deliberate yielding to the temptation to win a case . . . there have been rare instances of surprising behaviour by well-known barristers who would have been expected to know better [33]

We are given no clues as to who these mountebanks are. Solicitors are another matter. As noted elsewhere,[34] in the United Kingdom the legal profession is divided into a branch who undertake litigation only – barristers and one which is principally office-based – solicitors. Although, some of the latter do appear in the lower courts. Judges were traditionally drawn only from the barristers' branch while solicitors were regarded as the "lower branch" of the legal profession. In an early work Cecil devotes a couple of chapters to how unscrupulous firms of solicitors can "pad" their bills by adding motions and court appearances (and hence costs payable by the client) to a dispute – as well as accept specious cases. He bemoans this and suggests

> There should be some simple means of making solicitors themselves pay for frolics of this kind but there is not.[35]

The lower branch is subject to further negative comment in relation to their propensity to delay.

> It is, of course, necessary that the lists of cases should not be allowed to get into disorder by too many applications for adjournments. As, however, solicitors are officers of the court there should be little difficulty in making them behave themselves properly without prejudicing the litigants, who, after all, are the people to be mainly considered in Courts of Justice.[36]

He accepts that not everyone shares this rosy view of lawyers and centres one whole book on a notorious hater of lawyers, Major Claude Buttonstep whose family had in the past been brought to financial ruin through court cases. The Major "supported to the full the common but erroneous idea that the lawyers have no regard for the truth whatsoever."[37] Buttonstep had a clear view of the dispensability of lawyers

> The architect leaves you with the house, the accountant with a balance sheet, the doctor with a new tummy: all the lawyer leaves you with is a bill of costs. They're parasites.[38]

In his later work, he focuses, as we will see, on specific areas where ethical conflicts emerge such as the problem of the "guilty client," which is taken up next.

The "Guilty" Client

This is, of course a matter which is a persistent theme for the writers examined as it is the most frequently posed question of non-lawyers – how do lawyers deal with "knowing their clients are lying"? Cecil suggests at one point that there is no bar on putting forward your client's case without having to believe in it. As he puts it "hardly anyone would be defended if his lawyer had to believe in his innocence. [39]

More expansively in one of books from the early 1970s, he has his "everyman," Judge Henry Winthrup, expatiate on the notion of the "guilty client":

> "You can't know a man is innocent," said the judge, "unless you've committed the crime yourself and you knew that he had nothing to do with it. People are always using the word 'know' and they really mean 'believe'. When I was a barrister I was often asked: "What do you do when you know your client is guilty?" "Well, you can only know he's guilty if either he tells you he's guilty or if you see him commit the crime."[40]

He confirms this point in relation to civil litigation directly a couple of years later in an aside to the reader.

> contrary to what many members of the public think, a normal lawyer, whether counsel or solicitor, always prefers to advise settlement of a difficult case than to let his client take the risk of an expensive defeat. [41]

Anyone reading Cecil's work, then, is left in no doubt as to the position on the "I know my client is guilty" notion. There is no such thing and the title of Alex McBride's account of legal practice – *Defending the Guilty* – in the 21st century would have caused him serious disquiet.[42]

The Legal Profession and Some Shortcomings

Cecil is more than happy to interrupt his various tales to provide thoughts to the reader on any topic on which he feels strongly. He does not do this, however, through a discussion between any of his protagonists. One example involves his most serious case where, in a change from his minor civil disputes and petty crimes he is dealing with a murder case. In the middle of a tale about a judge accused of this most serious of crimes, Cecil breaks off to pay tribute to his fellow barristers:

> There is probably no profession where there is a greater friendliness between its members. At all legal gatherings judges and barristers mix on terms of easy familiarity and between [contemporary] Christian names are the order of the day. So when Benchers are together, views and confidences are exchanged with complete freedom.[43]

This echoes, almost to the letter his view of the Bar expressed in his 1975 autobiography.[44]

In a similar vein, in a 1967 story about a woman seeking to engineer a divorce with doubtful evidence,[45] he takes the opportunity to give his views on the rule that Senior Counsel must be accompanied by a Junior and the cost implications.

> There is at the present moment a move in some quarters to try to alter the rule by which a Q.C. must normally have a junior in every Court case. Of course it could be done. If it were, some cases would be done more cheaply and quite as well. Some cases would be wrecked at no less expense than if two counsel had been employed, while the bulk of cases would be done rather more cheaply and rather more efficiently. In the end the public will get the service it wants. If it wants the best service, it must pay for it. If it is satisfied with a workable, second-rate service it need not pay as much. The legal world will not come to an end, nor will judges, barristers and solicitors go on strike, if the movement towards lower cost and less efficiency is successful, but it will simply mean that our inevitably imperfect justice will become rather more imperfect. [46]

This two-thirds rule, in fact, was duly abolished in 1977, although Abel noted that it had little immediate effect.[47] Cecil's, perhaps understandable adherence to the "old ways" and innate conservatism also involves a touching faith in the meritocratic possibilities of the Bar. He suggested that to get on in law required only hard work. Apropos of nothing in particular, in a tale of revenge for murder, he addresses the questionable strategy of one woman who

> was very anxious for (her husband) to become a judge in due course, and she complained to him from time to time that he did not attend legal gatherings enough. She believed – quite wrongly – that, by associating regularly with the right people, (her husband) would increase his chance of promotion to the Bench. [48]

In a similar somewhat facetious vein, and not from personal experience, he took time out in a story centred around a serial blackmailer, to note that whilst it was "difficult to get on at the Bar"

> once a person who has the ability to succeed is established in prosperous chambers, he has only minor matters to worry about; such as seeing his wife and

children, getting enough sleep and indulging in any of those hobbies in which men in almost every walk of life (except that of the successful barrister) are able to indulge."[49]

Solicitors, as already noted, are on the receiving end of a good deal of criticism from the barrister Cecil. He resents the fact that solicitors who take competent counsel's opinion are protected against the risk of an action for negligence and notes that "it is a great temptation to a solicitor to avoid that risk where there is the least uncertainty about the answer to a legal problem, and quite often when there is not."[50] That said, the life a solicitor is described as far from thrilling by one solicitor speaking to two young women contemplating careers in law.

> The stories he told them about a country solicitor's life were not particularly exciting. . . . He never had any murder cases or anything of that sort; the only crimes he told them about were cases of no rear lamps on bicycles or, occasionally, chicken stealing. Alternatively, he told them about wills and leases and matters of that kind.[51]

Cecil's tongue-in-cheek assessment of the "lower branch" also appears within a sensitive exploration of a child custody dispute.

> We're the lower branch, you know. Very humble. But between you and me I don't know what we've got to be humble about. Our exams are harder and cover much wider ground. We usually spend five years in getting qualified, while a barrister spends only three. And, more important than that, we know something about the job before we qualified, while a barrister knows nothing. He learns it afterward. But the law's a funny thing.[52]

He does though recognise that solicitors have their uses. In a modest proportion of cases which are litigated they play a role of value. He breaks off from a divorce case conflict to reveal:

> Seventy-five per cent of cases would be decided in the same way by any judge, however good the advocacy on one side and however bad on the other. But twenty-five per cent is a considerable proportion and, if one in four cases can go wrong when it ought to go right, a great deal depends upon the knowledge, experience and ability of the solicitor in charge. . . . The non-lawyer might be forgiven for complaining that, if one out of four cases may be decided in the wrong way, it is not justice. Who said it was? Mankind can only aim at justice and, being fallible, must of necessity miss the mark from time to time.[53]

Cecil wrote, as noted, in a number of non-fiction locations advice to budding advocates.[54] Throughout his fiction, as well, he is more than happy to give advice on what skills are required by a good advocate. In a tale about the problems that would arise if people were kind to each other and conflict ebbed away, he opines thus:

> A trained advocate knows that if his client is in the right, he should not start his address to the judge or the jury by saying what a good case he has, but should build it up slowly, bit by bit, until it appears to be a very strong case from the facts which he has outlined. If a young barrister started his speech to a bad-tempered judge by saying that he felt sure his Lordship would have no difficulty in finding in favour of the plaintiff, without first telling him what the case was about, he would find if he did not actually lose a certain winner, he might only scrape home with some difficulty.[55]

He also advises on broader tactics in relation to the pros and cons of using a Magistrate's Court hearing to assess the credibility of likely witnesses in a story centred on the fallibility of such witnesses. As noted elsewhere,[56] magistrates have a role in determining whether there is a prima facie to answer and, if it is outwith their own powers, they can commit a defendant for trial to a higher court.

> That's a mistake some counsel make. They try to break up the witnesses in the Magistrate's Court and in some cases may do it pretty well. But the result is that, when the fellow's cross-examined at the trial, he's ready for it all. And it's amazing how telling points can be blunted or even eliminated in this way.[57]

The Justice System in Practice

Henry Cecil exhibited a strong faith in the operation of the justice system and was happy to explain how it worked in pre-Crown Prosecution Service days in a light tale of blackmail

> the authorities . . . consider first and foremost what evidence there is that a crime has been committed. If there is no reasonable evidence to lay before a magistrate or jury, then no prosecution will be undertaken, and if complaint were made in the House of Commons the Attorney General would explain that no case could be made out . . . if there is evidence to sustain a conviction the next question normally considered is whether a conviction is likely to be obtained upon that evidence. It is in the cases where the chances of securing a conviction are either small or no more than even that the difficulty arises. In such cases both the public good and the rights of the individual have to be considered most carefully.[58]

There is an interesting internal conflict in the outlook of Cecil on the operation of the justice system. In the later world of Cecil, miscarriages of justice simply do not occur in the view of a mysterious newcomer in a tale of middle-class paranoia and suspicion:

> We try to make it impossible to convict the innocent. In order to do that we have to make the meshes of the net so wide that a lot of guilty fish can swim out. This is most unfair on the public, but personally I've never been able to see an alternative. . . . The only way in which a respectable person ever runs the risk of being charged with a crime with which he'd nothing to do is if someone with a grievance against him tells lies about him or plants evidence on him.[59]

Well, hardly ever, as he observes in a tale centred on the ploys of a wife to clear her husband's name of a bank robbery by enlisting the assistance of the judge who tried the case

> Many people are rather sceptical of alibis and, indeed, some cynics say that they are never genuine. They argue that, if the accused really was somewhere else at the time when the crime was committed, he would never have been charged with it. But this implies that no innocent person is ever charged with a crime, and though it is a very rare occurrence, it does occasionally happen.[60]

Why the system works so well is, however, a bit of a mystery since Cecil himself, took a highly sceptical view of the reliability of witnesses. Cecil tells us directly, based, presumably on his own experience, in an otherwise dystopian account of a trouble-free world of harmony:

> I know that 9 out of 10 witnesses who honestly think that they've seen exactly how an accident happened, have simply heard a bang and looked up.[61]

The same thinking is revealed a year later in the judge's account of a trial about a traffic accident with conflicting stories from the parties involved and their independent witnesses. He notes:

> In fact what all those independent gentleman had seen was the resultant crash. They had heard a bang and looked up. But by the time they came into the court they had seen everything from start to finish.[62]

Cecil notes also that perjury is an issue for the justice system in a story about a motoring accident and resultant damages actions

> The offence of perjury strikes at the root of justice. But, in my opinion, many lawyers and laymen do not treat it seriously enough. . . . The amount of perjury

> committed in criminal trials is tremendous. Every day men and women are swearing what they know to be false. But prosecutions after a conviction or an acquittal of a man who has committed perjury in the witness box are extremely rare. . . . But while the solution in criminal trials is admittedly very difficult to find, that is no reason at all why in civil cases, when no man's liberty is involved, the danger of a man being charged with perjury should not be much greater.[63]

Writing at a time when capital punishment was still operating Cecil does raise a slight warning that all is not well with the justice system at all times in his comments on the appeal process in his account, mentioned above, of a judge seeking to discover whether his conduct may have caused a miscarriage of justice:

> An appeal can only be made to the House of Lords on a criminal matter if the Attorney General certifies that an exceptionally important point of law is involved and that it is in the public interest that an appeal should be brought. In a civil matter it is enough to get leave from the Court of Appeal or from the House of Lords itself, if either Court think that the justice of the case makes a further appeal reasonable. No important point of law need be involved. But, if the question is whether you should be hanged or sent to prison for life, only the Attorney General can send you to the House of Lords, and even he can't do so unless your case involves an exceptionally important point of law. This looks almost as though pure law is considered more important than life and liberty.[64]

There is a sense of fatalism in one of his pronouncements in his late middle period on the quest for justice. His message to reformers in a divorce story is somewhat bleak:

> Human justice will never be perfect even with the use of law reformers, ombudsmen and computers; even if you fuse the professions of solicitor and barrister; even if Parliamentary draftsmen are compelled to write in simple, intelligible English; even if judges have less holidays. Whatever improvements may be made, there will always be some injustice.[65]

Justice for the Poor

In the early novels the issue of moving away from the hit and miss operation of the Poor's Roll and providing statutory legal assistance cropped up in a story about the "black sheep" of a family reverting to type. Legal aid is noted as a welcome development being addressed by Parliament.

> As the years go on, more and more is done to assist impecunious litigants, and from the speeches made in Parliament by the large number of members of the

> Bar who, for one reason or another, take to a political career, it would seem that everything necessary is done to ensure that a man charged with a crime shall have adequate representation on his trial, however poor he may be.[66]

Cecil was, however, sceptical about the likely quality of the traditional form of assistance by way of the dock brief. Here an accused was entitled for a small fee to select representation from those barristers sitting in court who were free [67]

> Representation he can have – but adequate representation is another thing . . . counsel walk out – leaving behind them the following classes of counsel: (1) those who are already engaged on a case and can successfully plead this as an excuse for not accepting a dock brief; (2) those who are young and inexperienced and want a prisoner to practice on: (3) those who have failed at the Bar, and whose only work consists in dock briefs and "soup". "Soup" is the expression used for easy briefs for the prosecution, which are ladled out in rotation to members of a Bar mess.[68]

In later years one of Cecil's legal actors seems to have recognised the benefits of the system, albeit noting that others were excluded from litigation

> Legal aid is very useful and it's enabled a lot of people to be properly represented when otherwise they couldn't have been. But they are all people with low incomes and practically no capital. The rich and the poor are all right. It's the wretched man in the middle who gets into difficulties and the costs of litigation are no joke.[69]

He was not, however, necessarily always sympathetic to those whom he considers to be of the "lower orders," judging from this outburst in a tale of murder and sexual assault.

> It was one of those cases where the parties concerned were not far removed from the lower animals and were nothing like as pleasant as most dogs and most horses and some cats.[70]

To be fair, he is equally dismissive of those with money to burn in a light-hearted romp about a couple of rogues engineering a specious defamation action:

> They look upon it like the Archer-Shee case and don't mind what it costs them. The Archer-Shee case? Oh yes – you mean the case where a man called Rattigan appeared in some capacity. But there's nothing I can do. If they choose to make fools of themselves and ruin themselves into the bargain, that's not my fault [71]

Police, Prisons, and Prison Policy

As one would expect, perhaps, Henry Cecil has little problem with the police, other than the perennial complaint of their relative scarcity.[72] Although most of the views of Cecil are direct from the author, he does, one feels find a voice in Judge Ward in one of his later novels with an unusual critique based on the police's lack of intelligence. Talking to one of his neighbours, the judge, who lives in the village, which has welcomed an apparently respectable newcomer, explains

> On the whole the police are very good fellows, there is very little corruption among them and most of them are striving to do a very difficult job as well as they can. But unfortunately quite a number of them haven't a high enough standard of intelligence. So if you ask me what I would do if I were in authority the answer's quite simple. I should double the pay and raise the standard of entry. The Police Force would compete with the other Services and with the professions and other occupations for young men and women of good physique and a reasonably high standard of intelligence for entrants.[73]

He persists with this approach a couple of years later again through another fictional judge and makes explicit exactly with whom the recruiters should be competing. Here in another piece about blackmail his retired judge takes the view

> the great majority of policemen were people of integrity. But what they lacked on the whole was brain-power . . . (he) would have liked to see the present pay of the police doubled and the standard of entry made much more difficult. The police should compete for candidates with the Bar, solicitors, accountants, surveyors and businesses of all kinds.[74]

Prisons attract the harshest words for any aspect of the legal structure with Cecil lambasting politicians for their pusillanimity. This critique, in various forms, is a theme from his work in the early 1950s up until his final novels, as we shall see. In a narrative centred on a man seeking to remain in jail to avoid retribution from those whom he has cheated, he takes the opportunity to vent his views on prison.

> Albany is in one respect the latest disgrace in English prisons. It is a new prison but unlike its celebrated namesake in Piccadilly, it has no proper lavatories for the people for whom it was built, the prisoners. The disgusting slopping-out system still continues there. The Home Office and each successive Government appear to be determined that those who are convicted of crime shall not merely be punished, but degraded. . . . Unfortunately prison reform is not valuable from the party political point of view. The public at large does not much care what

> happens to prisoners inside prisons so long as they are not beaten up. And the continuation of the slopping-out system in Albany coupled with the failure to introduce the necessary legislation to get rid of the old prisons suggests that there is insufficient enlightenment amongst those in authority.[75]

The position of those on remand also attracted robust direct criticism somewhat oddly in a narrative about murder and sexual assault:

> It is not, however, in the public interest that the accused should be as uncomfortable as he is while awaiting trial. The manpower shortage and the acute lack of sufficient prison accommodation at present makes impossible any serious improvement of the position of a person awaiting trial in custody, but is to be hoped that the improvement of his position does find a place on the list of things to be done when the more urgent problems have been solved.[76]

The degrading nature of the whole system of incarceration is also expressed in vigorous terms through the mouth of a serial confidence trickster:

> He is taken from the dock to a cell below where he will be locked up. He has already been searched but he will be searched again to be sure he's not got any means of committing suicide. He will then be handcuffed to another prisoner and taken to the local prison. This may be several hours after he has been sentenced. Only if he is very lucky will he get a meal or even a cup of tea before he reaches the prison. On arrival at the prison he will be lined up with many others to wait the Reception procedure. He may be locked in a small room or box about four foot square to await this procedure. . . . Probably he will be locked in a cell with one or two others who may well have physical habits which he finds unacceptable and whose mental processes may differ greatly from what he is used to. The next morning he will be woken up at about six-thirty a.m. by a bell ringing on the landing. He will be expected to get up at once, wash in cold water, dress and make his bed. In due course he will take part in slopping out. For this purpose the cell will be unlocked and with all the other prisoners he will carry out his chamber pot.[77]

The same level of outrage is found in Cecil's final novel about a man who goes missing for years but reappears as if nothing had happened. A withering assessment is also provided by one of Cecil's jurors:

> To be deprived of one's liberty is a terrible thing in any event, but to be deprived of it in one of our prisons is quite appalling. You spend most of your time locked up in a cell, if you're lucky by yourself if you're unlucky with two wholly incompatible people. In many prisons there are still the most rudimentary sanitary arrangements. There is very little exercise and very little work. And when

> people use the expression "rotting away in prison" it doesn't seem to me at all too strong a phrase to use.[78]

He also adverts to the inherent danger of prison through the mouth of the errant husband:

> (prison) . . . is the one place where you're not safe at all. First of all, they know exactly where you are. Or, if your prison is changed, they can soon find out. And, unless you choose to ask for solitary confinement for the whole of your sentence, you haven't a hope of avoiding having your throat slit or your head bashed in. There are plenty of long-termers who are prepared to murder their fellow prisoners for a sufficient consideration.[79]

Miscarriages of Justice

The critical approach to the legal education and training and the operation of the legal system in the 1960s was not limited to journalists and scholars but also encountered within the profession. The trenchant polemic *Law Reform Now*, edited by Gerald Gardiner and Andrew Martin, drew attention to a range of issues in need of modification.[80] The prominent lawyers involved came from the same background and training as Henry Cecil but saw the world in a rather different way. Taken along with indirect critiques of the operation of the justice system revealed in various books on its operation throughout the 1960s and 1970s and a very different and less comfortable picture of the legal profession emerges.[81] In some instances the failure of the system seems to amount to a clear miscarriage of justice.[82] Sometimes biased and unsavoury "villains" like Lord Goddard are revealed.[83] The major culprit as a purveyor of injustice as Lord Chief Justice for Henry Cecil was not, however, Lord Goddard but Gordon Hewart. His critique when he was sitting as a member of the judiciary was slightly oblique. but there is clarification when we look at Cecil's autobiography and his post-retirement comments

> The last chance is what most criminals get when they appeal to the Court of Criminal Appeal . . . the Court of Criminal Appeal is their final fling. And in the bad old days of that Court, it was not much a fling.[84]

He went on to explain why the Court of Criminal Appeal was so flawed in the past

> Lord Chief Justice X . . . was a first-class example of the danger of making a man Lord Chief Justice until he has proved himself as a judge. It is an example which, it is hoped by many, will be remembered for ever . . . it was some time

> before the Court became what it is now, a Court for *hearing* as well as determining appeals.[85]

This seems to be, from its personal tone a reference to LCJs Cecil would have known – either Lord Hewart or Goddard. Gordon Hewart never sat as a judge before choosing to be become LCJ from being Attorney General in Lloyd George's Cabinet in 1922 at a time when the Attorney General had by tradition first right of refusal of the post. The highly controversial Lord Goddard sat as a judge from 1932 in the High Court, Court of Appeal and House of Lords before becoming LCJ in 1946 so does not readily fit the bill. In his 1975 autobiography Cecil clearly indicates that it was Hewart he had in mind whom he castigates as "a shockingly bad judge."[86] He was much more appreciative of Goddard – " a great Lord Chief Justice"[87] whilst, at the same time noting his technical shortcomings in the instructions he gave as to the meaning of "beyond reasonable doubt."[88]

As far as interference with the justice system it does make an appearance in the Cecil canon through characters both in the early work, middle period and at the end of his writing. In 1957 he opined through a less than reputable fraudster, Mr Richmond "It's terrible not to be believed. That's why innocent people have been convicted in the past – because no one would believe them."[89] In one rare instance he blames a policeman but with mitigating circumstances. He notes that the natural father of the child at the centre of an adoption dispute was in prison having been convicted of sexual assault and manslaughter of a small boy "due to evidence planted by a policeman whose judgment has been affected by his own son having once been frightened by a man."[90] One of his characters in his final novel makes the *prima facie* reasonable point that innocent victims should include the falsely accused.

> People are always talking about innocent victims. Girls who are raped, banks which are robbed and old ladies who are mugged and so on. But who are the real innocent victims? They are the raper (*sic*) who didn't, the robber who wasn't there and the mugger who didn't mug.[91]

This process, though, of somewhat dubious equivalence of victim and falsely accused is undermined as the character goes further. The speaker, Rosemary Clinch, of the Citizens' Protection Association, steps over the line into dangerous territory, when she goes on to suggest that "as a matter of fact, half the cases of rape aren't rape at all. The girls simply love it."[92]

Quite why Rosemary Clinch associates herself with this warped and specious perspective on rape is not revealed in this, the last and, to be fair, least convincing of Cecil's books.

Reforms of the Rules

Cecil does not always limit himself to defending aspects of the status quo or highlighting deficiencies in a general way. He does address issues of the day from time to time. For instance, the whole question of replacing litigation for accidents with some kind of insurance system as was encountered in New Zealand and which had been advocated by Jackson [93] found favour in Cecil's writings. Early on we find Roger Thursby, in his role as a judge, voicing such a view:

> Roger had formed the view that, in cases of personal injury, National Insurance should replace the present hit-and-miss form of judicial enquiry.[94]

Cecil much later dismissed the trial process as effectively a lottery in his tale about a conflict free society:

> Insofar as accident cases can be properly tried – and there's a great deal to be said for the toss of a coin being just as good a method and very much cheaper [95]

There was, though, as an alternative, he went on to suggest:

> Accident cases are, of course, in a class by themselves. They ought to be abolished and replaced by National Insurance. This has already been suggested more than once. It would relieve judges of the trial of many cases, so that it would become possible for legal business to be despatched satisfactorily without the appointment of a large number of new judges, and the consequent additional expense to the public.[96]

He retained this stance in a later work with very similar views being expressed, on this occasion by a judge playing detective in a blackmail scenario:

> The truth about the cause of an accident very often never comes to light and (the judge) believed that as soon as the courts ceased to pursue the slippery eel of the truth in that sphere the better.[97]

The solution again was to be entrusted to the State and that "National Insurance, in (the judge's) view, should replace the hit-and-miss methods of purporting to ascertain liability.[98]

Legal Education

The impact of the rules about pupillage and the problem of underemployment in the profession is noted in Cecil's statistics on likely income in the first years of a young barrister's career.[99] The social implications of this receive no comment. The process is merely compared to equivalent trade apprenticeships. It might be suggested that Cecil's approach was simply a product of his times and that this lack of critique can be attributed to the benefit of hindsight. That would, however, ignore the other contemporary perspectives on the legal profession which are available. Cecil's fiction has little time for academic study. We discover that Jurisprudence and Roman Law are dull and irrelevant.[100] When Cecil was writing there was no equivalent of Continuing Professional Development for newly appointed judges.[101] He implies that the proper training of barristers is far from adequate in his account of being left with limited instructions and given no proper supervision beyond "just tell him the tale, tell him the tale."[102] It is worth noting that at the time of writing the problem of inadequacy of training is claimed to still be an issue over half a century later. In March 2022, a solicitor who runs The Secret Trainee Twitter account has spoken of the pressure on criminal trainees to undertake work for which they are unprepared.[103]

Judges and the Art of Judging

There is a whole range of issues which crop up throughout the fictional work of Henry Cecil concerning judges and process of judging. In this text, I focus on the principal areas of the role of judges, their appointment and the qualities Cecil tells us made a good judge. Judging and the role of the judiciary in the legal process, then, is the issue on which Henry Cecil expends more of his time than on any other single topic. Indeed, in *Alibi for a Judge* in a book centred on the attempts of a judge to undo the harm he has wrought by his impatience in court, there is a chapter entitled "On Judges." Here Cecil devotes the complete nine-page chapter to the merits of the British system of judicial appointment from the practising Bar. He succinctly lays out the central but limited role of the judge:

> It has frequently been said that a judge should hold himself aloof from the struggle going on in Court between the advocates. Of course sometimes he has to blow the whistle when there has been an infringement of the rules, or when someone has been hurt, but otherwise he should leave the battle to the advocates.[104]

The judge needs to be above the fray and not be concerned about the consequences of his action so that having made up his mind "he should give his decision and go to the theatre"[105] and not worry since a judge who constantly worries about his decisions is not usually a good judge.[106] The qualities, then required for a good judge, were simple and exemplified in one of his judicial characters, Mr Justice Short, the judge in a case involving a cunning fraudster:

> He was everything the English public rightly thinks a judge should be. Quiet on the bench, courteous, judicial, a sound lawyer, patient, with a controlled sense of humour.[107]

He reiterated this notion of a Weberian "ideal type" judge with a stress on the role of the evaluation of evidence some fifteen years later in a tale of a robber evading justice by appearing to be a perfect gentleman. Introducing one of the characters in the story places this judge in context estimating him to be in the "lower half of the league table."[108]

> There are various types of judges. The best type never comes to a final conclusion until he's heard the whole of the evidence and the arguments. . . . The worst type of judge comes to an early conclusion when there has been insufficient evidence and insufficient argument.[109]

On this theme of "good judging" Cecil offers this pen portrait of the range of deficiencies to be found in the judiciary in one of his more outlandish explorations of English eccentrics falling out over minor matters such as lawnmowers lent and never returned

> There are, of course, a few judges who do behave like the schoolboy and cannot resist the temptation to intervene, but they form the minority. . . . He had appeared before the rough and ready, the over-technical, the talkative, the too silent judges. . . . the over-anxious, the judges who never sat after lunch if they could avoid it, the sarcastic, the too-kindly judges who were prepared to put their hands in richer people's pockets to pay poorer people, whatever the merits might be, and so on.[110]

A good judge will have positive characteristics and operate as impartially as is possible, which Cecil points out in a mid-period blackmail story:

> On the whole judges try to control their likes and dislikes. Those who hate motorcycles, try hard to decide fairly any accident case which involves such a vehicle. Judges who are allergic to noise do not automatically grant injunctions to restrain defendants from carrying out some noisy operation, which the judge himself could not bear to have next door. But they are only human and, for example, a judge who is devoted to animals might, at any rate unconsciously, decide a case where cruelty to animals is involved rather differently from a judge who was not interested in them.[111]

Another theme which recurs is the difficulty of predicting which members of the Bar are likely to make good judges and which will make poor judges. In an early work a barrister's wife opines about his suitability for the Bench in a tale centred on revenge for a claimed miscarriage of justice in a murder trial:

> . . . you'd be a very good appointment.
>
> That's a thing no one can say. That's why there are bad appointments. You get a man who's first-class at the Bar but makes a rotten judge. And you get a man who isn't much of an advocate and only has a moderate practice who'd make a first-class judge, if only they knew it. . . . Surprise appointments which turn out well and expected appointments which turn out badly.[112]

Related to this imponderable is how anyone can tell who is a good judge and who is merely adequate. In a work from the late 1960s, where a judge is blackmailed into ensuring a criminal is found not guilty, Cecil muses on a "grading system."

> It is a pity that judges cannot have labels, like hotels, with "recommended by so-and-so" etc., etc. If the idea appeals to the publishers of the Law List (or some less reverential body) they might compile each year a list of all the judges with all the virtues and imperfections shortly described. And perhaps one year a class B judge would be promoted to class C. How would this do? "It is worth a detour off the Strand to see Mr Justice Grain at work. Good simple judgments. Friendly and comfortable. But the service is a little erratic. Class B, sometimes Class C."[113]

In this respect he foreshadowed both the Chambers UK Legal Guide,[114] and the evaluation of University Law Schools, which began in the mid-1980s.[115] Once Judge Leon had reached the end of his judicial career, he felt free to comment on the need for judicial courtesy and civility in the Courtroom. He took up the theme of how the accused should be addressed in a mid-period blackmail story:

> It is quite true that today many judges will treat an unconvicted prisoner with proper courtesy, though there are still a few who insist on calling him by his surname without the prefix of "Mr", whereas they treat other witnesses with ordinary politeness.[116]

It was a theme which he took up again in his next fictional outing through the lazy, but loveable fraudster Harry Woodstock:

> Just because one or two judges didn't know how to behave and called all male witnesses "mister" except the prisoner, whom they called by his bare surname,

> some of the newspapers have run amok. They sometimes put in a "mister" and sometimes don't. Does it depend on the amount of the sentence?[117]

It received a degree of "Establishment" support with which Cecil expressed his approval in a late novel about a robbery and a stranger coming to a prosperous village with no "background":

> Owing to the unsatisfactory behaviour of one or more judges in insisting upon calling people charged in front of them by their surname without any prefix, *The Times* suddenly took it into its head not only that this conduct was wrong (as I think it was) but that *The Times* itself should always be courteous in referring to anyone by name, whatever they may have done.[118]

That said, there are other failings which afflict a Bench drawn from people who are used to acting as advocates for one side or the other which Cecil adverts to in the romp about neighbours appearing to fall out irreconcilably over trivialities:

> But in a country such as England, where every judge has been an advocate, often an outstanding one, it is perhaps rather surprising that so many of them are able to keep silent from the moment they get on the bench.[119]

Henry Cecil, though, saw no great need for a formal set of rules to guide judges such as was found in the United States. The "chaps" could be relied on and such things as the various modern Bench Books[120] would have no doubt been seen by Cecil as unnecessary. He opines this is the context of a mid-period tale in which a man, with a hatred of lawyers, is inveigled into litigating solely so that his sons can marry two female lawyers without incurring his displeasure:

> the behaviour of English judges is regulated by tradition and, although it is true that very occasionally an English judge will break one of the rules laid down for his American brethren, most judges instinctively know how to behave. [121]

One element which does not appear extensively but is nonetheless of significance is the notion of the judge as facilitator of justice. It ties in with the "welfare approach" which Cecil himself adopted in his work as a County Court/Circuit judge.[122] In an imagined "purgatory" in his dream, a judge is upbraided for his narrow "legalism" and lack of concern with "justice":

> Do you know how much harm you did in your court by deciding cases according to pure technicalities and by not helping people to comply with the technicalities and so to have the case decided on the merits? . . . I was there to judge, not to

> help. A party hires an advocate to help . . . Parliament is to blame, not me . . . if Parliament wanted me to administer palm-tree justice, it should have said so.[123]

The fictional judge adopts the defence that his cruelty has led to the legislative reform of free legal aid

> And as for my treatment of litigants in person, didn't that perhaps accelerate the passing of the Legal Aid and Advice Act? If every litigant had been nursed and coddled by me, there wouldn't have been half the complaints about injustice, and you might never have had free legal aid at all. I'll warrant there were plenty of complaints about me. You don't get reforms until people cry out for them. I made them cry out.[124]

In one of his last tales, as so often, on blackmail, Cecil concludes that on the whole the public is well served by the judiciary:

> All Her Majesty's judges invariably tell the truth in public and almost invariably in private. That is not say that some of them don't tell lies for other people's benefit. Ordinary social lies are told by almost everyone. . . . One of the reasons for the high reputation which English judges have is the complete trust which most people put in their integrity.[125]

The critical analysis of Griffith[126] and particularly the embarrassing findings of McConville and Marsh exposing the myth of an independent judiciary[127] would undoubtedly have made unwelcome reading to Henry Cecil.

Gender and Diversity

Henry Cecil's novels reflect both the times when he was in active practice at the Bar as well as the times in which he wrote and was sitting as a judge. For one thing his tales are almost entirely bereft of female lawyers. In most of his work there are no female barristers, solicitors nor judges.[128] The first hint we get of the female sex is with Roger Thursby's girlfriend in *Brothers in Law*, Sally Mannering. From her lowly secretarial position in barristers' Chambers, she expresses a vague aspiration, albeit in relation to the junior branch of the legal profession

> I like the law, and who knows, I might become a solicitor myself in the end, if I were good enough[129]

At the very general level of relations between men and women in his first published work there seems to be a recognition that, *inter alia*, marital unhappiness leads to murder[130] that it affects both sexes[131] it may lead to blackmail[132] but that it can be solved by divorce.[133] He is even more explicit in another early work centred on blackmail where there is a recognition of the ever-present threat of mariticide

> people in the so-called civilised countries do not often even consider killing other people who are in their way, except, of course, on the grand scale during a war. The main exception to this apparent moderation on the part of human beings exists in the case of husbands and wives . . . murder between husband and wife (. . . goes on regularly and usually undiscovered),[134]

These relationships operate in a male-centred world where men are driven by their nature into extra-marital relationships. A character expresses this view in the middle period of his writings when dealing with divorce:

> You see, I am a normal man and, whether you like the idea or not, man is a polygamous animal.[135]

The same stance is also found at the end of his career when telling a tale of a disappearing husband's return

> Although many of them may not realise it, the greatest triumph of a wife is to keep for herself alone a husband who has the normal polygamous instincts of a man.[136]

I Married the Girl was one of Cecil's more unusual novels which he published under a pseudonym to assess its quality. His publishers suspected his hand in the book and only paid a very modest advance. It was not a success.[137] It duly appeared under his own name some 13 years later. The narrator here expresses this kind of tendency to male promiscuity

> Some women complain that there are men who undress them with their eyes. I'm afraid I'm much worse than that, I hope I don't make it obvious.[138]

This brings to mind the words of President Jimmy Carter[139] who opined at one stage in his career such a similar tendency towards adultery

> I've looked on a lot of women with lust. I've committed adultery in my heart many times[140]

Violence and Domestic Abuse

The notion of woman as the likely object of rampant male desire is also encountered, albeit in the mouth of the antediluvian ex–Indian Army character, Colonel Brain, in an early and strange treatment of vigilantism, when advising a timid young man about his love life

"Hug 'em and hope,' repeated the colonel. 'The direct assault. Like all the best plans, simple. It's got me through several campaigns. Not without a scratch here and there, I'll grant you, but, on the whole, with success."[141]

This contrasts with the later appreciation of the oppression of women at the hands of the justice system when they resist such attacks. A judge muses on the dilemma he had got himself into when innocently helping the wife who had enlisted his support to free her husband. He started to wonder whether the whole thing was a blackmail trick, and he would end up in a court case

What about the woman who committed suicide when the charge of rape she had made was dismissed? May she not have had a clear conscience and been unable to stand the verdict of acquittal which reflected guilt on her?[142]

Cecil further recognises the problems faced by abused women in marital relationships where signs of physical abuse could be crucial when we find a semi-retired solicitor cogitating upon how he had been forthright and direct during the days of his active practice. Then he had crudely enquired of any client claiming her husband had been guilty of cruelty "Where did he hit you and who saw the bruises?"

(The Solicitor) of course, realised that it was not essential in law for a husband to hit his wife in order to be guilty of cruelty. But he also knew that anything short of physical violence usually meant simply that the parties did not get on well together. He further knew that such was the view of his Bench. A couple of black eyes, a bruised arm, and an independent witness to at least one of them – not just 'my mum' who had always hated the man anyway – and (the solicitor) could almost guarantee success.[143]

That said, Cecil does express some male chauvinistic doubts about the depth of sisterly solidarity in general, albeit in 1960 through his strange male protagonist, the serial monogamist, Douglas:

quite a large proportion of womankind have friends who are no friends. They lunch with them, shop with them, go to the theatre with them and even impose them sometimes on their husbands, but they don't really like them. This is something in the feminine make up which I no longer try to understand. I have tried.[144]

Gender and the Legal Profession

The invisibility of the "second sex"[145] is recognised in Cecil's work. In his advice in his 1958 guide to entering the law, *Brief to Counsel,* Cecil advises against women going to the Bar.[146] If they must be lawyers then the solicitors' branch is safer. By the time he came to update the guide in 1972 the advice remains the same noting

> . . . very few (women) have gained success, and it does not appear that the road is becoming much easier. Although the fact that there is now one woman High Court judge, three women Circuit judges and one woman magistrate should give a little encouragement to women.[147]

In his fiction he stresses again that sexism is rife. His male protagonist seeking a divorce discovers

> that the law is much more interested in men than in women. It is indeed only recently that women have been recognised as separate individuals and even now the law does not appear to think much of them.[148]

He takes this view on the basis of how women's roles were treated in the divorce process.[149]

The most radical approach, where two female lawyers feature at the core of a narrative, occurs in a tale of man with a fierce antipathy towards lawyers being conned by his two sons out of his phobia. The female lawyers – a barrister and a solicitor – lack agency. They are playthings of their paramours. They do, however, have connections – their father is a High Court judge. Their novelty is in their appearance alone. They are playing at being lawyers just as they would have played at running a clothes boutique or antique shop if their father had not guided them into his own profession:

> So Prunella went down to her first county court, and she created quite a stir in the robing room. She was quite the prettiest girl that had been to Ladbroke County Court, and there were two of her, for, before she robed, no one not intimately acquainted with them could have told the difference between the two sisters.[150]

> Jane had been qualified three years before she briefed Prunella in a High Court case . . . she was now in practice entirely on her own, with only a boy of sixteen to help her, and clients were not as many as they might be. But her father still gave her and Prunella a small allowance, and they enjoyed playing about with the law.[151]

Furthermore, in *A Woman Named Anne* as late as 1967, not only are there are no female legal protagonists, but a central narrative driver is the extent to which the male barristers are swayed by the attractiveness of the witness of the title.

Miscellaneous Observations

Cecil's fiction is full of observations on aspects of the legal system generally including some issues whose significance, at the time, was far from prominent. For instance, he addresses the issue of vigilantism and "self-help" in the legal system from his earliest work where it seems that taking direct action against miscreants is justified on balance[152] to a more considered consideration of moral relativism in connection with killing. He notes in a tale of an accidental death of someone on a set of unlit stairs:

> But, apart from murder between husband and wife (which goes on regularly and usually undiscovered), premeditated murder for the sake of removing someone who is a nuisance or danger is extremely rare.[153]

In the quite serious early work on the theme of a vigilante killing of someone who has escaped the clutches of the law by being found not guilty by a jury, he takes up the same theme.

> It makes such a difference how and when you killed. If you kill the right person at the right time, we are publicly acclaimed as a hero. But mistake the person or the time you will be very likely be hanged.[154]

Despite accepting that the public is involved in killing people through the medium of a judge, jury, and hangman,[155] he draws the line at approving of the person responsible for the killing of man suspected of rape and murder but found not guilty by the courts.

> Much as I admire his public spiritedness, he oughtn't to have done it. Where's your law and order? Much more important than a few people's lives. If one were allowed to kill undesirables, no one would be safe.[156]

The leader writer of the fictional London Clarion newspaper in this tale of vigilantism – one of Cecil's most seriously themed works – expresses the matter thus

> Once private individuals are permitted to take the law into their own hands, it is the end of civilisation as we know it. So start the secret societies which, however laudable their objects may be in the beginning, end by being tyrants and thugs of

> the worst description. We want no Ku Klux Klan in this country. We should not need it. Let the police force be overhauled.[157]

It is left to a letter writer to the Clarion to express the "crime limitation" argument.

> Of course I agree that private execution or vengeance cannot ordinarily be allowed, but the exception proves the rule. The police failed, other women would have been killed, they were saved by the act of a public benefactor.[158]

This is one of the rare examples where we find opposing views expressed in the fiction of Henry Cecil. He also suggests that the courts also have an entertainment value which is not to be undervalued. He notes in relation to a ruse dreamed up by a couple of conmen and their wives resulting in defamation litigation:

> They had introduced into the case a large variety of subjects which many members of the public and all the popular newspapers love. There was a wealth of headlines from which editors or sub-editors could choose. Kisses and corsets, games under the kitchen table, the trusting wife, the beautiful next door neighbour, they were all there and many other things besides. Small wonder that all the parties concerned were approached outside the Court while the jury was considering its verdict.[159]

Not only were members of the public entertained but there were no losers in this set-up. As he observed, only slightly tongue-in-cheek, one suspects:

> It was really quite an achievement and, when you come to think of it, no one was any the worse off. The judge and the jury would have had to try another case if they hadn't tried that one. So they lost nothing. Counsel and solicitors were not only paid their fees, but had some useful advertisement. So they gained. The newspapers got what they wanted and were very willing to pay the price asked. Those members of the public who liked reading about kisses and brassières and so on had their fill of entertainment. No one lost, some people gained, while the conspirators made over £2000.[160]

Looking to the future we find the most unlikely source for a view of the future in the shape of the permanently intoxicated denizen of the legal profession, solicitor, Mr Tewkesbury opining that this will involve computers having a major role

> "mark my words, the day will come when the law will be one vast slot machine" . . . automatic judges, my dear sir, No barristers or solicitors. You

> just put down your statement of the case, the other side puts down his, push 'em in the machine – pull the lever and, after a few minutes' calculation, the answer comes out on a ticket. No long arguments, no lawyer's fees, all done by the State.[161]

The 21st-century Transport Appeals Tribunal system fits quite neatly into this description with its use of written evidence only submitted electronically.

CONCLUDING REMARKS

As the above has, hopefully, made clear, the views and perspectives which are expressed by Henry Cecil are almost always in the form of direct addresses to the reader and are usually unconnected with the narrative theme of the story. It is very much as though Cecil, when encountering a theme as a storyteller or actor, breaks off and confides his own views to the audience. Then back to the plot. In the final chapter, I seek to disentangle the twin themes of entertainment and instruction within the various writers including Henry Cecil. What is interesting is the consistency of Cecil's views over the period of his writing. The political scientist Harold Laski suggested that judges form their ideas at some point in their lives and they remain fixed.

> It is the judge's experience of life that determines his attitude to the problems of law. Most people's philosophy, both in its conscious assumptions, and its much more significant unconscious prejudices, is fairly fixed at 40; and 30 years later, the average judge will belong to a generation of which the general outlook is very different from his own.[162]

Hence judges will be criticised for having the ideas of a generation ago. Cecil seems to embody the same kind of role. His rosy view of many aspects of the justice system are very much located in the interwar period when, it seems, the profession was enjoying a steady flow of work and positions in Chambers were easily come by, even for those without existing connections in the legal profession.

Henry Cecil's work embodies a desire to amuse and secure publication on the one hand and the impetus to inform and educate on the other. We find these two driving forces most potent over a considerable period of time. The writer expressed it in his autobiography and, hopefully, this examination of his writings has made clear the full nature and extent of his pedagogic aims. His most celebrated work, *Brothers in Law* combines these dual goals perfectly as he saw it.

> The book was mainly written for the purposes of entertainment but some of it was also intended as propaganda.[163]

APPENDIX 1

Details of All Henry Cecil Publications

Books and works for the theatre

Title and year	*Principal areas of legal conflict*	*Principal protagonists*	*Themes and issues raised in text*	*Comments*
1. Full Circle (1948) -nine short stories	Murder; Blackmail; Theft; murder; murder; burglary; blackmail; murder; fraud; murder;	Centred around stories told to students by a law professor who has suffered a head injury	Legal ethics Gender relations	Based on stories told to soldiers during World War II – to provide some entertainment on s troop ship. Most end with a last page twist
2. The Painswick Line (1951)	Fraud Libel	C of E vicar tips horses and his daughter is accused of fraud Judge's "rogue" son in sub-plot about libel	Family traits and their unpredictability	Last-page twist in diffuse first novel
3. Ways and Means (1952)	Libel	Two couples engineer libellous comments from prosperous villagers	Happy middle-class village setting	Law being used by genial fraudsters to fund a comfortable lifestyle
4. No Bail for the Judge (1952)	Murder	Alleged murder by a judge of a prostitute and the elaborate means of finding the true killer using a criminal	Dangers of circumstantial evidence as basis for conviction highlighted	Almost an Alfred Hitchcock film – but Audrey Hepburn became "unavailable", and the project failed to materialise
5. Natural Causes (1953)	Blackmail Libel Wrongful dismissal	Newspaper publisher tries to silence critics using the law including his own solicitor	Power of "big money" buying legal immunity	Precursor to modern press barons abusing their positions

(*Continued*)

Title and year	*Principal areas of legal conflict*	*Principal protagonists*	*Themes and issues raised in text*	*Comments*
6. According to the Evidence (1954)	Murder Sexual Assault	Man "known" to have raped and murdered women but found not guilty by a jury is killed by the protagonist and he escapes without any sanction	Vigilante killing approved in these circumstances. Use of the "double jeopardy" rule – no retrial after acquittal – now partially abolished by the Criminal Evidence Act of 2003	Theatre version revamped as a much more light-hearted comedy thriller with MI5 elements – see B below
7. Brothers in Law (1955)	Divorce Fraud Libel	Experiences of a trainee barrister muddling his way through minor litigation	Dock brief system covered along with challenge to jury membership of a relative	Exposed the woeful training available to trainee barristers Cecil's commercial breakthrough
8. Friends at Court (1956)	Bribery	Centred on one case of bribery by hoteliers of the police	Beyond reasonable doubt	Brief re-appearance of "scallywag" from BIL, fraudster, Mr Green
A. No Bail for The Judge (10 March 1956)	Theatrical version of 4. above			
B. According to The Evidence (19 May 1956)	Theatrical version of 6 above			light-hearted comedy thriller with MI5 elements
9. Much in Evidence (1957)	Fraud	Fraudster stages burglary of large sum of insured cash and successfully sues insurance company who reject his claim.	Very elaborate plot-driven tale with hugely improbable coincidences. Minimal didactic elements	Double twist in tale plot
C. Natural Causes (11 May 1957)	Theatrical version of 5. above			
D. Much In Evidence (27 July 1957)	Theatrical version of 9. above			
10. Sober as a Judge (1958)	Fraud Libel Damages Blackmail	The court from the judge's point of view of some minor cases	Moral integrity of the judiciary	Rehash of themes from BIL about trainee inexperience

Brief to Counsel (1958)	Advice to would be lawyers			First of four editions of a book last published in 1982 with Cecil's name still on the cover – he died in 1976.
11. Settled Out of Court (1959)	Murder	"Retrial" of man convinced he was convicted by perjured evidence	Reliability of witness evidence	Highly theatrical – see below at E. Jon Breen's choice as "best Cecil novel".
E. Settled Out Of Court (14 March 1959)		Theatrical version of very theatrical book – 11 above	Co-written with William Saroyan (author of The Human Comedy)	Premiered at the Strand Theatre, London, 10 October 1960
12. Alibi for a Judge (1960)	Robbery	Judge turns detective, with the help of the convicted man's wife, in seeking to right a wrong caused by his own unfairness in court	Judicial conscience at doubtful behaviour in court is principal issue	Seems almost written for the theatre – see below at F.
13. I married the girl (1960) Clifford Maxwell	Divorce	Strange absence of any obvious legal theme	Serial monogamist looking for the "perfect" partner until the last page	Cecil seeking to find out if he is being published because of past success – not a good idea
F. Alibi For A Judge (2 April 1960)				Additional jeopardy of judge in the hotel bedroom of the convicted robber's wife
14. Daughters in Law (1961)	Fraud Defamation	Two brothers conspire to show their prejudiced father that lawyers are not all crooks by concocting a wheeze involving an apparently duplicitous 3rd party	Lawyers as sharks Women lawyers make an appearance	Not exactly tokenism but the women lawyers lack agency Twist in the tale
G. Daughters in Law* (2 September 1961)	Theatrical version of 14.			
ii. Not Such an Ass (1961)	Series of tales about how the law has been "saved" by bold judges in the past			

(Continued)

Title and year	*Principal areas of legal conflict*	*Principal protagonists*	*Themes and issues raised in text*	*Comments*
15. Unlawful Occasions (1962)	Blackmail Libel	Supposed blackmailer dupes a number of worthy people into defaming him and sues for defamation Pools win sub-plot	Moral duties of those involved in joint enterprises like pools syndicates	A strangely intriguing plot
H. Unlawful Occasions (8 December 1962)	Version of 15.			Saturday Night Theatre radio play available on YouTube
16. Independent Witness (1963)	Dangerous driving	Motor accident in which an MP is on trial for dangerous driving	Witness credibility	Twist in the tale
17. Portrait of a Judge (1964) Collection of 22 short stories - 13 of them "legal"	Murder x 3 Perjury Damages Fraud Revenge	Will scam Judicial style x 3 Alibi False "verdict"	Double jeopardy rule	Highly variable in quality and length – from 3 pages to 20 with a median of 12
iii.Tipping the Scales (1964)	Account of corrupt and doubtful judges in the past			
18. Fathers in Law (1965) aka A Child Divided (US)	Adoption Blackmail	Adoption practice where the natural parents change their mind.	Adoption rights	Absence of usual humour on a sensitive subject
iv. Know About English Law (1965)	Primer for young adults on the key features of English Law			
v. A Matter of Speculation: The Case of Lord Cochrane (1965)	Revisiting a 19th-century case where a prominent sailor was accused of manipulating the price of stocks and imprisoned			More recent re-assessments are still divided between if this was a miscarriage of justice
19. The Asking Price (1966)	Blackmail Murder or accidental death?	57-year-old man "forced" into marriage with 17 year old neighbour who dies on their honeymoon	Societal attitude to "sugar daddy" syndrome	Very odd
20. A Woman Named Anne (1967)	Divorce	Divorce of a woman who wishes to marry another but whose husband resists the process	Oblique critique of the "fault" based divorce Sexism of male barristers	Very theatrical - set almost entirely in the courtroom

I.The Disagreeable Man (13 September 1967)	Adapted from the novel Ways and Means – above at 3.			Radio play, TV film from 1953 (30 minutes)
21. No Fear or Favour (1968) [aka The Blackmailers (US)]	Blackmail	Judge who doubts he could ever be a victim is blackmailed through his daughter being kidnapped to secure a not guilty verdict	A longer version of one of his 1964 short stories	Not one of his merry diversions Twist in the tale
22. Brief Tales from the Bench (1968) Mixture of 8 partly true and entirely fictitious short stories - solutions in an Appendix	Contempt of court Duty of schools to pupils Perjury Standards in hotels – to gain publicity Civil and criminal standards contrasted in a shoplifting case Scheme to divest a man of assets pre-divorce backfires Two lovers fall out and dispute about existence of a sum paid as an investment Dispute about whether a suit fitted or not – double twist ending			A novel approach mixing fiction and fact-based storylines
23. Tell You What I'll Do (1969)	Avoiding retribution by staying in gaol.	Con man pleads guilty to stay in jail to avoid the gangsters whose money he has purloined Subplot about a prosecution for shoplifting	Jail conditions not an issue – see above	Limited humour and social issues
vi. The English Judge (1970)	Hamlyn lectures on English judges and their role in the legal system			

(Continued)

Title and year	*Principal areas of legal conflict*	*Principal protagonists*	*Themes and issues raised in text*	*Comments*
24. The Buttercup Spell (1971)	Fantasy about a magic, but legal substance that makes everyone act reasonably and its practical consequences		The need for strife without which nothing would get done	A short story idea fleshed out beyond its capacity Not published in the United States
25. The Wanted Man (1972)	Robbery	Stranger turns up in a village – is he actually respectable or a bank robber?	Policing and its problems	Another "thin" piece with a predictable twist in the tale – extended version of 1964 short story
26. Truth With Her Boots On (1974)	Blackmail	Judge asked to lie on behalf of a friend feels he must retire early and start investigating miscarriages of justice.	Moral sentiments in action in tale of codes of conduct from an earlier era where judge unable to tell a "white lie" and remain a judge	Not published in the United States
vii. Learn About English Law (1975) revised edition of Know About English Law (1965)	Updated version of the 1965 book above at iv.			
viii. The Trial of Walter Rowland (1975) Celebrated Trials Series	Reassessment of a man hanged when another man confessed to the crime. Despite the confessor later being convicted of murdering in the same way Cecil thinks the Rowland verdict safe			

J. No Fear or Favour (5 July 1975)				Radio play version of 21. above
ix. Just Within the Law (1975) (autobiography)	Very sparse details of many aspects of his life and time and very little on his writings			
27. Cross Purposes (1976)		A couple win the football pools and seek to help friends and family with wacky and unusual consequences	Moral code determines that the couple return money won through an undetectable scam	Not published in the United States Not any legal elements.
28. Hunt the Slipper (1977)	Divorce Wills	A man who has mysteriously disappeared shows up 7 years later as his wife is divorcing him. Elaborate ruse involving bank robbery and gangsters.	The problems of a dead man being alive	Plot unusually improbable even for Cecil and not a fitting end to his writing career.

APPENDIX 2

Henry Cecil's Fictional Work Publishing History

Title	*Publisher and year*	*Reissued 1*	*Reissued 2*	*Reissue 3*
1. Full Circle	1948 Chapman and Hall	1958 Pan	1965 Penguin	*2000 House of Stratus*
2. The Painswick Line	1951 Chapman and Hall	1964 Penguin	1982 Ian Henry	*2000 House of Stratus*
3. Ways and Means	1952 Chapman and Hall	1961 Michael Joseph	1963 Penguin	*2000 House of Stratus*
4. No Bail for the Judge	1952 Chapman and Hall	1955 Pan	1964 Penguin	*2000 House of Stratus*
5. Natural Causes	1953 Chapman and Hall	1956 Pan	1964 Penguin	*2000 House of Stratus*
		1964 Michael Joseph		
6. According to the Evidence	1954 Chapman and Hall	1957 Pan	1965 Penguin	*2000 House of Stratus*
		1963 Michael Joseph	1979 Ian Henry	
7. Brothers in Law	1955 Michael Joseph	1962 Penguin	*2000 House of Stratus*	
8. Friends at Court	1956 Michael Joseph	1962 Penguin	*2000 House of Stratus*	
9. Much in Evidence	1957 Michael Joseph	1962 Penguin	*2000 House of Stratus*	
10. Sober as a Judge	1958 Michael Joseph	1962 Penguin	*2000 House of Stratus*	
11. Settled Out of Court	1958 Michael Joseph 1961 Companion Book Club	1963 Penguin	1991 International Polygonics	*2000 House of Stratus*
12. Alibi for a Judge	1960 Michael Joseph 1961 Companion Book Club	1963 Penguin	1991 International Polygonics	*2000 House of Stratus*

(Continued)

Title	*Publisher and year*	*Reissued 1*	*Reissued 2*	*Reissue 3*
13. I Married the Girl	1960 Michael Joseph – sub nom Clifford Maxwell	1973 White Lion – sub nom Henry Cecil		
14. Daughters in Law	1961 Michael Joseph	1963 Penguin	1991 International Polygonics	*2000 House of Stratus*
15. Unlawful Occasions	1962 Michael Joseph	1964 Penguin	*2000 House of Stratus*	
16. Independent Witness	1963 Michael Joseph	1965 Penguin	1977 Ian Henry	*2000 House of Stratus*
17. Portrait of a Judge	1964 Michael Joseph	1968 Sphere	*2000 House of Stratus*	
18. Fathers in Law US Title A Child Divided (1966)	1965 Michael Joseph	1968 Sphere	1977 Magna Large Print	*2000 House of Stratus*
19. The Asking Price	1966 Michael Joseph	1969 Sphere	*2000 House of Stratus*	
20. A Woman Named Anne	1967 Michael Joseph	1968 Sphere	1993 Academy Chicago Publishers	2000 *House of Stratus*
21. No Fear or Favour US Title Blackmailers	1968 Michael Joseph	*2000 House of Stratus*		
22. Brief Tales from the Bench	1968 BBC	*2000 House of Stratus*		
23. Tell You What I'll Do	1969 Michael Joseph	*2000 House of Stratus*		
24. The Buttercup Spell	1971 Michael Joseph	*2000 House of Stratus*		
25. The Wanted Man	1972 Michael Joseph	*2000 House of Stratus*		
26. Truth with her Boots On	1974 Michael Joseph	*2000 House of Stratus*		
27. Cross Purposes	1976 Michael Joseph	*2000 House of Stratus*		
28. Hunt the Slipper	1977 Michael Joseph	*2000 House of Stratus*		

(Continued)

NOTES

1. In Cecil's entry in the *Dictionary of National Biography*, HFR Keating notes that this prestigious award received no mention in Cecil's autobiography – Cecil (1975) – https://www.oxforddnb.com/search?q=Henry+Cecil+Leon&searchBtn=Search&isQuickSearch=true (accessed 24 January 2024).

2. Cecil (1975b) at p. 131 (Chapter 11).

3. *Fathers in Law*: Amazon.co.uk: Henry Cecil: 9788129102768: Books (last accessed 10 March 2024).

4. Cecil (1975) at 137.

5. Sunday Times review of *Alibi for a Judge* (1960) by crime writer and scholar Julian Symons.

6. Cecil (1958).

7. *Brothers in Law* (1955).

8. Loc cit at 142–146 – "it is not your duty to try to procure the acquittal of a guilty man but to do the best you properly can to secure the acquittal of a man who tells you he is innocent" – at 144.

9. Loc cit at 160–162.

10. Loc cit at 86–97.

11. Harvey (1958).

12. Pritt (1966).

13. Loc cit at 105.

14. Cecil (1964) per Foreword of Lord Devlin at 9.

15. The annual Hamlyn Lectures were inaugurated in 1949 by Lord Denning. The Hamlyn Trust website indicates that the Trust was created by Miss Emma Hamlyn in memory of her father, a solicitor and Justice of the Peace in Torquay. The object of the Trust is to further knowledge and understanding of the law, including "the comparative jurisprudence of the chief European countries," among the people of the United Kingdom, "to the intent that the people of the United Kingdom may realise the privileges which in law and custom they enjoy . . . and recognise the responsibilities and obligations attaching to them." The Trust's objective is achieved primarily by an annual series of public lectures by distinguished judges, legal practitioners, academic lawyers and other eminent speakers. Henry Cecil put his own gloss on the purpose of the annual lectures as being "to show to the people of Great Britain how lucky they were with their standard of justice compared with that of other European countries" – Henry Cecil (1970) (Preface at 8). Fellow Hamlyn lecturers prior to Henry Cecil included Judges like Lords Devlin and Kilbrandon and Sir Robert Megarry as well as distinguished academics like Professors Glanville Williams, TB Smith and CHS Fifoot. More recent luminaries include Dame Hazel Genn and Professor Alan Paterson and most recently online Eleanor Sharpston, Kate O'Regan and Lord Thomas of Cwmgiedd.

16. Abel-Smith and Stevens (1967 and 1968).

17. Zander (1968).

18. Cecil (1970) – see Chapter 1.

19. Cecil (1965) Chapter 22 and particularly 202.

20. Dale (2006).

21. Cordingley (2007).

22. Cecil (1965) at 57; Cecil (1974) at 54.

23. Per Sir Kenneth Branagh who paid tribute to him, saying, "He was a national treasure, a great actor and a wonderful man" – quoted in his Obituary in *The Daily Telegraph*. London. 18 February 2013.

24. Available on YouTube and as downloads or casettes.

25. Henry Cecil Archive – McMaster University, Hamilton, Ontario. Along with the drafts and revisions of the books and plays, there is extensive correspondence between Cecil and his British and North American agents about the sales and income from these works. This greatly exercised him and financial issues dominate the correspondence in his archive.

26. See Appendix 2, *Fiction Publishing History*.

27. http://www.houseofstratus.com/our-books (accessed 24 January 2024).

28. Kynaston (2007) at 19.

29. Robson (1996) at 203.

30. The Confession (Full Circle) (1948).

31. The Dream (Full Circle) (1948).

32. Portrait in Silk (Full Circle) (1948).

33. Unlawful Occasions (1962) p. 66.

34. See Introduction to the English Legal System Appendix.

35. The Painswick Line (1951) p. 139.

36. Portrait of a Judge (The Application) (1964) p. 64.

37. Daughters in Law (1961) per protagonist Major Buttonstep p. 20.

38. Loc cit p. 24.

39. Friends At Court 1956 p. 37.

40. The Wanted Man (1972) p. 129.

41. Truth with Her Boots On (1974) p. 14.

42. McBride (2011).

43. Alibi for a Judge (1960) at 77.

44. Cecil (1975) at 8–9.

45. A Woman Named Anne (1967) passim.

46. A Woman Named Anne op cit p. 105.

47. Abel (1998) p. 100.

48. Settled Out of Court (1958) p. 53.

49. Unlawful Occasions (1962) p. 20.

50. Alibi for a Judge (1960) p. 68.

51. Daughters in Law (1961) p. 35.

52. A Child Divided (1966) per Mr Luttrell p. 22.

53. A Woman Named Anne (1967) p. 9.

54. Cecil (1958); (1965) and (1974).

55. The Buttercup Spell (1971) p. 55.

56. See Introduction to the English Legal System Appendix.

57. Independent Witness (1963) p. 20.

58. Unlawful Occasions (1962) p. 144.

59. The Wanted Man (1972) p. 58 per Mr Partridge.
60. Alibi for a Judge (1960) p. 9.
61. The Buttercup Spell (1971) p. 109.
62. The Wanted Man (1972) at 88
63. Chapter 3 Perjury (*Brief Tales from the Bench*) (1968) p. 40.
64. Alibi for a Judge (1960) p. 62.
65. A Woman Named Anne (1967) p. 9.
66. The Painswick Line (1951) p. 21.
67. The system before Legal Aid was introduced – see Brothers in Law (1957) and The Dock Brief aka Trial and Error (1962).
68. The Painswick Line op cit p. 22.
69. Truth With Her Boots On (1974) per solicitor Mr Groaner p. 87.
70. According to the Evidence (1954) p. 114.
71. Ways and Means (1952) p. 175 – a jokey reference to Terence Rattigan's fictionalisation of the Archer-Shee case in the play *The Winslow Boy* (1946) – two film versions in 1948 and 1999.
72. Tell You What I'll Do (1969) p. 136.
73. The Wanted Man (1972) p. 39.
74. Truth With Her Boots On (1974) per retired Judge Julian Whitehillt p. 115.
75. Tell You What I'll Do (1969) pp. 20–21.
76. According to the Evidence (1954) p. 120.
77. Cross Purposes (1976) per conman Edward Livermore pp. 44–45.
78. Hunt the Slipper (1977) p. 105.
79. Loc cit p. 116.
80. Gardiner and Martin (1963).
81. Abel Smith and Stevens (1968); Zander (1968).
82. Kennedy (1961).
83. Yallop (1969).
84. Alibi for a Judge (1960) p. 128.
85. Loc cit pp. 129–130.
86. Cecil (1975) at p. 62.
87. Loc cit at p. 76.
88. Loc cit at p.77.
89. Much in Evidence (1957) p. 79.
90. Fathers in Law (1965) p 127 (US title A Child Divided) (1966) p. 128.
91. Hunt the Slipper (1977) p. 83.
92. Ibid.
93. Jackson (1964) Chapter 7.
94. Sober as a Judge (1958) p. 11.
95. The Buttercup Spell (1971) p. 104.
96. The Buttercup Spell op cit p. 110.
97. Truth With Her Boots On (1974) p. 89.
98. Op cit p. 90.
99. Cecil (1958) pp. 18–19.
100. Chapter Eighteen (Full Circle) (1948).

101. Alibi for a Judge (1960) p. 13.
102. Brothers in Law (1955) at p. 26 : see also Cecil (1975) p. 27.
103. Scottish Legal News March 3 2022.
104. Alibi for a Judge (1960) p. 17.
105. Ibid.
106. Ibid.
107. Much in Evidence (1957) p. 70.
108. The Wanted Man (1972) p. 94.
109. The Wanted Man loc cit p. 93.
110. Daughters in Law (1961) p. 123.
111. Unlawful Occasions (1962) p. 109.
112. Settled out of Court (1958) p. 156.
113. No Fear or Favour (1968) p. 116.
114. Chambers publishes an Annual Guide – see https://chambers.com – legal guide based on the profession's own evaluation of the prestige of individuals and firms. Appearance here is highly valued by those who appear.
115. There have been a number of versions of academic rankings carried out by specialist peer review panels. These were carried out on behalf of the four UK Higher Education funding bodies at the time – Higher Education Funding Council for England, Scottish Funding Council, Higher Education Funding Council for Wales and Department for Employment and Learning Northern Ireland. This was named the RAE (Research Assessment Exercise) and carried out and reported in 1986, 1989, 1992, 1996, 2001 and 2008. It was replaced by the REF (Research Excellence Framework) in 2014. It is undertaken on behalf of Research England, the Scottish Funding Council, the Higher Education Funding Council for Wales and the Department for the Economy, Northern Ireland. It reported in 2022.
116. No Fear or Favour (1968) p. 157.
117. Tell You What I'll Do (1969) p. 160.
118. The Wanted Man (1972) p. 154.
119. Daughters in Law (1961) p. 122.
120. These include the Crown Court Bench Book (HMSO) which advises on the whole trial process; there are other volumes available down to Tribunals operating such matters as social security benefits.
121. Daughters in Law (1961) p. 149.
122. Cecil (1975) pp. 160–61.
123. Daughters in Law loc cit pp. 126–27.
124. Loc cit at 128.
125. Truth with her Boots on (1974) p. 22.
126. Griffith (1975).
127. McConville and Marsh (2020).
128. No female legal protagonists in Full Circle (passim) (1948); The Painswick Line (passim)(1951); Ways and Means (1952); Natural Causes (1953); No Bail for the Judge (1952); According to the Evidence (1954); Friends at Court (1956); Much in Evidence (1957); Unlawful Occasions (1962); Independent Witness (1963); Portrait of a Judge (1964); Fathers in Law/A Child Divided (1966); The Asking Price

(1966); A Woman Named Anne (1967); No Fear of Favour (1968) [US The Blackmailers]; Tales from the Bench (1968).

129. Brothers in Law (1955) p. 132.
130. The Name (Full Circle) (1948).
131. Not on the Menu (Full Circle) (1948).
132. The Catch (Full Circle) (1948).
133. Music for All (Full Circle) (1948).
134. Natural Causes (1953) p. 93.
135. I Married the Girl (1960) p. 15.
136. Hunt the Slipper (1977) p. 1.
137. Cecil (1975) at 141–2.
138. I Married the Girl (1960) p. 19 of 1973 reissue.
139. 39th U.S. President 1977–1981 – see Bird (2021).
140. Atlanta Constitution (Sep 22 1976).
141. According to the Evidence (1954) p. 74.
142. Alibi for the Judge (1960) p. 172.
143. Independent Witness (1963) p. 68.
144. I Married the Girl (1960) p. 50.
145. de Beauvoir (1949).
146. Brief to Counsel (1958) p. 160.
147. Cecil (1972) p. 169. Although Cecil cannot be entirely blamed for it, the 3rd edition which appeared in 1982 and was revised and edited by Circuit judge His Honour Edgar Dennis Smith takes a similarly pessimistic view – Cecil 1982 at p. 169.
148. I Married the Girl (1960) (per Douglas, the narrator at p. 73).
149. Ibid.
150. Daughters in Law (1961) p. 43.
151. Daughters in Law loc cit p. 61.
152. The Liberty of the Subject (Full Circle) (1948).
153. Natural Causes (1953) p. 93.
154. According to the Evidence (1954) p. 32.
155. Op cit p. 42.
156. Op cit p. 49.
157. Op cit p. 61.
158. Op cit p. 62.
159. Ways and Means (1952) p. 89.
160. Op cit p. 92 – equivalent in 2023 £47,000.
161. Much in Evidence 1957 (per Mr Tewkesbury p. 83).
162. Laski (1925) p. 550. For a critical comments on the methodology of such views, see Robson (1979) *passim.*
163. Cecil (1975) at 29.

Chapter 3

Hastings Draper and Julian Prescot

INTRODUCTION

In the immediate postwar era, there were two writers who seemed to take inspiration from the success of Henry Cecil and produced two series of books dealing with day-to-day legal practice. One was a London-based barrister Roderic Jeffries writing as Hastings Draper. The other was a Blackpool solicitor, John Budd who took the pseudonym, Julian Prescot. Between them they added a further dozen books to the legal sub-genre of vocational comedy. This includes many books on doctors,[1] vets,[2] teachers[3] and academics[4] but only a single one, so far as I can ascertain, on dentists.[5]

RODERIC JEFFRIES

Roderic Jeffries was a barrister who practised at the Bar for some three years between 1952 and 1954 and then moved into writing. The son of the well-established author, Graeme Jeffries,[6] born in London in 1926, he became a merchant seaman. He worked initially in 1943 for the New Zealand Shipping Company as an apprentice and sailed to Australia and New Zealand. He later transferred to the Union Castle Company to visit a different part of the world.[7] He returned to England in 1949 where he was admitted to the Honourable Society of Gray's Inn and read for the Bar at the same time as he began to write. He was called to the Bar in 1953, and after the year of pupillage, practised law for a few terms. Three comic legal novels were published in 1956, 1958 and 1961 featuring his rookie barrister, Alan Pace.

THE TRIALS AND TRIBULATIONS ALAN PACE, BARRISTER

Given the greater obscurity of his comic legal work it is worth rehearsing his novels tracing the struggles of the young lawyer, Alan Pace. In contrast to the verse musings of Horace Rumpole,[8] there is only one poetry quotation within these books.[9] Alan Pace and his wife inhabit a run-down cottage in a smartish suburb of London in all three novels. Like the time lock in 1940 in Walmington-on-Seà,[10] and in many British radio soaps [11] the events and encounters of Alan Pace are preserved in aspic firmly around the mid-1950s. Lots of clients may have married, divorced or been acquitted but time has more or less stood still. He is, however, gradually building a practice and, one might have reasonably expected in due course, a few further entries from the Pace *curriculum vitae*. As we shall see, there are interesting and arresting reasons for the halting of the cycle.

The three Draper books featuring barrister Alan Pace consist of a series of episodes in the style of Henry Cecil. The tone is light. The young couple are not well off but they both have private incomes and "deprivation" means running low on gin.[12] Cigarettes are constantly on hand to smoke while worrying about the lack of money. Some of the humour derives from the location of the cottage of the Paces amidst wealthy neighbours including solicitors and bankers. The episodes are highly visual, and they call to mind what was to become a standard television sitcom in their structure. For instance, typically, early on, Alan Pace is rude to a pompous middle-aged man, by denying him his regular seat on the morning train into town. They part with the bumptious younger man glad to have got one over on the older man who has not received his expected deference. The latter, in fact, ends up failing to catch the train, after leaving the carriage to remonstrate with the guard.[13] Their wives – neither engaged in waged work nor childcare – meet quite independently. The older wife, hearing of the plight of the younger couple is sure that her solicitor husband will be able to put some work Pace's way and invites them round for cocktails that evening. The classic end of a half-hour sitcom scene arrives with Pace discovering the identity of the new neighbour – none other than the pompous middle-aged man from the train – a solicitor. The solicitor himself is not there in person his wife explains as he is not feeling well after a "dreadful" incident involving being deprived of his seat in the train by some "fresh faced young man." The chapter ends abruptly there with the clear message that what could have been a valuable source of case referrals for the impecunious barrister will now not come to fruition following this incident.[14]

In our introduction to the world of Alan Pace, the major narrative element is a civil action by an eccentric millionaire businessman against a company for a misleading advertisement. The principle involves one of the first things which first-year law students studying contract learn about,[15] namely the difference between an offer and a "puff." The principle, as outlined in all English law contract textbooks is that there is a difference between a promise to pay in the event of conditions being met and a mere "puff."[16] For the plot to "work" there have to be a number of elements – the client with bottomless financial resources, a firm of solicitors with no scruples about not advising him to give up on what is a laughable claim and a young barrister prepared to accept these doubtful instructions. The litigation has shades of AP Herbert's Albert Haddock about it.[17] There is also the fortuitous insistence by the rich litigant that Alan Pace be his barrister because he has chanced to see him in action in court in a very minor landlord and tenant case seemingly not being overawed by an unpredictable judge.[18]

The book ends on a high note for our hero with him being promised work from the solicitor neighbour, Steven Curry, as his price for silence about the traffic offence which Curry commits at the end of the breach of contract trial. In his haste to get to court, Curry has run into the car of Pace's unscrupulous instructing solicitor.[19] This latter solicitor's firm normally likes to instruct a barrister who pads out the case with multiple motions and appeals to increase the fees of all the lawyers. Pace refuses to do this, and they seek to sack him. This unethical action comes to light and they are forced to instruct Alan Pace even though he will not swell their costs by spinning out the litigation with protracted procedural points.[20] Pace is more than happy to have his witness silence "bought" with the promise in the last paragraph of the book of "plenty of briefs" from Steven Curry's firm – the major concern throughout the Draper novels being the scarcity of work for unconnected young barristers.

> You need a little help in the business world, I will see you're sent plenty of briefs because that's the only way in which young counsel can make their mark.[21]

What strikes one reading these books is the similarity of style and the mixture of comic storyline and the indirect commentary on the English legal system portrayed by Henry Cecil. They also prefigures the triple elements of John Mortimer's *Rumpole* stories with Case-Chambers-Home."[22] With Draper's work we encounter the amateurism of the training and the limitations of the market for legal services as well as a hint of the darker side of the ability of lawyers to stray from the path of righteousness, a feature largely missing from Cecil's lawyer portrayals.[23]

HASTINGS DRAPER ON THE LAW AND JUSTICE SYSTEM

The approach to a view on the English justice system and comments on it are generally rather more oblique in the writing of Draper than was noted in

Cecil's work. The issues which are raised emerge in the narratives and characters rather than in the comments made by the author to the reader. There are four principal themes which are worthy of note along with some issues which are touched on briefly.

The Bar as a "Closed" Profession

This is the serious underlying message from the first outing of Alan Pace. We meet the freshly qualified barrister, without connections within the legal profession, struggling to gain any work at all in postwar London.

> Alan Pace was not yet a successful barrister. That is to say, no close relative of his was a solicitor nor had he had the forethought to marry a solicitor's daughter.[24]

He works in Chambers where many of those are starved of paying work and where a large private income[25] or even a small private income is the order of the day.[26] The context is a legal profession split into office-based solicitors and barristers appearing as advocates in court. For barristers to work on behalf of an individual, they had to be referred by a solicitor.[27] The process by which solicitors might be encouraged to favour one set of Chambers over another,[28] is only mentioned once in the sad account by the Chief Clerk of his recent entertaining of someone from a firm of solicitors which has produced a very limited "payback."

> Blotches and Haksworth. I met the managing clerk two days ago and treated him to three pints of best mild and bitter in the Crypt . . . when I offered him the third pint I had something more than a two guinea[29] brief in mind.[30]

The solicitor then supervises contact with the barrister. It is made clear that work is at a premium and that many fall by the wayside.

> but because he had been unable, or unwilling, to cultivate solicitors, he had failed to receive any worthwhile work and, finally, had to leave.[31]

That said, the qualities likely to lead to success are dismissed by Draper in a throwaway line as having little to do with skill or innate ability

> Because he was not very clever, and possessed a skin impervious to verbal darts however strongly barbed, he was obviously destined to be a success at the Bar.[32]

As a barrister, then, to obtain work representing clients a barrister had to be instructed by a solicitor. Until he has experience, no-one is likely to provide him with work. Without work he cannot gain experience. The picture for him and similar colleagues is bleak since "To those without influence, the bar offered but one Hope – luck."[33]

Pace and his wife have just had to leave London to rent a decrepit cottage in the suburbs to save money. Hastings sets the scene in the barristers' Chambers with the other individuals at various stages in their legal careers/non-careers. These loose amalgams of individual lawyers share clerks who arrange fees and liaise with instructing solicitors. The clerks also recommend another member of Chambers if the barrister sought by the solicitor is unavailable. The status of clerks is adjudged to have risen from its interwar position as we find Pace musing.

> He thought how accurate a guide to social differences the car was. Before the war, barristers drove cars, solicitors' clerks used public transport. Nowadays, barristers used public transport, solicitors' clerks drove cars.[34]

Most of the junior barristers in Chambers find work in short supply, lacking either brilliance, or more importantly, family connections. There is one ray of hope which receives a number of mentions but which occurs on relatively few occasions in these books. A client in the waiting room of a solicitor's office is described thus:

> The man was obviously poor, but since the introduction of legal aid that had ceased to be an insurmountable difficulty.[35]

There is also a possibly tongue-in-cheek suggestion about the income guarantee element of the Beveridge Welfare State introduced in the 1940s providing income security from "cradle to grave."[36] This had, however, led to a diminution of crime – stemming, as is implied, from poverty.

> Beyond this hall were two courts only one of which was now used because with the virtual abolition of poverty there were fewer cases to be tried. This explained why the legal profession as a whole was highly suspicious of the welfare state.[37]

There is, however, an upside to the Welfare State which Draper notes in his account of Alan Pace's career sometime later in his third appearance.

> Legal aid enables anyone to have a go, and to the newly qualified, or not so successful, barrister this is an excellent thing. A few undefended divorces a day keep the debts at bay[38]

There is also a useful combining of products of the Welfare State with legal assistance and medicine free at the point of use which might save our impecunious barristers. Presciently, in view of the kinds of claims experienced by Britain's National Health Service in the 21st century,[39] he notes:

> In allowing people the joys of free operations for all sorts of novel and interesting complaints, the National Health Scheme had, in conjunction with Free Legal Aid, greatly widened the field for lawyers in the medical world:[40]

Alan himself has faith in the system's ability to produce a modicum of justice and notes that the ambience of the Court tends to achieve results

> even in the relatively short period Alan had been at the bar, he had learned the difference between the story told to the solicitor and typed out as a proof, and the evidence given in the witness box. Sometimes it almost seemed as though the taking of the oath had an effect.[41]

Amongst the other characters we encounter are pompous overweening Senior Counsel, manipulative Barristers' clerks, and grumpy judges. There are also litigants with quirky cases with very limited prospects in the style of AP Herbert. It is also reminiscent of the world of Horace Rumpole some 25 years later. We find out little, however, about the other barristers with whom Pace is quartered and where they fit into the higgledy piggledly world of legal practice.

The Costs of Going to Law

Although Draper's perspective and critique of the legal process and profession derive more from the narrative arcs and issues which Alan Pace encounters rather than adopting the Cecil style of editorialising, he does indulge in a certain number of "asides to the audience." For instance, we learn about unscrupulous solicitors in two of the books where they exploit their clients by extending litigation unnecessarily. The author does not comment on these actions as Cecil would no doubt have done. He lets the actions speak for themselves for the most part. He does, however, allow himself a number of sly scathing assessments of the venality of the legal profession in general.

> The two men carefully wrote on the pads before them: "one telephone call, Stone and NoDoze." The costs of the case must not be overlooked.[42]

This, in the context of a firm of solicitors who are unscrupulous in their desire to string out the cases with delaying tactics to swell their fees but is described as part of the lawyers' craft in general.

> Engraven on every lawyer's heart lies the motto: "more haste, less feed."[43]

Delay and wasting time were not something which were of concern to the legal profession in general as opposed to the firm of chiselling lawyers who instruct our protagonist. In a passage recalling the opening paragraphs of *Bleak House*,[44] Draper describes the courts' operations in almost Dickensian terms.

> The days passed and in the law courts, the Old Bailey, the Assizes, the quarter sessions, the stipendiary magistrates' courts. justice was done. . . . The Temple [one of the Inns of Court] had many too many mouths to feed in relation to the work that came its way. The carrion-crows of the legal profession plucked the monetary carcasses of their clients.[45]

The underlying theme is reinforced in Pace's later encounters where his Head of Chambers reminds him that money is a crucial element in the search for justice.

> Never forget this most important practical rule of law, . . . a man who fights the case because of the principles involved can safely be charged twice as much as anyone else.[46]

We are informed of the disjunction between cases coming to the attention of the legal profession and reaching the Courts in a relatively rare Draper "aside."

> Since few litigants ever knew what they were arguing about, it had been decided by certain rules of the Supreme Court – themselves a delightfully fruitful source of further litigation – that before the parties came to court they should set down there numerous complaints on paper. It was this paperwork that was the bread-and-butter of all junior counsel, since well over ninety per cent of all cases were settled before they came to court.[47]

The process of law, as was made very clear in *Jarndyce v Jarndyce* a century earlier in *Bleak House*, could be a long and winding road. It seems that little had altered in the interim. Noting that medicine had no use for a patient once they had died, we learn that,

> The law does not recognise such waste, and rightly so, since who is to say whether the dead are really alive, or the live are really dead. . . . One could always appeal. At practically every stage of a case one can appeal, and if one is a citizen filled with a zest for battle, then one can lodge many and varied appeals, and appeal the appeals, and have such skirmishing among the ramifications of

procedural law that by the time the actual case is heard nobody can remember what was the original bone of contention.[48]

There is, though, a distinction between the "sharp" practice of drawing out matters and breaching the rules of legitimate conduct

> Every trade or profession has its black sheep . . . the proportion of counsel who "arrange" is relatively small and not very flourishing, . . . [it consists of] Direct bribery of the solicitors' Chief Clerk and "kickback" . . . secondly an acceptance, without reservation, of any instruction from this solicitor as regards the conduct of the case.[49]

We see an attempt to impose on the barrister a time-wasting course of conduct by withdrawing instructions from one barrister and giving them to a more pliant and less principled advocate.[50] We learn of the rule which says one counsel cannot take another's brief unless the other agrees. In this instance, we see an example of ethical conduct at the Bar, when the preferred barrister known for complying with "time wasting" tactics, actually refuses the brief.[51]

Judges and the Courts

There are a number of comic judges with whom our protagonist must contend. They are a mixed bunch They include the independent minded and dispassionate,

> Mr Justice Tenby was everything that a judge should be. He had a long, lean, sardonic face and he spoke with sarcasm. He took no notice of anybody or anything, least of all the strictures of the Court of Appeal or Divisional Court. He ruled his court with a rod of iron. He would pronounce a judgement in Tort, or send a man to hang with equal ease and fluency. If he did not like a person he made no secret of that fact.[52]

Few were people one would choose to appear before and most appear to be somewhat dyspeptic.

> He wondered if Mr Justice Blue had become cantankerous because he was a judge, or whether he'd been appointed a Judge because he was cantankerous.[53]

Others sitting on the Bench have their own peculiarities. Even when Alan has a case which offers the "scope for some good and pretty legal argument,"[54] he is thwarted

> It was a pity it was before a County Court judge. Such gentlemen, being short tempered, fidgeted when any argument lasted five minutes, became impatient at the ten minute mark, and downright rude after a quarter of an hour.[55]

There are, however, parts of the justice system where justice appears to be absolutely absent in the Draper view of things. He notes enigmatically at one point

> In those Magistrates' Courts ruled by Justices of the Peace justice was rarely done.[56]

It is only later that we learn why these unpaid lay people are unable to provide what the professional judges manage. In an aside worthy of Henry Cecil himself, Draper opines through our protagonist the following assessment

> . . . You mustn't be rude about the magistrates courts–the average Englishman dotes on them.
>
> Until the day he comes before one and discovers that a bench of civilians concerned with their own pomp and ceremony and who lean on their Clerk for advice – possibly a local man with strings to pull – are quite incapable of doing justice as we know the word in the High Court.[57]

The problem seems to stem from their tendency to convict as opposed to a jury who are much more malleable and subject to persuasion.

For those judges who were unable to function effectively but who did not recognise their own failing powers and writing at a time before a compulsory retirement age was introduced,[58] Draper notes

> If everyone else knew that his memory and hearing were becoming dimmed, he did not . . . and in order to remove Mr Justice Carpet from a position in which he could do so much harm, he was made a Lord of Appeal in Ordinary [judge in the supreme appellate court – then the House of Lords – now Supreme Court].[59]

The notion that the supreme appellate court was filled with time-serving incompetents draws at least some of its force from the operation of the doctrine operating until 1966 that the then House of Lords judicial division could not revisit and overturn its own decisions as well as some of the personnel.[60] As is noted elsewhere in this text its composition and appointment process has been radically altered since Draper made his comments.[61]

Women and the Law

The idea of the male bastion that was the law in the 1950s being threatened by the encroachment of women results in no "editorial" comments from Draper. The issue does not appear at all in the novel, *Wiggery Pokery* from 1956. In Draper's first novel a major missing feature is women legal professionals.

There is only a spinster barrister's clerk and non-waged wives in this world of male barristers.

In his second story *Wigged and Gowned* from 1958 we see the issue of women in law from the point of view of the principal affected parties – the various male barristers. We learn in these books several things about male-female relationships rooted in the notion of women as subservient. From knowing that a woman's happiness can be bought with the promise of a dinner and a new dress,[62] we progress to an understanding that when our protagonist is a rich and successful barrister, his wife's ambition is to be bought "a new washing machine."[63]

Apart from their being consigned to the role of housewife – not uncommon in the 1950s and part of the reasoning behind pay disparity between married men and single men and women[64] – women are alleged to have a special character making them unsuited to decision-making. Alan's Head of Chambers expresses himself clearly in crude essentialist terms:

> What motivates a woman? It's either her unreasoning instinct or her unreasoned intuition. So what happens if she's judging a law case? One of two things. Either she hears the case and by the time it's finished has forgotten what's gone before and find for the party she instinctively prefers; or she intuitively makes her mind up at the very beginning and not even the last trumpet would make her change it.[65]

This notion of the apparently irrational and unhinged is encountered in a case prior to the second wave of feminism where a woman juror insists on finding against Pace's Head of Chambers for a reason quite unconnected with the evidence

> He referred to us as Gentlemen of the jury. He deliberately insulted me and all my sisters. . . . He is a perjurer and blasphemer and all he works for bears his mark of evil, corruption and rottenness.[66]

Keen to get away to carry on with their lives the other 11 members of the jury are finally prepared to go along and find the accused not guilty.[67]

In *Wigged and Gowned*,[68] the major focus is on relations with women, specifically a newly qualified blonde barrister, Caroline Welber. At the time of writing and during the years of Hastings Draper's practice as a barrister in the mid-1950s, the number of woman barristers practicing was some 64 out of a Bar of 1,000. The first woman QC was only appointed in 1949 and she remained the sole female QC for the decade of the 1950s.[69] The first female High Court judge in England was appointed in 1965.[70] As for the rest of the legal profession, progress was slow and meant that by 1968 women comprised less than 10 per cent of solicitors. [71]

The time being the 1950s, the nearest Alan Pace gets to infidelity is that of the mind in the style of US ex-president Jimmy Carter.[72] Caroline Welber is the junior barrister in the major case with which the second book was concerned. This again involves a rich eccentric – golf-mad Jonathan Green – who keeps absent-mindedly marrying women without, apparently, remembering to obtain a divorce from the incumbent wife. This time, however, we are dealing with crime. Green has been charged with bigamy and Alan Pace is the junior counsel. The major theme throughout this second outing is the role of women in the legal profession. The Head of Chambers, Oliver Hunt, has had a traumatic experience when appearing in the past before a female magistrate. This fills him with fear when the judge in the bigamy trial, Mr Justice Blue dies in the luncheon interval and a newly appointed judge appears for the new trial. This turns out to be Mrs Justice Jelph, the first female High Court judge to be appointed in England. Here Draper anticipates history as the first female High Court judge, Elizabeth Lane was not appointed until 1965.[73]

Fortunately Hunt's nemesis, the oily and manipulative Reggie Aiden rubs the judge up the wrong way and incurs her displeasure in his confusion as to how to address her and by referring to her as a "woman judge." Things are resolved neatly when a combination of the intuition of Pace's spectator wife Belinda and her insistence that Alan put the points she thinks are pertinent along with the unconventional non-legalistic approach of the new judge produce a surprise victory for the defence and an end to the ill-fortune of Head of Chambers, Oliver Hunt, when women are involved in his trials.

The last time we encounter barrister Alan Pace he is still making his way in the legal profession but with gaps in his work diary. This time, in *Brief Help* from 1961 the major narrative driver continues to be women and their status. The background story centres on the supposed "wandering eye" of the protagonist, Alan, and the problems he encounters in trying to maintain a mask of innocence in relation to his dealings with the by-now married Caroline Welber. She has married the golf-mad eccentric Jonathan Green but now, three years on, wants Alan Pace to act for her in her divorce.

In the meantime, in a run of farcical cases, from which Pace is distracted by these issues in his personal life, he manages to lose cases which he should have won but where losing the court battle means winning a wider war. In one instance he asks the one question the solicitor has warned him not to ask, which exposes his client's knowledge of the terms and conditions under which he lodged four dozen kippers at a left luggage office which have been lost. A *deus ex machina* rescues Alan's error when the terms and conditions which appear to give all the rights to the other party mean that the opponents are in fact owners of the now-found kippers. These ageing kippers, however, have contaminated forty tons of butter of another depositor. Alan's additional question has brought into play the terms and conditions which, by luck, removes responsibility from his client.[74] By the same token, he causes a client charged with unlawful imprisonment to lose his case and be liable in damages. At the last moment, having won over the jury he snatches defeat from the jaws of victory by asking an additional unnecessary question as to the state of the fire escape down which the imprisoned individual could have escaped. This would have been dangerous as it was rotten. This turns out, however, to be a saving of his client whose story is bought up by the papers and he makes far more money through increased visitor numbers to his stately home than he would have had he not been convicted. The instructing solicitor is exceedingly pleased.[75] Finally, in a case highly reminiscent of one of AP Herbert's *Misleading Cases*,[76] he acts for a person who takes actions against a politician who promised to reduce local taxes if he got into office. He is elected and the local taxes are, in fact, raised. The claim is that the vote was obtained under false pretences in terms of the Corrupt Practices Prevention Act. He loses the case but unwittingly saves his client since, we are led to understand, a person who allows himself to be so affected would also be guilty of the offence of bribery.[77] A clear pattern is established in the final outing. Pace appears to be developing into a poorer less persuasive advocate than when he started out on his career.

The major part of the final book, though, involves a series of misunderstandings and misperceptions around Pace's denials that he has met Caroline and his lies to his wife about her. All these meetings are, of course, completely innocent, but, egged on by his Head of Chambers, Oliver Hunt, who fancies himself as some kind of latter day "fixer" figure in the mould of PG Wodehouse's Jeeves,[78] Pace resorts to a variety of fictions and misrepresentations. At one juncture he claims to have had lunch not with Caroline but a fictitious woman whose name he makes up, whom he describes as looking like the "back end of a bus." This person turns out to exist – the name being buried in his subconscious – and to be someone he played with as a boy. She is, of course, stunningly beautiful. This is discovered, and it comes back to haunt him. Like the first two books, the book concludes with a "major" case. In *Brief Help* this involves the divorce of Caroline Green, née Welber, for desertion by her husband. The grounds are explained

> Desertion has to be without cause and for a period of at least three years immediately prior to the petition. There has to be separation and an intention to the desert, and both elements must be present. Separation is a question of fact.[79]

As a result of the distracted incompetence of Alan Pace, evidence emerges that, during the required minimum period of three years of the so-called desertion there were several periods of reconciliation. The couple end up together at the end of the book effusively thanking Alan for bringing them to their senses. It was, it turns out, all a way of Caroline getting her rich but occasionally cheeseparing rich husband to pay her a decent allowance. He agreed to her terms late in the action provided that the divorce did not go through. The book ends with Alan and his wife Belinda happily together with the would-be solver of all marital problems, Oliver Hunt still phoning in improbable belated schemes of reconciliation. The apparent simplicity of women and their happiness at their secondary role in life are shown here to full effect. To this we are also led to understand they are also cunning and manipulative into the bargain.

Prescient Issues

Some notions are present which we might imagine emerged in the 1970s with hard-hitting police dramas showing that not all police were avuncular figures in the style of traditional friendly "Bobby" George Dixon.[80] Police evidence is, here in the 1950s looked on with some scepticism, at least by juries

> Normally, Counsel did not attack a witness so directly, even if the said Counsel were greatly annoyed, because if he did, the jury automatically sided with the witness in his capacity as Traditional British Underdog, kicked around yet once again. But when a policeman was a witness, the psychology was different! The uniform became English Officialdom, the most legitimate of targets for all, a veritable Aunt Sally and everyone thoroughly enjoyed the sight of a police witness being proved an imbecilic liar. Of course, once the same policeman was out of the box, he ceased to be Officialdom and was once again the Friend of the People.[81]

Although, as Draper enigmatically observes, only a friend of "some of the people."[82]

Some matters which are briefly mentioned, have come to form a major issue in later thinking about the criminal justice system and whom it protects. A colleague enquires whether another barrister is available. The language and approach are interesting to us 60 years on with paedophilia the major factor in the kind of "self-help justice" vigilantism encountered in Britain,[83]

> I wanted a word with him about a case of I have. Most peculiar affair – my chaps been had up for running after little girls. I just can't understand it since he's a man of over sixty. . . . Can you follow why a man does such a thing.
>
> Alan considered the question, slowly shook his head. He could understand normal human passions . . . yet in a case like the present one he also was at a loss.[84]

Apart from the caricatured feminist juror noted above,[85] a couple of other incidents show how ideas have altered. A nit-picking solicitor, Hipscord, is the channel through whom we learn of the dangers of tobacco smoke[86] and of the benefits of a meat free diet.[87] In Pace's world everyone smokes and Hipscord is presented as a pain in the neck evangelist. His day is yet to come. Rather less forward looking is the view we are provided on the supposed benefits of Empire, albeit at a time when British colonial rule was under severe challenge with independence movements from Cyprus to Kenya resorting to armed struggle to persuade imperial Britain to grant self-government.

> He'd been a judge in one of the colonies that had newly found independence: the rulers had deported all those Europeans who had assisted the country to progress to a state of balance on the plea that they were responsible for the country's previous backwardness.[88]

Some comments are even more questionable, and probably tongue in cheek, as where the existence of undefended divorces supports young barristers and hence a flow of people into the judiciary.

> Indeed, since our democracy needs an independent judiciary now more than ever before in order to combat the growing power of the executive over the legislature, it can truthfully be stated that undefended divorces are an absolute necessity to the well-being of our state.[89]

SUMMARY

Having established a more leisurely pace than the rapid rise and career success of Henry Cecil's Roger Thursby, Roderic Jeffries might have been expected to go on producing novels charting the legal life of Alan Pace for some years. This did not occur. After *Brief Help* there is nothing more from the pen of Hastings Draper. Perhaps Roderic Jeffries had returned to lucrative legal practice? Possibly the sheer volume of Cecil's work and his successful translation to stage, screen and television had exhausted the market demand for light legal procedurals? In fact, Jeffries simply shifted his emphasis from the legal profession to crime fiction and went on to produce some 186 books, none of which return to the English courts in comic mode[90] but are principally located abroad where Jeffries moved.[91]

His legal novels are set at the same time and in the same milieu as mid-period Cecil. There are several themes which immediately suggest themselves in contrast to the world of Cecil. Firstly, the role of women is very different. In the legal world of Henry Cecil women make only the rarest of appearances as legal protagonists. There are the sisters, Jane and Prunella Coombe – solicitor and barrister – whom we came across in *Daughters in Law*.[92] Rather than being heroic protagonists, however, they are the innocent dupes of the Buttonstep brothers. By contrast, Hastings Draper features women judges and women barristers in *Wigged and Gowned* from 1958. The lawyers' wives are, of course, for the 1950s, not surprisingly, located in the home rather than engaged in waged work. It is not simply that Draper has women in the picture in a somewhat different way from his contemporary writer Cecil but also the role of women is discussed much more extensively. The vehicle for the discussion of women's role is the misogynistic Head of Chambers, Oliver Hunt. He is the catalyst for a discussion of what women can or cannot add to the practice of law. His misogyny is not, however, merely, a knee-jerk reaction to the female sex. He has suffered reverses whenever he has appeared before women magistrates. This provides the opportunity for our main protagonist, "everyman" Pace, to provide the platform for a more nuanced view of a legal world with women in it.

There is also the question of the nature of the legal profession. The principal issue which all the books illustrate is the need for a substantial private income to be able to practice at the English Bar of the 1950s. This is achieved through our "unconnected" barrister making his way more through luck and "niceness" rather any great skill or application. There is also a neat contrast with his relative success as compared with the other members of the Chambers who lack his luck. There is also the issue of race which we find very briefly in the work of Mortimer [93] but which is absent from Draper. Although Britain experienced race riots in 1958 in Nottingham and Notting Hill and had racist political parties commanding attention in by-elections,[94] the issues of immigration and race were rather later in appearing in both novels[95] and film.[96]

As noted above, the loss to the literary world of Alan Pace was not, on the face of it, due to any factor other than the writer's desire to work in other genres producing police procedurals and thrillers. It is perhaps to be regretted that his keen critical eye was not caste over the developments and changes in the decades from the 1960s onwards given the tone and prescience of this out-of-character aside towards the end of his final light legal comedy:

> Most forms of legal actions have decreased in numbers due to the fact that the class of person who used to enjoy going to law can no longer do so owing to the effects of constant inflation, and the companies which might have taken such people's places seem to prefer to waste their money on esoteric or erotic advertising. Divorce provides the exception. Legal aid enables anyone to have a go, and to the newly qualified, or not so successful barrister, that is an excellent thing. A few undefended divorces a day keep the debts at bay.[97]

Hastings Draper's adventures of Alan Pace do provide readers with a sharper and more critical viewpoint of the legal profession and the issues of gender and class in postwar Britain to contrast with the rather blander version which we get from an initial reading of his contemporary in writing, Henry Cecil.

The three Pace novels are courtroom comedies. They proceed, though, at a quite leisurely pace. They would certainly have allowed the spawning of further works of fiction, TV and radio series and films without too much effort. Between his first appearance in *Wiggery Pokery* in 1956 and his final appearance five years later in *Brief Help*, Alan Pace has gone from being a struggling young barrister with financial and marital problems to being a struggling young barrister with financial and marital problems. There has been no change in his status as a very junior barrister. He and his wife have produced no children. They inhabit the same run-down cottage in the same suburb of London. Like the time lock in Walmington-on-Sea and in many radio soaps noted above,[98] the events and encounters of Alan Pace are preserved in aspic firmly in about 1955. Lots of clients may have married and divorced but time has more or less stood still. He is, however, gradually building something akin to a practice and like the fans of Henry Cecil, one might reasonably have expected in due course a further entry from the Pace *curriculum vitae*. Given his greater recognition of the impact and emerging role of women in the profession it is to be regretted that his eye was not cast over the law in the ensuing decades.

JOHN BUDD

The life and times of John Budd are even less well documented than those of Roderic Jeffries. Born in 1913, John Budd was a partner in the solicitor's firm, J Budd and Co. in Blackpool. This was a family firm and included his cousin William Aldred. The founder's name is still in existence in Blackpool at the time of writing under the umbrella of Blackhurst Budd. John Budd became a Coroner until his retirement. His parents were a violinist Victor (1885–1981) and children's clothing maker Ellen (1887–) John was renowned for being one of the last to wear a bowler hat – once the mark of the professional man/solicitor. The books were set in Blackpool and it has been suggested that it was possible to recognise the characters from his books.[99] The town has a Tower and a Golden Mile like Blackpool.[100] He produced ten books in what has been called the "established genre of vocational comedy."[101] These were almost all centred in the same solicitor's office in an unnamed provincial town. They trace the life of the solicitor Julian Prescot from his days as a young apprentice solicitor in the family firm through being made a partner and then over the years. The books are set in an unspecified era. John Budd wrote a 200-page book every year for 10 years between 1958 and 1967. All but one were books with "case" in the title and were in the light comedic vein. As a keen racing man and owner of horses he produced one other work of fiction about horseracing in 1966 with the unusual title of *The Krakatoa Colt.* It features as its protagonists the lawyers whom we know from the "case" series so that this maintains readers' interests in familiar legal characters although it is only tangentially a light legal comedy.

More than any of the other writers in this study the books follow a straightforward narrative. They are essentially anecdotal and judging by the reaction of critics had the ring of authenticity about their subject – which unlike all the other writers concerned the practice of a provincial solicitor in England rather than a barrister appearing in court. The very first page of John Budd's first venture into writing about the world of provincial solicitors reminds us of the very exclusive company we are in. In order to become a solicitor at the time Budd was writing qualification involved working without pay for five years after paying a premium of £300–£6,000 at 2024 prices. Budd's protagonist, Julian Prescot, is fortunate that he can enter a firm where his uncle is a partner and which bears his own name, having been founded by his own grandfather. In his first book, *Both Sides of the Case* (1958), we are taken through the five years of Julian's training as an articled clerk. As noted elsewhere,[102] this was at one time the standard route into the profession in England. In 1922 some 83 per cent of solicitors entered the profession this way rather than obtaining a law degree and completing a shorter practical apprenticeship. It was not until the 1960s that the figure of graduate solicitors in England and Wales rose above 50 per cent.[103]

His firm places him in various departments, from the family section through civil litigation and criminal defence work to wills and conveyancing. During this time, we encounter a variety of characters with problems ranging from excessive sexual demands by a husband to disputed paternity claims and nullity for non-consummation. The people whom Julian encounters are dealt with sketchily in a few pages. Rather like some of the incidents in Alan Pace's career, they make nice vignettes for a television adaptation. For instance, in his first brush with criminal defence work, he is perplexed by the language of his safebreaker client and the mystery of who Peter is. Peter, of course being the term for a safe and other words like "screwing" and "nicked" all add to Julian's confusion. Also, when working in the matrimonial side of the office his reticence means he is loath to directly ask one young woman about any affairs she may have had before her husband deserted her. Known as the "discretion" question this admission used to involve the court being asked to exercise its discretion and overlook the "matrimonial offence" of adultery if it did not itself contribute to the desertion. Swayed by the beauty and demure appearance of his client, Julian does not feel able to put the "discretion" question. It is the client who asks him why he has not asked this question and then proceeds to fill a full sheet with her various affairs. A valuable lesson learned. On this theme of the televisuality of the incidents in Julian's life, we have him being asked to make up the numbers in an identity parade. The result is inevitable but, of course, he is a solicitor and beyond reproach and the real criminal is caught in a police "sting" a few nights later.[104]

Julian also discovers the wiles of another of the firm's specialists who deals with personal injury cases including skimming a little from settlements by way of a tip for excellent service. The same man is keen to sniff out "malingerers" with dubious claims. One such device involved a woman who claimed to have been traumatised by a wasp served in a hotel's food. Keen to avoid publicity, the lawyer arranges for a second medical opinion at a location some miles away providing generous expenses to the potential litigant. Suckered into the trap the woman duly avails herself of the expenses to eat a slap-up lunch and her bluff is effectively called and her false claim exposed.[105]

In the subsequent outings with our protagonist, we find him in *The Case Continued* (1959) expanding his work in the field of criminal defence. In the year after qualifying, he gets to deal with the "dross" in the form of

> cases involving clients who tended to be unbalanced, impecunious, or unpleasant, not only lent spicy variety to my professional life but kept the cranks who are to be found among any legal clientele away from my colleagues, so enabling them to concentrate on the weighty cases that brought in the costs.[106]

He can observe a whole host of different approaches to court practice ranging from the defence by an accomplished solicitor of a drunk driver whose smell of alcohol, slurred speech, illegible writing, falling over and furry tongue are all "explained away."[107] His work involves him in matrimonial work as well as the juvenile court which affect his view of the punishment process, as noted below. He learns how to trim as where he loses clients with horses by defending someone accused of cruelty to horses by promising not to take such defence work in the future.[108] All does not go swimmingly though. Julian has the embarrassment of being conned into defending an upmarket sex worker.[109] The book is peppered with humorous vignettes as when he takes on a case involving Donald McGill type "seaside postcards,"[110] when a betting tip is accidentally passed to a magistrate[111] and when a newspaper appeal to save three redundant coal horses takes off.[112] By the end of the book, though he has collected a coterie of loyal clients and is made a partner in the firm.[113]

His career continues on an even keel and the next books take us through the day-today work of a young solicitor; although as we shall see, the emphasis changes from the collection of everyday incidents to rather more focused single theme stories. His next book, though, retains the collection approach. In *Case Proceeding* (1960), there is a parade of interesting issues typical of a the work of a provincial solicitor's. These range from the mundane motoring, assault[114] and illegal street trading cases[115] to more unusual issues – a damages claim for an escaped bull having impregnated a neighbouring herd of cows,[116] keeping a common gaming house[117] and bigamy.[118] Some cases seem from the pages of crime fiction although as Scots writer William McIntyre has effectively demonstrated identifying the real and fictional stories is no easy task. McIntyre records the publishers' doubting reaction to his fact-based tales and praise for the realistic material concocted from his imagination.[119] Julian encounters a serial will-maker who visits a number of solicitors' offices to make a will.[120] Their safes are subsequently burglarised and despite what appears compelling forensic evidence, with the assistance of Julian, the testator avoids conviction. He also provides help to a pools winner who is the victim of a range of scams.[121]

Julian's legal life by the time of his fourth book, *Case for the Accused* (1961), has taken on a familiar pattern:

> For me, Monday and Friday in the magistrates' court at the bottom of South Kemp Street meant a heavy heterogenous list likely to contain anything from minor mayhem to careless motoring; Tuesday – Black Tuesday as I call it – was domestic day, devoted almost exclusively to the problems of marriage gone awry ; Wednesday was usually reserved for long committals; while on Thursday afternoons, prodigal sons and delinquent daughters passed in sad procession on their way to the juvenile court.[122]

Early in his career he discovers that the cases he is involved in result in a problem of public reputation when defending people charged with unpopular actions such as living off immoral earnings and child and animal cruelty.[123]

> If a lawyer consents to act in cases of certain type he quickly finds himself falling under cloud of personal opprobrium which has done nothing to deserve.[124]

The approach and material in *Case for the Accused* (1961) is a continuation of the ordinary and the unusual, although there is more coverage of the latter. So we find alongside accident cases where the client's limp disappears after the court decision[125] and where a client's son committed multiple motoring offences to impress a girl[126] to the rather more intriguing notion that adultery in a motorcycle sidecar might be possible.[127] Some novel defences are encountered and succeed in Julian's defence work. A small pugilistic client is found not guilty of assault when his dog was called a "miserable little mongrel"[128] and the victim loses the sympathy of the jury. Another campaigner against drink who is charged with drink driving benefits from a finding that the sample has been affected by her being diabetic.[129]

Similar kinds of matters and approach are encountered in *Case for Trial* (1962). Again, the book consists of a series of small cases which come across Julian's desk as a solicitor in private practice. None are earth-shattering but they give a flavour of the daily round in a small town. We have him defending a range of clients from a charge of indecent assault by taking a 15-year-old's measurements for an alleged possible film role[130] to the illegal sale of alcohol in a cafe[131] youths aged 12 and 13 "playing at bank robbers"[132] and cruel treatment of an old dog.[133] There is also a foretaste of his later works when he deals at length with the phenomenon of "mock auctions" and the criminal implications.[134] One area which particularly exercises Julian at this time is the crime of underage sex.[135] This leads to some editorialising on this as is noted below which captures neatly a misogynistic victim blaming perspective.[136] There is also room for humorous civil work with a prize boar failing to perform when out to stud.[137] and a slip and fall claim by the person charged with maintaining the slippery floor.[138]

There is, though, a change of style in the books from 1963 onwards. The focus shifts away from the career of Julian Prescot. In *Case for Hearing* (1963) we have interlinked narratives centring on two families. One is a loveable rogue, window-cleaning burglar Wally Sambrook who somehow manages to avoid the long arm of the law represented by a Detective Inspector Drax. The matters are complicated by the fact that the son and daughter of the two sides of legality become a romantic item. There is a series of escapades in which the burglarising window cleaner, Wally always seems to avoid apprehension. His solicitor, Julian, reports these various scrapes but we hear almost nothing of anything else the lawyer is involved in other than a bigamy case.[139] Matters with the policeman/rogue are finally brought to head when their offspring elope to Gretna Green and their relationship collapses when the pregnant ex-amour of the boy appears. The only thing we discover about Julian Prescot in this volume is that he has a hobby – winter wildfowling.[140]

This shift in approach is even more marked in *Case for Court* (1964) Julian plays the role of reporter in a long-drawn-out tale about the difficult relationship between a newcomer to the town and a well-established but unscrupulous solicitor. This the only one of Prescot's books which is précised in Jon Breen's *Novel Verdicts.* This "guide to courtroom fiction" provides thumbnail sketches of "trial fiction" books.[141] As he notes, the book is centred on the attempt by a young solicitor who moves into Prescot's town to take over the business of a retiring lawyer. Another pompous solicitor in town resents the incomer and is particularly exercised when he becomes involved with his own daughter. He gets up to all sorts of ruses to harm the young man's budding practice. It is never entirely clear why he is so exercised as his own practice is thriving. There is a resolution when the two combatants are each defending a husband and wife in a murder case using the "cutthroat defence." Each blames the other. All the evidence points to the wife although it seems as though the husband has "set up" the wife to take the fall. One expects some kind of Perry Mason denouement but it all fizzles out at the end with the young upstart producing no "rabbit out of the hat" and leaving town. Breen notes this "genuinely surprising conclusion is truer to real life than fictional formula."[142] It is, nonetheless, a bit of damp squib for the reader who has been duped into thinking the underdog will surely at last have his day.

The focus on matters other than the life and work of provincial solicitor Julian Prescot is also found in his eighth offering. *The Case Re-opened* (1965) has him, instead, recount the more dynamic and unconventional career of another new solicitor in town, Jack Paxton-White. The raffish character replaces Julian again as the central character in the book. What we hear about is how before the Second World War entry into the law was effected. Not only did the aspiring lawyer receive no payment but was required to pay a sum of money for the privilege of working as an "articled clerk" in a law office. The sum for the stamp for the articles alone was £80 (£4,700 at 2024 prices).[143] Jack was an acquaintance last encountered in Brussels during the war.

In what appears to be a complete shift away from the "cases" series, the next offering from Julian Prescot was *The Krakatoa Colt* (1966), which derives from John Budd's own ownership of race horses. In this story we have a revised version of Julian Prescot's entry into the law. Before he had considered the legal profession, we are told he had been a keen amateur jockey riding under National Hunt rules. As a boy his ambition was to win the Derby.[144] In this telling he qualifies in 1939 and then spends six years in the army before returning to practice in 1945.

> I came back to a legal world very different to the one I had left behind me six years before. Lawyers seemed to be working like galley-slaves: the stream of conveyancing was already in heavy spate, for the men returning from the services were queueing up to buy homes; divorce work was going ahead under full sail on the troubled seas of separation and wartime infidelity; so that instead of dropping back into the old, leisurely routine I found that there there was more to do, less staff to do it, and that I was working a great deal harder than I'd ever worked before.[145]

He kept up his interest in racing and managed to attend some meetings. Along with his horse-mad Aunt Clara, Jack Paxton-White and fellow solicitor Harry Pemberton he forms a syndicate to buy a horse and run him in the Derby. This forms the gist of the book, and we end with the success dreamed of as a boy – winning the Derby albeit as an owner rather than a jockey. Matters of legal practice do not feature other than context for him having money to invest in horseflesh.There is the question of an attempt to nobble their horse before the race. This book, then is more Dick Francis[146] than Henry Cecil.

Julian Prescot's final novel at the age of 54 was ostensibly a return to the world of solicitors in *Case Counterfeit* (1967). This time, however, it is a thriller, and we have shifted to clients of the firm of a new lawyer, Frank Strickland. He is the family solicitor for the Montague family. They have in their home a valuable painting which cannot be sold as it is part of the estate which is entailed.[147] The story revolves around the attempts to raise money for the estate and the discovery that the painting may be a fake. Although the book is technically part of the "cases" series it does not have any of the features of the earlier books and is a "whodunnit" of sorts.

JULIAN PRESCOT'S STYLE

Prescot employs quite elaborate language and makes a range of obscure literary and historical references absent from any of the other writers in this field. The unusual language may be a creature of its time or simply reflect this writer's limited vocabulary, but it includes "erubescent"[148] "extravasate,"[149] "cloacal,"[150] "adamantine,"[151] and "cynosure."[152] Some are, however, of use such as the case involving a "monorchid" Sealyham dog,[153] discovering what the terms "living tally"[154] and "Burma"[155] mean. The same may be said of the historical references which may reflect a more literary age. These include an adolescent delinquent referred to as "a budding Gezinck"[156] and the "Procession of Sirdar."[157] There is mention of George Cruickshank,[158] Dendy Sadler,[159] Harpagon,[160] King David and the Shunammite,[161] Dunmow Flitch,[162] Murat,[163] La Salle,[164] Marengo,[165] Fouquier Tinville[166] and Dragonetti.[167] There are also references which might be familiar to a niche legal audience such as Sergeant (sic) Buzfuz from Pickwick Papers,[168] Sir Edward Marshall Hall[169] who died in 1927 as well as "Dodson and Fogg tricks."[170] Non-English phrases are mentioned but not translated such as the Latin "melius est petere fontes (quam sectari rivulos – not completed in the book)"[171] nor the French derived "autrefois acquit."[172]

PRESCOT'S ISSUES

In addition, as far as editorialising is concerned, these occur on a few topics on a one-off basis. For instance, in relation to defamation he notes,

> Usually there is only one piece of advice that one can conscientiously give to a client who instructs one to issue a writ claiming damages for defamation. That advice can be crystallised in the simple injunction, "Don't".[173]

He also tells the readers about the final remedy when a debtor will not pay, although he does not express a view on whether jail for debt is a good idea:

> The judgement summons is the last hope of the creditor who has tried all other remedies and failed to obtain satisfaction: when an execution has proved abortive; bankruptcy proceedings, for one reason or another, are impracticable; all other known means of enforcing a judgement have been tried and found wanting, the creditor issues his summons calling upon his debtor to appear before the court and to show cause why he, the debtor, should not be committed to prison for making default in payment.[174]

There is a fine sense of the problem of a solicitor having to be a master of a whole range of laws which can be changed and whose meaning is never constant anyway. He explains to his mother that he has had to deal with a case about the protections afforded to tenants by the Rent Acts. Since he has just qualified as a lawyer, she is at a loss to comprehend this as "surely every solicitor should know everything there is to know about the Rent Acts? I thought cases about them cropped up almost every day"[175] Julian's remarks are prescient:

> I don't suppose many High Court judges know all there is to know about them. In fact it was a judge who once described them as a tangled welter of chaotic verbiage that were rapidly consigning many of Her Majesty's judges to an untimely grave. I suppose I shall get the hang of them in time. The trouble is, they'll probably be repealed before I do.[176]

Throughout the years of Julian Prescot's life as a solicitor, though, a number of issues do recur.

Expenses

Julian is advised in two ways on this issue. From the civil side he is advised "always deliver your bills of costs while the tears of gratitude are still in the clients' eyes."[177] When working on the criminal defence partner, however, the idea of gratitude is firmly in the background. As he learns though "The first principle of criminal practice is cash on the counter. You must have cash down . . . the chances are that when a criminal case is over the client will have tears in his eyes not because he's full of gratitude for what you and counsel have done for him but because he's going to prison."[178] As he complains when his principal is often out of the office he has to apply "the first principle . . . when it came to the question of costs to stipulate, quite firmly, for cash on the counter."[179]

Criminal legal aid and civil legal aid are, it seems, two very different animals – "in civil cases given under the Legal Aid and Advice Act . . . solicitors and counsel get eighty-five per cent of their full fees,and legal aid in criminal cases under the Poor Prisoners Defence Act, where if one does the work properly, one gets so little that the case usually results in a dead loss."[180]

Criminal Guilt

The notion that the police are usually right in their actions is found in Budd's Prescot. As he observes

> I discovered that the majority of cases that come the way of the solicitor-advocate are lost long before the client comes in to consult him . . . the majority of cases we were retained to deal with in the Magistrates' Court involved nothing more than a plea in mitigation.[181]

The problem for any defence lawyer was the high level of credibility of the police:

> Blake is no ordinary witness. As a former police officer his evidence will be accepted without question. In fact, counsel for the Crown accept what he says and won't even bother to cross examine.[182]

That said he expresses his doubts about juries and their effectiveness:

> Juries often acquit the guilty, where the offence is not brought home to the accused beyond all doubt, but I had never yet known one convict a client who was innocent.[183]

Prescot, though, has doubts too about the true "guilt" of young men charged with underage sex and again sees such events as part of the dark female arts of seduction.

> The average calendar usually contains half a dozen cases relating to young men charged with having relations with girls below the age of consent, and it is extremely easy for the layman to get the erroneous impression that the world of to-day contains an unduly high proportion of youthful satyrs who go around challenging the chastity of any girl below the age of 16.
>
> In fact, as anyone who practises criminal law well knows, the girl herself is often largely to blame. The modern young miss of fifteen is rarely an

unsophisticated child in need of statuary protection; in fact one finds that long before she is out of the schoolroom she is physically and emotionally mature and all too eager to play the role of huntress to any attractive masculine quarry who comes her way.[184]

Punishment

Early on in the series Budd expresses great faith in the possibilities of guidance and the value of the Probation service in securing rehabilitation and avoid recidivism:

> My work in the juvenile court brought me into constant touch with probation officers, so much of whose work consists of plucking youthful brand from the burning, and it didn't take me long to reach the conclusion that whatever public money is laid out on the probation service is money that could hardly be better spent. A long criminal record often builds up in a well-defined progression; the offender begins on the lowest run of the wrongdoer's ladder with a period in an approved school; then, a few offences later, he finds himself in a Borstal institution; and ultimately, on reaching criminal maturity, he gravitates to one of Her Majesty's prisons. His first terms of imprisonment are usually short ones, but the longer he goes on offending the longer his sentences become, until he finally reaches the age of thirty and some judge, deciding that reformation is now out of the question, passes a sentence of eight years or so of preventive detention.[185]

It is not simply the desire for providing a more fruitful path away from a life of "crime – prison – crime – prison ad infinitum" but the recognition that this makes little economic sense for society:

> A confirmed offender of this kind, in a criminal career perhaps extending over thirty or forty years, inevitably costs the State many thousands of pounds. But if a probation officer who can catch the young offender at the very beginning of what might otherwise be a long criminal career, and can contrive to nip his anti-social tendencies in the bud, then he effects an enormous financial saving and turns a potential State liability into an asset in the shape of a useful and self-supporting citizen. A good probation officer, in receipt of a modest salary, saves that salary many times over if his efforts are crowned by success in only a small proportion of the cases he deals with; in fact, the incidence of success in probation cases is remarkably high.[186]

It is worth noting that he also expressed a view which does not ring true to those reading it over 60 years later:

> The juvenile court also has to deal with a sprinkling of sexual offenders – usually accused of indecent assault – and I rapidly came to the conclusion that

> most of my young clients are motivated more by a misplaced sense of curiosity than by anything else . . . who has become aware of certain essential biological differences between the sexes, and has proceeded to a fumbling and empirical investigation.[187]

The success of this as a defence in the 21st century seems improbable, and it is hard to imagine anyone putting it forward. The perspective on rape and sexual assault, perhaps, reflects the time of writing in relation to the reaction to women's complaints in this field.

> The man who is charged with rape, however, is rarely the sensual brute he sounds, and the incidence of acquittal in cases of rape is remarkably high. Quite often the girl concerned is a fully consenting party to all the preliminary intimacies, and although she is quite prepared to bring her partner to boiling point – and to keep him there indefinitely – she's often all too ready to blame him when he suddenly boils over.[188]

So the explanation for rape is to blame the victim. As he goes on to explain to a client who had sex with a man she met in a pub and with whom she later had sex against her will. Her change of mind, however, had come to late:

> Her alleged retraction of consent would appear to have been made too late, and in circumstances in which no normal man could have been reasonably expected to act upon it. I suggested she had been playing with fire and had only herself to blame because she had been burned; and that no reasonable jury could possibly convict in the light of the evidence which had been given.[189]

Equally questionable is the "tough" line taken on domestic matters where Budd distinguishes between "real cruelty" and imagined matrimonial wrongs

> Experience of the real cruelty one so often encounters in cases dealt with by the domestic court tends to make one impatient with the women – and they are legion – who haunt solicitors' offices to seek advice upon their imagined matrimonial wrongs. I soon came to know all too well the client who comes in, tells you that she has issued a summons against her husband for persistent cruelty, and then – when asked to give some details – trots out to a disconnected mass of trivia that doesn't amount to cruelty at all.[190]

He provides a single example of a client who has "married beneath her" and who resents her husband's lack of ambition along with his doing the football pools and going out for a drink on a Saturday to a club where she would not be seen dead. Julian advises her that her claim that this amounts to mental cruelty is not well founded. Her husband in fact welcomes release from his wife which with Julian's assistance he secures.

Legal Aid and the Impecunious Client

Julian Prescot sees the emergence of legal aid as a welcome development in the context of a client base who are keen to have their solicitor bear the burden of their legal worries:

> The men and women who come into a lawyer's office for advice care little for legal erudition; in any event, few understand it. What they need is someone to whom they can chat as a friend, someone who can reduce a legal problem to simple and easily comprehensible terms, someone who will imbue them with confidence and send them away with the comforting assurance that they have transferred a difficult personal problem on to sturdy professional shoulders well able to bear the burden.[191]

In his next outing he expands on this notion where Julian's mentor observes that

> A solicitor shouldn't be someone who, from Olympian heights, dispenses advice like some oracle to the lesser mortals below. He's there to help human beings with human problems, to inject confidence into the faint-hearted, and comfort into those in distress. He should make their burdens his burdens, and – wherever possible – look upon those who come to consult him not so much just as clients but his friends.[192]

As for those who have limited means we learn the benefits of the assistance available to enable lawyers to come within the budgets of such clients. That said, he tempers his acceptance of the legal aid system with a certain degree of petulant frustration

> It was all very well for a beneficent and enlightened legislature to decree that any citizen who needed it should be entitled to free legal advice. But advice is seldom welcome, and those are need it most usually like it least. The soul-destroying reality is that so many of those who come in for advice are determined not to accept it unless it happens to coincide exactly with what they want to hear. Without the foolish and the stubborn the lawyer would have a great deal less to do.[193]

There is, though, an acceptance that those with limited means are not to be denied legal assistance simply on account of lack of funds.

> Unfortunately, they're always some clients in every practice who haven't two pennies to rub together, who stand in dire need of professional help, and simply have to be helped whether they can pay one or not. Clients like that – almost always – seemed to find their way to me, and if it came to a choice whether I was going to take a fee or whether the client, his wife and children, were likely to go short of a dinner, I plumped for the dinner every time.[194]

Sexuality

Julian Prescot writes during an era in which same-sex relations between men were criminalised as well as crudely stereotyped.

> The homosexual, charged with gross indecency or – more rarely – with something worse, is perhaps the easiest type to detect on sight: his voice, his manner, his walk, all betray him within two or three minutes of walking into one's room.[195]

The issue is only mentioned on a couple of occasions and in a less than empathetic stance. He adverts to the need for any gay client to hide and certainly not to flaunt their sexuality before the court.

> magistrates will take appearance into account. So if one is defending a homosexual for an offence like gross indecency, and he trips mincingly into the witness-box and pleads not guilty and in a falsetto that would have done credit in another age, to one of the castrati, then one realises that – in racing parlance – the accused is starting under seven-pound handicap.[196]

He appears delighted to have obtained an acquittal of a man for whom on the evidence a "conviction for a particularly unpleasant offence was absolutely inevitable"[197] when the accused "when called upon to plead – boomed 'not guilty' in a rich and sonorous bass, as patently virile as the bellow of an Andalusian bull. When they heard that voice the twelve members of the all-male jury sat up smartly in the jury-box, exchanged significant glances among themselves which said, quite clearly, 'The owner of a voice like that a queer? Perish the thought!'"[198]

Apropos of nothing in particular, he mentions a case in which he is involved as part of a tough day:

> It had been an exhausting afternoon: I had taken a particularly unpleasant proof of evidence from a homosexual charged with gross indecency.[199]

The same distaste is expressed in connection with a client on a charge of gross indecency which he describes as "an unpleasant little case"[200] and quotes approvingly what a barrister had said in mitigation "surely the hand of the potter folded when he was fashioned."[201]

Barristers

They receive quite fair treatment at the hands of John Budd. He bemoans, however, the excess number of those seeking to make a career as advocates. Through the mouth of Julian's mentor on criminal defence matters the problem is discussed.

> The Bar's the most heartbreaking profession in the world, and yet year after year attracts hundreds of youngsters who just haven't got what it takes. It's difficult enough for the talented ones. How on earth the others can ever hope to make a go of it I just don't know. I'm speaking of those – and there are plenty of them – with no voice, no confidence, and no flow of words. They may possess plenty of brains, unlimited courage, and lots of perseverance, but unless they have the essential equipment of the advocate, they can never really hope to succeed.[202]

As he explains when discussing the ancient system of conducting criminal business in England and Wales prior to 1970.[203]

> At and behind the advocates' table were no less than three tightly packed rows of wigs – mostly very white ones – and glancing at them quickly I realise that prisoners were heavily outnumbered by members of the bar. I thought again, as I had thought so often before, that anyone minded to become a barrister should pay a visit to any busy quarter sessions, on the opening day, to see something of the overcrowding that prevails in the profession he has chosen.[204]

Prescot, himself by way of a bald statement does, however, note the lack of self-awareness of some of those who are members of this branch of the legal profession and the need for forbearance by solicitors.

> Sometimes, for example, a young and earnest member of the Bar sits down after haranguing a jury for an hour and twenty minutes and turns round to his instructing solicitor, sitting on the bench behind him, with a self-satisfied smile which says "And what do you think of that? They tell me that F.E. Smith used to be rather good, but I flatter myself that even he couldn't have touched that peroration.' The solicitor probably returns a nod and a smile intended to indicate the speech was very good indeed. To tell a well-meaning young man who was called, perhaps, only six months before, that he has been prosy and long-winded; that he could have said everything he had to say in ten minutes; that he's taxed the patience of the judge to the uttermost and bored the jury to tears into the bargain may be – and often is – all too true. But to say so would

> be cruel, and good manners demand that one should, at least, give some outward and visible sign of acquiescence although honesty demands dissent. [205]

This situation can be avoided by taking care in selecting the appropriate counsel when these are called for. He discovers that there are horses for courses ranging from divorce and running-down cases to jury specialists and those good at settling.[206]

He even learns that his partner selecting a female barrister is not based on her personal appearance but rather on her having come first in the Bar Finals, being the author of a major text on Chancery pleadings and an author of numerous articles in the *Law Quarterly Review*.[207] There is, though, a suggestion that the reputation of the senior branch is to some extent less than merited

> To a jury about to be empanelled it must seem that the case they are to hear is just beginning, and that it is going to be fought out by the grave-looking gentlemen in wigs and gowns deployed in readiness before them. The jury, of course, are in error. The probability is that the case has been lost long ago by some sober-suited solicitor standing unobtrusively by. It is he who has laid the foundations, he who has done all the patient work of preparation, he who has forged the weapons of law and fact which counsel is about to wield [208]

He also reveals that knowledge of the approach of different barristers can yield results where, for instance, he succeeds in settling a doubtful damages case by arriving in court with lots of law books as the barrister on the other side "tends to settle everything – bad cases as well as good ones – and he's simply no stomach for a really intricate legal argument."[209]

The Work of Solicitors

There are a variety of different elements in his life and aspects of the work of a solicitor which he finds worthwhile and which make practice somewhat satisfying.

> Adoption cases are, perhaps the most rewarding form of work that a solicitor is called upon to do: the part he plays is a small one, but to watch a childless couple walk out of court with a baby that has become legally theirs only a moment or two before, is to be present at an instant of such happiness that I often felt I should pay the proud parents a fee for letting me share it.[210]

This is not to say that all elements of the proximity to clients' lives are quite so positive.

> Because so much of the evidence given in the domestic court is painful, squalid and unpleasant, the cases are heard *in camera*, and the Regulation of Reports

> Act prevents the publication in the press of anything beyond the bare bones of the proceedings. The unpleasantness of the hearing is heightened when one remembers the parties, glowering at one another from opposite end of a long table, are two people who – once upon a time – swore to love and cherish one another for the rest of their lives.[211]

Slightly disconcertingly, in one of his final works, Prescot seems to admit that sometimes the success of lawyers is down to *chutzpah* since clients have no idea whether their case is a good one or not

> Most clients like a fighter, and whether that is . . . lost or settled they are usually no complaints so long as they feel someone has been fighting their battles every inch of the way.[212]

SUMMARY

Prescot's style is conversational but includes the citing of actual cases[213] and statutes.[214] As noted, there is occasional obscure and obsolete language and literary references prefiguring John Mortimer's highly performative approach. Discussing the excellent location chosen by his grandfather for his office he notes,

> He must have selected the spot with the same care that the young Napoleon bestowed upon the plateau of Montenotte.[215]

Describing the town's brothel, he refers to it as "its maison Tellier."[216]

Like his barrister counterpart, Roderick Jeffries, he abruptly ceased his fiction writing on legal issues with *Case Counterfeit* in 1967 seemingly when appointed Coroner for Blackpool and Fylde.

CONCLUDING REMARKS

For very different reasons, these two writers ceased producing these kinds of books after five and ten years respectively. They both focus principally on the early years of a young lawyer. In the case of Hastings Draper, he moved on to other forms of fiction in the form of crime procedurals and thrillers. The sense that he had perhaps done all he could with his chosen topic is a not unreasonable inference. After all he had followed the advice "write what you know about." His inclination was perhaps to tales of the imagination. The same might be said of the Julian Prescot books. He also ceased to write about life as a young lawyer. In his case his focus changed to stories about those observed by the increasingly inconspicuous lawyer narrator. The same thing can be observed in the way in which Henry Cecil shifted through the life and times of Roger Thursby in three books before moving on to a range of different scenarios. After these long-running works of Cecil what was needed was another long-term commitment to the sub-genre. This task was left to our next author, the prolific John Mortimer.

APPENDIX

Bibliography of Roderic Jeffries (Hastings Draper)

Jeffries also wrote under the names of Peter Alding, Jeffrey Ashford, Hastings Draper and Graham Hastings. Under the name Roderic Graeme he continued the Blackshirt series begun by his father Graham Jeffries, who wrote as Bruce Graeme.

"ENRIQUE ALVAREZ" NOVELS

Mistakenly in Mallorca (1974); *Two Faced Death* (1976); *Troubled Deaths* (1977); *Murder Begets Murder* (1979); *Just Desserts* (1980); *Unseemly End* (1981); *Deadly Petard* (1983); Three and One Make Five (1984); Layers of Deceit (1985); Almost Murder (1986); Relatively Dangerous (1987); Death Trick (1988); Dead Clever (1989); Too Clever by Half (1990); Murder's Long Memory (1991); A Fatal Fleece (1992); Murder Confounded (1993); Death Takes Time (1994); An Arcadian Death (1995); An Artistic Way To Go (1996); A Maze of Murders (1997); An Enigmatic Disappearance (1998); The Ambiguity of Murder (1999); An Artful Death (2000); Definitely Deceased (2001); Seeing is Deceiving (2002); An Intriguing Murder (2003); An Air of Murder (2003); A Sunny Disappearance (2005); Murder Delayed (2006); Murder Needs Imagination (2007); An Instinctive Solution (2008).

OTHER NOVELS BY RODERIC JEFFRIES

Evidence of the Accused (1961); Exhibit No. Thirteen (1962); Police and Detection aka Against Time! (1962); The Benefits of Death (1963); An Embarrassing Death (1964); Dead Against the Lawyers (1965); Police Car aka Patrol Car (1965); Police Dog (1965); Death in the Coverts (1966); A Deadly Marriage (1967); A Traitor's Crime (1968); Police Patrol Boat aka River Patrol (1969); Dead Man's Bluff (1970); Trapped (1972); The Riddle in the Parchment (1976); The Boy Who Knew Too Much (1979); Voyage

Into Danger (1981); Eighteen Desperate Hours (1982); Missing Man (1982); Peril at Sea (1983); Sunken Danger (1985); Meeting Trouble (1986); The Man Who Couldn't Be (1987)

AS PETER ALDING

The CID Room aka All Leads Negative (1967); Circle of Danger (1968); Murder Among Thieves (1969); Guilt Without Proof (1970); Despite the Evidence (1971); Call Back To Crime (1972); Field of Fire (1973); The Murder Line (1974); Six Days To Death (1975); Murder is Suspected (1977); Ransom Town (1979); A Man Condemned (1981); Betrayed by Death (1982); One Man's Justice (1983)

AS JEFFREY ASHFORD

Counsel For the Defence (1960); Investigations Are Proceeding aka The DI (1961); The Burden of Proof (1962); Will Anyone Who Saw the Accident aka: Hit and Run (1963); Enquiries Are Continuing aka The Superintendent's Room (1964); The Hands of Innocence (1965); Consider the Evidence (1966); Forget What You Saw (1967); Prisoner at the Bar (1969); To Protect the Guilty (1970); Bent Copper (1971); A Man Will Be Kidnapped (1972); The Double Run (1973); The Colour of Violence (1974); Three Layers of Guilt (1975); Slow Down the World (1976); Hostage To Death (1977); The Anger of Fear (1978); A Recipe For Murder (1980); The Loss of the Culion (1981); Guilt With Honour (1982); A Sense of Loyalty (1983); Presumption of Guilt (1984); An Ideal Crime (1985); A Question of Principle (1986); A Crime Remembered (1987); The Honourable Detective (1988); A Conflict of Interests (1989); An Illegal Solution (1990); Deadly Reunion (1991); Twisted Justice (1992); Judgement Deferred (1993); The Bitter Bite (1994); The Price of Failure (1995); Loyal Disloyalty (1996); A Web of Circumstances (1997); The Cost of Innocence (1998); An Honest Betrayal (1999); Murder Will Out (2000); Looking Glass Justice (2001); A Truthful Injustice (2002); A Fair Exchange is Robbery (2003); Evidentially Guilty (2004); Deadly Corruption (2005); Illegal Guilt (2007)

AS RODERIC GRAEME

Concerning Blackshirt (1952); Blackshirt Passes By (1953); Blackshirt Wins the Trick (1953); Salute To Blackshirt (1954); The Amazing Mr Blackshirt

(1955); Blackshirt Meets the Lady (1956); Paging Blackshirt (1957); Double For Blackshirt (1958); Blackshirt Helps Himself (1958); Blackshirt Sets the Pace (1959); Blackshirt Sees It Through (1960); Blackshirt Finds Trouble (1961); Blackshirt Takes the Trail (1962); Blackshirt on the Spot (1963); Call For Blackshirt (1963); Blackshirt Saves the Day (1964); Danger For Blackshirt (1965); Blackshirt at Large (1966); Blackshirt in Peril (1967); Blackshirt Stirs Things Up (1969)

AS GRAHAM HASTINGS

Twice Checked (1959); Deadly Game (1961)

NOTES

1. Most notably in Britain Richard Gordon's doctor series ran to 18 books between 1954 and 1970 starting with *Doctor in the House* (1952) and finishing with *Doctor in the Soup* (1986) with numerous film and TV spin-offs.

2. Sunderland-born vet Jim Wight (1916–1995) produced some eight books between *If Only They Could Talk* (1970) and *Every Living Thing* (1992) also with extensive film and TV versions. He took his pseudonym, James Herriot from Chapelhall's Birmingham City goalkeeper Jim Herriot (1939–).

3. Errol Braithwaite's *To Sir with Love* (1959) and Bel Kaufman's 1972 *Up the Down Staircase* join the earlier Miss Read novels as light reflections on the trials and tribulations of teaching.

4. Along with David Lodge's campus trilogy *Changing Places*, *Small World* and *Nice Work*, there is the timeless *Lucky Jim* (1954), the remarkably prescient *Coming from Behind* (1983) from Howard Jacobson and Malcolm Bradbury's *The History Man* (1975).

5. Matthew Finch *Dentist in the Chair* (1955) – which led on to two British comedy films with this dental background – *Dentist in the Chair* (1960) and *Dentist on the Job* (1961) starring Bob Monkhouse and Ronnie Stevens – in the *Carry On* vein.

6. He also wrote under the pseudonyms "Bruce Graeme," "Peter Bourne" and David Graeme. Born in London in 1900 he served in the Queen's Westminster Rifles in 1918. He was also a film producer and reporter. He died in 1982 – https://www.fantasticfiction.com/g/bruce-graeme/ (last accessed 21 December 2021).

7. https://www.fantasticfiction.com/j/roderic-jeffries/ (accessed 12 March 2022).

8. See Chapter 4.

9. Though I am young, I scorn to flit on the wings of borrowed wit. – The Shepherd's Hunting (1615) George Wither – Draper (1958) at 102.

10. *Dad's Army* – Jimmy Perry and David Croft – ran from 1968 until 1977 with Hitler poised to invade Britain throughout. No mention was ever made in the series of how the war was going. See https://www.dadsarmy.co.uk/, and https://www.comedy.co.uk (accessed December 6 2023).

11. The long-running *Archers* series from May 1950 in Britain typically has seen characters age rather slower than standard chronology. See http://www.thearchers.co.uk/ and (accessed 6 December 2023).

12. Draper (1956) p. 68.

13. Draper op cit p. 23.

14. Draper op cit at p. 59.

15. *Carlill v Carbolic Smoke Ball Company* [1893] 1 Q.B. 256.

16. Carlill op cit per Lord Bowen at p. 266.

17. See Chapter 1.

18. Draper (1956) at p. 35.

19. Draper op cit at p. 209.

20. Draper op cit at p. 114–15.

21. Draper op cit at 215.

22. Mortimer (1994 b) p. ix.

23. *Pace* his drunken comedy solicitor Mr Tewkesbury, who makes a major appearance in *Much in Evidence* (1957).

24. Draper (1956) at 7.

25. Draper (1958) at 46.

26. Ibid.

27. See Introduction to the English Legal System Appendix.

28. This is a highly prominent feature of Peter Moffat's TV series *North Square* (2000) tracing the lives of half a dozen barristers in a set of Chambers in Leeds where none have any "connections" – see https://www.imdb.com/title/tt0267201/.

29. Traditional sum of money consisting of £1 1/- the number of pounds is matched by the number of shillings so that 20 guineas would be £20 and 20 shillings – as there are 20 shillings in a pound this would be, in effect, £21 – almost never encountered since decimalisation in Britain on 1 February 1971. The sum is kept alive in popular culture by the two classic horse races – the 1,000 and 2,000 guineas run annually at Newmarket, Suffolk, England in the Spring.

30. Draper (1958) at 28.

31. Draper (1961) at 138.

32. Draper (1958) at 70.

33. Draper (1956) at 15.

34. Draper (1961) at 21.

35. Draper (1956) at 24.

36. Abel-Smith (1992).

37. Draper (1958) at 34.

38. Draper (1961) at 168.

39. In 2021–22, the cost of settling negligence claims was £13.6 billion of which legal fees amounted to £639.5 million – NHS Resolution Annual Report 2021–22 at p. 23 – available at https://resolution.nhs.uk/wp-content/uploads/2022/07

/NHS-Resolution-Annual-report-and-accounts-2021_22_Access.pdf (last accessed 12 April 2023) – for the covid affected later data see https://resolution.nhs.uk/wp-content/uploads/2023/07/NHS-Resolution-Annual-report-and-accounts-2022_23-3.pdf at p. 19.

40. Draper (1958) at 70.
41. Draper (1956) at 128.
42. Draper op cit at 61.
43. Draper op cit at 147.
44. Dickens (1853).
45. Draper (1956) at 92.
46. Draper (1958) at 5.
47. Draper (1956) at 62.
48. Draper loc cit at 86.
49. Draper loc cit at 116.
50. Draper loc cit p. 114-5.
51. Draper loc cit at 120.
52. Draper loc cit at 174.
53. Draper (1958) at 171.
54. Draper (1961) at 12.
55. Ibid.
56. Draper (1956) at 92.
57. Draper loc cit at 145.
58. Judicial Pensions Act 1959 set it at 75 – later under Judicial Pensions and Retirement Act 1993 – retirement at the age of 70/72 – now increased back to 75.
59. Draper (1958) at 165.
60. Statement to the House; Judicial Precedent 26 July 1966 by Lord Chancellor Lord Gardiner.
61. See Introduction to the English Legal System Appendix and Conclusions.
62. Draper (1958) at 58.
63. Draper (1961) at 113.
64. Seccombe (1986) on the emergence of the "male breadwinner" role in 19th-century industrialisation.
65. Draper (1958) at 11.
66. Draper loc cit at 107.
67. Draper loc cit at 112.
68. Draper (1958).
69. Heilbron (2013).
70. Acland and Broomfield (2019) at Chapter 6 – for other judicial firsts see p. 63.
71. Acland and Broomfield op cit at Chapter 2 (barristers) and Chapter 3 (solicitors).
72. President Jimmy Carter stated in an interview with *Playboy Magazine* in 1976, "I've looked on many women with lust. I've committed adultery in my heart many times. God knows I will do this and forgives me." http://www.notable-quotes.com/c/carter_jimmy.html.
73. Acland, L and Broomfield, K (2019) at p. 78.

74. Draper (1961) at 71.

75. Draper (1961) at 109.

76. Uncommon Law (1935) Case No 42 R v George, Macdonald, Maxton and Others (p. 275).

77. Draper (1961) at 144.

78. Wodehouse (1915–1974) – the fictional valet of Bertie Wooster who appears in many books and short stories and is able to extricate Bertie from many scrapes over the years – mainly matrimony with a range of "unsuitable" prospects.

79. Draper (1961) at 159.

80. Turnbull (2014) at 67 – re-shown on the *Talking Pictures* TV channel in Britain in 2024.

81. Draper (1958) at 98.

82. Ibid.

83. Robson (2022) in Robson and Spina at p. 67.

84. Draper (1961) at 116.

85. See footnote 66.

86. Draper (1961) at 91.

87. Draper loc cit at 173.

88. Draper loc cit at 171.

89. Draper loc cit at 168.

90. Breen (1999) notes that there are court scenes in thirteen of the Jeffries thrillers – 119–122.

91. The Internet suggests that Jeffries left the Bar in 1953 after losing all of his first seven cases. "The books he wrote were published throughout the world, in many languages, and were adapted for radio, television and film. He married and lived in Mallorca." *Roderick Jeffries: Golden Age of Detection* http://gadetection.pbworks.com/w/page/7930853/Jeffries%2C%20Roderic (accessed 5 December 2023) – see Appendix to this chapter.

92. See Chapter 2.

93. Rumpole's first appearance is to defend a young Afro-Caribbean man in "Rumpole and the Confession of Guilt" (TV play, BBC, December,1975). The story appears in book form in The Collected Rumpole Volume 2.

94. The ex-leader of the British Union of Fascists, Sir Oswald Mosley stood in Kensington North – near Notting Hill – in the 1959 General Election. His policies were centred on the issue of immigration, and he called for forced repatriation of Caribbean immigrants as well as a prohibition upon mixed marriages. Mosley's final share of the vote was only 8.1 per cent – Barberis, McHugh and Tyldesley (2005) at 191.

95. *Pace* McInness (1957), (1959) and (1960).

96. Robson (2002).

97. Draper (1961) at 168.

98. See notes 9 and 10.

99. It was possible in those days to recognise some of the characters on which he based his stories per Derek Hartshorn – https://www.facebook.com/groups/blackpoolhistory/posts/1381525958699407/ – last accessed 19 July 2024.

100. Prescot (1958) at 129.
101. Prescot (1967) per dust cover blurb.
102. See Introduction to the English Legal System Appendix.
103. Sampson (1965) at 166.
104. Prescot (1958) at 105–10.
105. Prescot loc cit at 67.
106. Prescot (1959) at 184.
107. Prescot loc cit at 18 ff.
108. Prescot loc cit at 73 ff.
109. Prescot loc cit 133–44 – albeit offered a “freebie” by way of a tip.
110. Prescot loc cit at 34.
111. Prescot loc cit at 155.
112. Prescot loc cit at 83.
113. Prescot loc cit at 201.
114. Prescot (1960) at 35.
115. Prescot loc cit at 42.
116. Prescot loc cit at 21.
117. Prescot loc cit at 35.
118. Prescot loc cit at 122.
119. McIntyre (2013) – appendix to electronic version.
120. Prescot (1960) at 68–69.
121. Prescot loc cit at 75–79.
122. Prescot (1961) at 9.
123. Prescot (1959) at 71.
124. Prescot loc cit at 69.
125. Prescot (1961) at 17.
126. Prescot loc cit at 129 ff.
127. Prescot loc cit at 11 – accepted by the magistrates – loc cit at 18.
128. Prescot loc cit at 205.
129. Prescot loc cit at 53 and 187.
130. Prescot (1962) at 22.
131. Prescot (1962) at 24.
132. Prescot (1962) at 160.
133. Prescot (1962) at 194.
134. Prescot (1962) at 59 ff.
135. Prescot (1962) at 89.
136. See note below – 184.
137. Prescot (1962) at 166 and 173.
138. Prescot (1962) at 44.
139. Prescot (1963) at 85.
140. Prescot loc cit at 77.
141. Breen (1984) and (1999).
142. Breen (1984) at 144 and Breen (1999) at 179.
143. Prescot (1965) at 10.
144. Prescot (1966) at 5.

145. Prescot loc cit at 33.

146. (1920–2010) Jockey and author of books about racing and mainly on skulduggery and crime on the Turf starting with *Dead Cert* (1962) and ending with *Crossfire* (2010). Latterly, from 2007 these were collaborations with his son Felix who continues to write these using the description "a Dick Francis novel."

147. Entail or fee tail was a process whereby it was possible to ensure that an estate should not be broken up or sold off by the heir but passed on to the next generation *ad infinitum* intact. It became impossible to limit ownership in this way after the Law of Property Act 1925 although existing entailed estates were not affected.

148. Prescot (1959) at 27.

149. Prescot (1960) at 42.

150. Prescot (1963) at 26.

151. Prescot ibid.

152. Prescot loc cit at 34.

153. Prescot (1962) at 176 – the same issue affecting Adolf Hitler in the popular wartime refrain known as The River Kwai March – sung to the tune of the Colonel Bogey March.

154. Prescot (1960) at 58 – an old term for living together as man and wife without marrying – which by 2021 had reached some 24.3% of couples. Superseded by "cohabiting."

155. Prescot (1960) at 149 – Be Undressed and Ready My Angel – a cousin of the Alan Bennett Norwich telegram sketch from Beyond the Fringe (1960) – which suggests that Burma stands for Be Upstairs Ready My Angel.

156. Prescot (1959) at 58 – a reference to the brothers Willem and Johann Gezinck who were Dutch percussionists at the end of the 19th century – they match only one Google search – a review of the Ring Cycle in the Independent – 12 October 1994.

157. Prescot (1964) at 9 – a reference to a person of high rank in India as well as a commander of the Anglo-Egyptian army, aka Sardar.

158. Prescot (1960) at 9 – George Cruikshank (1792–1878) – caricaturist and book illustrator.

159. Ibid and Prescot (1966) at 149 – Walter Dendy Sadler (1854–1923) – painter whose works include "In the solicitor's office" and other legal scenes such as "Country clients" and "The right of way lawyer."

160. Prescot (1960) at 79 – the miser in Molière's "L'Avare" (The Miser) – oddly the client referred to was a gullible winner of the football pools of over £1.3 million (at 2024 prices) who kept being fleeced.

161. Prescot (1960) at 147 – on a relationship with allegedly no consummation due to the man's advanced years – like Abishag who was selected to keep King David warm in old age – 1 Kings 1.2.

162. Prescot (1960) at 133 – this refers to a practice mentioned in Piers Plowman and Chaucer of providing a side of bacon to married couples who could swear to not having regretted their marriage for a year and a day. The practice was revived, and elements still survive in Great Dunmow in Essex.

163. Prescot (1961) at 62 – French military commander and statesman Joachim Murat (1767–1815) who played a major role in many battles in service of Napoleon.

164. Prescot ibid – French cavalry General Antoine-Charles-Louis, Comte de Lasalle (1775–1809) killed at the battle of Wagram.

165. The name of Napoleon's horse – named after the Battle of Marengo (1800) in Piedmont against Austria.

166. Prescot (1961) at 182 – French lawyer Antoine Quentin Fouquier de Tinville (1746–1795) – prosecutor of the Revolutionary Tribunal during the Revolution and Reign of Terror – himself guillotined by order of the Revolutionary Tribunal.

167. Prescot (1962) at 13 – Domenico Dragonetti was an Italian double bass virtuoso (1763–1846).

168. Prescot (1959) at 114.

169. Prescot (1964) at 9.

170. Prescot loc cit at 37 – a reference to the legal firm in Charles Dickens' *Pickwick Papers* in the case of *Bardell v Pickwick.*

171. Prescot (1960) at 28 – it is better to go to the fountain head than to follow streamlets from it.

172. Prescot loc cit at 19 – i.e., double jeopardy.

173. Prescot loc cit at 55.

174. Prescot loc cit at 75.

175. Prescot loc cit at 198.

176. Ibid – by the time the book was published the controversial Rent Act 1957 had started the process of repealing the Rent Acts – for how this policy fared see Robson and Combe (2019) chapters 1 and 13.

177. Prescot loc cit at 68.

178. Prescot loc cit at 91–92.

179. Prescot loc cit at 145.

180. Prescot loc cit at 96.

181. Prescot loc at at 140–41.

182. Prescot (1961) at 38.

183. Prescot loc cit at 200.

184. Prescot (1962) at 86.

185. Prescot (1959) at 67.

186. Prescot ibid.

187. Prescot loc cit at 66.

188. Prescot (1962) at 135.

189. Prescot loc cit at 141.

190. Prescot loc cit at 121.

191. Prescot loc cit at 145.

192. Prescot (1960) at 213.

193. Prescot (1962) at 57.

194. Prescot (1959) at 187.

195. Prescot (1958) at 154.

196. Prescot loc cit at 156.

197. Prescot loc cit at 157.

198. Ibid.

199. Prescot (1960) at 17.

200. Prescot (1961) at 180.
201. Prescot loc cit at 181.
202. Prescot (1958) at 161–62.
203. See Introduction to English Legal System Appendix.
204. Prescot (1961) at 165.
205. Prescot (1959) at 42.
206. Prescot loc cit at 102 ff.
207. Prescot loc cit at 102.
208. Prescot (1961) at 61.
209. Prescot (1960) at 50.
210. Prescot loc cit at 170.
211. Prescot (1959) at 119.
212. Prescot (1967) at 7.
213. *Singleton v Ellison* [1895] 1 Q.B. 607 – there needs to be more than one person operating to amount to a brothel; *R v Taylor* May 15 1950 disapproving *R v Treanor* 1939 27 Cr App R 35 – on bigamy and the availability of the "seven years absence rule" a second time – cited in Prescot (1960) at 138.
214. Unlawful Games Act 1541 and Gaming Act 1845 cited in Prescot (1960) at 46.
215. Prescot (1961) at 62 – a reference to Napoleon's first army command at the Battle of Montenotte fought on 12 April 1796 between the French and Austrians in the French Revolutionary War.
216. Prescot (1958) at 110 – a reference to Guy de Maupassant's *La Maison Tellier* short story collection including the eponymous tale of a brothel from 1881.

Chapter 4

John Mortimer

The Rumpole Years, 1975–2007

INTRODUCTION

John Mortimer has a rather richer legal pedigree than any of the other authors in this study. Born in 1923 he was the son of a successful barrister and spent a significant part of his life practicing as a barrister himself. His fictional output was extensive, only exceeded in this area by Henry Cecil. He was also the most written-about of the comic legal authors under review with no less than four volumes of autobiography[1] and two biographies[2] covering his life and careers as lawyer and author as well as many articles.[3] His close colleague, fellow barrister, Geoffrey Robertson, has suggested that John Mortimer as a campaigner "helped to achieve the abolition of the death penalty and of the censorship of the theatre by that doltish establishment figure, the Lord Chamberlain."[4] As a barrister the cases he took such as *Last Exit to Brooklyn*, *Oz*, *The Little Red School Book* and *Inside Linda Lovelace* are credited with ending "censorship for the written word."[5]

THE RUMPOLE PHENOMENON

John Mortimer has enjoyed a rather less circuitous route to his past and present reading public. There was an all too brief glimpse into the work of a struggling young barrister in his second novel, but the majority of the book concerns the troubled love ambitions of the main protagonist, Ransom.[6] Mortimer continued to write plays and books with commercial and critical success throughout the 1950s and 1960s. He adapted his 1953 book, *Like Men Betrayed* for the radio in 1955. His plays also proved popular. One, in particular, *Dock Brief*, was originally broadcast on the radio in May 1957. It was adapted for television later that year and then for the stage in the following year. The works *Dock Brief* and *What Shall We Tell Caroline* played as a Double Bill in the West End in 1958. A feature film version of *Dock Brief*, starring Peter Sellers, premiered in 1962.

Mortimer's first comic legal book, *No Moaning of the Bar*, was published under the name of Geoffrey Lincoln in 1957. It was a tongue-in-cheek guide to the reality of being a barrister – how to deal with managing clerks, what to do with stone deaf witnesses; what not to say to Judges and the much-debated question of whether it is necessary to know any law to be a successful barrister. Parts had appeared in the pages of the humorous weekly magazine, *Punch* and contained some 25 pen-and-ink sketches by the author. More than any of the other early writings of Mortimer it can be seen as a first attempt at the voice of Horace Rumpole.

There is general agreement in the various versions about his genesis. Rumpole was an extension of the two earlier slightly shabby lawyers he conceived for radio in *The Dock Brief* and on TV in *Infidelity Took Place*. Mortimer undertook the commission from Irene Shubick to write a play for the BBC's Play for Today in 1974. Shubick, the producer who brought Rumpole to the screen,[7] recalls that before he wrote the play, they agreed Rumpole's broad outline. Born in 1910,[8] he was educated at public school and Oxford.[9] With his call up delayed for medical reasons he was able to take advantage of the lack of competition and achieve success in the Penge Bungalow Murder case.[10] Subsequently married to the Head of Chambers' daughter he lapsed post War into being an Old Bailey hack.[11] Mortimer suggested in 1994 that he was always looking for an insurance policy for his old age

> I'd wanted to write about a detective, a Sherlock Holmes or a Maigret, to keep me in my old age. Then I thought of making him a criminal defender, in honour of the Old Bailey hacks I'd known and admired.[12]

The play appeared on television on 16 December 1975. With the BBC unwilling to take a chance on a series, the producer took it in 1976 to Thames Television where it remained for 7 series.[13] The books which followed were novelisations of the screenplays which according to Mortimer were "written quite rapidly"[14] This publishing phenomenon lasted some 30 years. All featured tales of Horace Rumpole and one was in fact the writing up of the Penge Bungalow Murders, which the old defender referred to in many of his stories. All were published by the Penguin publishing house and continue to be available in bookshops as well as online. He has come to be the "epitome of the English Barrister" and in the view of one American commentator a reliable guide to the English system's operation

> While other lawyers come and go through the television courts of the world,[15] Rumpole, perhaps because he was created and written by practicing English barrister John Mortimer QC, is still the character lawyers love in their hearts and who they happily watch because all of the legal content is right.[16]

There has also been established a clear perception that Rumpole is irreverent and loves tweaking the tail of The Law.

> His delight comes from combat, from advocacy, from tearing paper to distract the jury as the prosecutor speaks. To undo the state and its minions, in all their power, glory and complacency, is his sweetest joy.[17]

In the novelisations of the TV series we find Rumpole delivering speeches in the form of "what I didn't say" in place of his highly critical internal unspoken monologues in which he casts doubt on the judges and other professionals.[18]

The impact of John Mortimer's creation, ageing junior barrister Horace Rumpole, appears to have been significantly greater than the legal characters of other British writers. He has inspired clubs around the world[19] as well as some serious scholarly analysis.[20] His creator, not being noted for a consistent relationship with actuality in his recollections,[21] does appear to have always been clear that he envisaged Rumpole as a conduit for his own world view.

> Horace Rumpole . . . is very unlike me, being a far more stoic and single-minded person than I am. However, he has this great advantage – he does say a good many of the things I think and if I said them they might sound rather leftish and off-putting, but when given voice by Rumpole they become crusty, conservative and much more appealing.[22]

RUMPOLE AND HIS CHARACTER

As mentioned, John Mortimer wrote at different times of how he perceived his character as an insurance policy for his old age,

> I wanted a sort of detective, who could be the hero of a number of stories but whose personality and approach to life were more important than the crimes with which he was concerned.[23]

It seems that, whilst this notion may have been present in Mortimer's subconscious, it was not until the success of the TV series that Rumpole transformed into the insurance policy. If he had been conceived as a hero of a number of stories the age of Rumpole was ill-chosen. Mortimer confirmed that this was an error he regretted.[24] Rumpole starts out in 1975 aged 67[25] and 5 years at least later after Nick has been to university and got a job as a lecturer in Baltimore he is in his 67th year of life[26] and by 1995 he is a mere 74.[27] Such minor details were a result of Mortimer's speed of writing due to his many commitments[28] and he is not alone in this.[29]

Rumpole is no master of law, but rather only persuasive rhetoric – and increasingly, in later outings, detecting. He does not keep up to date with matters legal or stylistic. When Rumpole pontificates on the value of a person's good name by quoting the line "he who steals my purse" from Shakespeare's *Othello*, his client is less than impressed

> "Oh for heaven sake, Rumpole"! Peppiat was impatient. "They gave up quoting that in libel actions 50 years ago."[30]

There are times when the reputation and skill of Rumpole are not expected to shine, as when he wins acquittal for a client accused of murder and finds his client desolate.

> With his acquittal, he has learned that his brothers framed him for a crime one of them committed, and chose Rumpole as the barrister – seedy, with an ancient wig and a tattered hat – who would insure a conviction.[31]

His practice is wide and varied and, we learn, includes affray,[32] warehouse-breaking,[33] receiving,[34] theft,[35] fraud,[36] actual bodily harm,[37] grievous bodily harm,[38] breaking and entering,[39] manslaughter,[40] living on immoral earnings,[41] dangerous driving,[42] taking and driving away[43] and housebreaking.[44] Another apparently recurrent issue is indecency and gross indecency,[45] which the apparently sexless Rumpole, for some reason, longs for in lean times.[46] He relies on a minor crime family for a steady supply of cases,

> Such support and comfort has, for many years, been furnished for me by the Timson's, an extended, intricate and perpetually expanding family of South London villains , whose turnover of crime though never of a sensational or particularly ambitious nature, shows commendable industry. Armed robbery, murder, mayhem or serious fraud are out of the Timpson's league. The most simple breaking and entering, burglary, and the taking and driving away of clapped-out Cortinas are their bread-and-butter, receiving stolen jewellery their occasional slice of cake. If your telly, your video and your microwave mysteriously leave home while you're away for the weekend, 10 to 1 some Timpson has got it and is disposing of it at a knock down price in the saloon bar of the Needle Arms.[47]

Whilst we hear about the Penge Bungalow murders frequently[48] what we actually get in the books and television shows on which they were based is often rather less dramatic as the Appendix demonstrates. Overall, there are indeed some 21 murder cases but they are outweighed by over 50 non-murder issues. These range from theft and robbery (10), fraud (7) and blackmail (3) alongside a host of matters which occur only once[49] and matters which appear to be about murder but are not.[50]

THE RUMPOLE CANON

Mortimer, then, gave us many pages devoted to the working days of his selected insurance policy, the ageing Old Bailey hack, Horace Rumpole. His exploits ended up appearing in 62 short stories as well as 3 novels written over 31 years. They amount to some 3,371 pages. The first nine books are faithful adaptations of 44 previously screened 1-hour television episodes.[51] There are, in addition to the adaptations of the seven TV series and a special feature length episode,[52] a further 6 stories adapted from radio broadcasts published along with the original Play for Today adaptation.[53] There are some 19 Rumpole tales published in three books after the TV series came to an end in December 1992.[54] In addition, there is a collection of 7 magazine and newspaper stories with a Christmas theme.[55] Finally there are three short novels featuring Horace Rumpole.[56]

Rumpole during this period does not seem to age which is not unusual in fiction, of course. In terms of chronology, there is in the first book and its TV series a shift from the early 1970s to the early 1980s but thereafter it is all a bit vaguer. The kind of career progression which one can see in Henry Cecil's Roger Thursby trilogy does not occur. There is no taking silk, being elected Head of Chambers or even a Circuit Judgeship, although these tantalise his wife Hilda, if not Rumpole. He remains how he started out – at the end of his career. He starts and stays on the brink of retirement, albeit for an impressive 15 years on television and 31 years in print. During this time the pupil Phyllida Trant becomes a Q.C. and in due course a High Court Judge. The books, like their television originals, are set more of less contemporaneously. There are spasmodic references to social and political events and developments. It would seem, on the face of it, that anyone seeking to trace detailed changes in the legal, social and political landscape in Britain between the mid-1970s and 2007 would find only limited assistance in the world of Rumpole. Mortimer, however, took a rather different view congratulating himself on how he can range across new issues as they present themselves and he is able to keep "the old barrister" fresh and up to date.

> I think this is because you can take today's events – social workers snatching children for suspected devil worship, the Court of Appeal having to eat the words of previous judges, the suggested reforms of the legal profession – and

> the slender difference between actors and barristers and write a Rumpole story about them.[57]

There is a little bit of context at the start of the TV series with the culture clash of early 1970s hippiedom and the brutal world stemming from Edward Heath's call for people "to stand on their own feet, to accept responsibility for themselves and for their families . . . and less government."[58] We find the counterculture represented in a story set "in the early 1970s when Flower Power flooded the country with a mass of long hair, long dresses and the sweet smell of the old quarter of Marrakesh"[59] Apparently with Rumpole having added nothing to his starting age of 67, we find mention of the 7/7 suicide bombings of 2005 and him grappling with newfangled notions like Continuing Professional Development in one of his final outings in 2006[60] and Marketing Managers for barristers' Chambers[61] – albeit one still using a flip chart in the 21st century.

Perhaps surprisingly too, Rumpole does not have *wide-ranging* comments on the workings and defects of the legal system. That is not say there are not extensive comments. Like Rumpole, however, they are rather repetitive and limited in their scope. The downside of Rumpole as a conduit which Mortimer alluded to above is that Rumpole is a conservative wedded to the existing order. There is a whole host of "dogs that do not bark" compared, for instance, with Henry Cecil, as we shall see.

Mortimer seemed aware of these limitations right from the very start. In fact, the original screenplay for the Play for Today, *Rumpole of the Bailey*, ends with Rumpole's son asking who Rumpole is. The reply is a fascinating description of the facade Rumpole presents to the world rather than anything else.

> Everyone down the Bailey knows me. I'm an amiable eccentric who drops ash down his waistcoat and tells the time with a gold hunter and calls Judges old sweetheart. Also I recite Wordsworth in the loo.
>
> That's who I am isn't it?[62]

Years later this same theme re-emerges when we find Rumpole forced to ruminate on whether he has become a "character." His "endearing features" have transformed him into a collection of traits rather than anything else. Hilda observes acidly about Rumpole's loutish behaviour at a restaurant with a Michelin star, on behalf of whose owner he is due to appear

> You did it because you have to be a "character," don't you? Wherever you go. Well I don't know if I'm going to be able to put up with your "character" much

longer . . . You have to be one all the time, don't you? . . . with your cigar ash and steak and kidney and Pomeroy's Ordinary Red and your arguments.[63]

This leads Rumpole to evaluate himself

> On the way to my place of work I spent an uncomfortable quarter of an hour thinking over what She Who Must Be Obeyed had said about me having to be a "character". It seemed an unfair charge. I drink Château Thames embankment because it's all I can afford. It keeps me regular and blots out certain painful memories such as a bad day in court in front of Judge Graves, an old darling who undoubtedly passes iced water every time he goes to the Gents. I enjoy the fragrance of a small cigar. I relish an argument. This is the way of life I have chosen. I don't have to do any of these things in order to be a "character". Do I? [64]

Linked to this is his style in court. Rumpole gets warned by a judge as to his demeanour – "You mustn't think of this Court simply as a place of entertainment, Mr Rumpole 'The Judge had, perhaps, put his finger on a flaw in my character."[65]

This was, however, something which Mortimer the advocate regarded as crucial in certain types of jury trial. Quizzed on his own style of advocacy by American Robert F Hanley, his response was clear.

> *Hanley* . . . Did you use your fantastic sense of humor (*sic*)?
>
> *Mortimer* Oh, absolutely. Particularly in obscenity cases. In these cases, the first thing I did was to make the jury laugh. The great object of the judge and prosecutor was to stop the jury from laughing. The prosecution and court want to treat these so-called porno magazines with the height of seriousness.[66]

RUMPOLE AND HIS "REPUTATION"

Rumpole, for his part, has a reputation for both success and being on the side of the unprivileged. We hear about this but do not observe it all that frequently. His forensic success is limited although many clients escape the wrath of the law through happenstance.[67] As Mortimer always wished, however, his major source of success is as a detective, with the assistance of Ferdinand Isaac Gerald (Fig) Newton.[68] There is talk of the level of Rumpole's success. One tells him "I told Superintendent Gannon I couldn't have a better brief, Mr Rumpole. Not one with your talent for acquittals."[69] Some are clearly bemused by this apparent success and say so – "I told him that, for some reason, you had a remarkable record in securing acquittals.[70] This seems strangely at odds with his propensity to rile the Establishment.

> All right, Mr Rumpole. You're out to protect the underdog, I understand that. I might say that I find it very sympathetic. You attack the establishment. Tease the judges. Give the police a hard time. Well, doesn't my daughter deserve defending as much as any of your clients?[71] . . . Well, I admired the fact you were always on the side of the underdog. You stopped the judges sending everyone to the nick. You showed up the police. You stood up for the underprivileged.[72]

> We knew you'd have the right attitude, Mr Rumpole. Men like the good doctor come here and everyone is against them. The government, the opposition, most of the public and the newspapers. You speak up for them.[73]

Rumpole is, in reality, prepared to act in defence of anyone.

> How do you feel about defending blackmailers? Much as I feel about defending anyone. Glad of the money.[74]

He also has doubts about the source of his "reputation" as a champion of the poor and unprivileged musing "I don't know where everybody got the idea that I only act for underdogs?"[75] He is, also, prepared to dissemble to obtain work.

> "And you couldn't have thought of anyone better." I was determined to give a passable imitation of someone who had the law of breach of confidence and the European Convention on Human Rights at their fingertips.[76]

Rumpole, "having scraped a 4th in law,"[77] (or in another tale a 3rd[78]) certainly reflects Mortimer's own thoughts on the value of the law degrees available when he studied at Oxford in the 1940s. Mortimer's own degree was, it seems, a special unclassified wartime award recognising, *inter alia*, his work in the Crown Film Unit. [79] It has also been suggested that it was "a poor Class III, equivalent of a 2:2 today."[80] Given that he was sent down in 1942 for writing Wildean letters and then went to work for the Government in the Crown Film Unit, the confusion is understandable.[81] Mortimer himself suggested that he "got a 'war degree.' It was given with no ceremony and luckily for me there were no classes. It was just one more utility BA 'in a nutshell.'"[82] Whatever the degree, it left him disillusioned with the benefits of the academic study of law.

Whilst Mortimer's own studies did indeed include Roman Law, there was also coverage of libel, slander and other areas of tort as well as land law.[83] Again the idea that the syllabus was only about how to manumit (free) slaves or adopt a Senator is "good copy" but far from the reality.

> It has always been my view that knowing too much law is not only no help but also a considerable handicap to the courtroom advocate. Juries, on the whole,

> have little interest in freeing slaves or the Roman law governing the ownership of chariots.[84]

Rumpole, however, went on to have a certain degree of self-confidence in his early years

> I had managed to win a reasonable number of taking and driving aways, actual bodily harms and minor indecencies around a number of fairly unsympathetic courts.[85]

She who knew him best had a more modest view of his talents, noting that "we all know he's not exactly Gregory Peck reborn."[86]

THE RUMPOLE STORY APPROACH

The very essence of the vast majority of the Rumpole canon is that it comes in the form of the short story. Each one is self-contained. There are no running plot lines. Each story is free-standing. The characters who people the life of Rumpole are consistent and some develop. Some like Hoskins and Uncle Tom remain as unchanging extras. Each of the major members of Chambers establishes their character in each story. Regular viewers will have a good idea how they are probably going to react to various events. This works as a device on television. When the series were transmitted at the end of the twentieth century, television series watching involved a run of half a dozen programmes shown weekly. There were few video recorders and no box sets when Rumpole's first three series were shown. Establishing the Rumpole "character" and the tics and habits by which he became known was a weekly event. Reading this in print is a little less satisfactory and repetitive.

Apart from his occasional forensic ability, there is a significant role in Rumpole's cases for detective investigation as Mortimer desired. We find this not only in the work carried out by the private detective Fig Newton but by Rumpole himself. He does this in relation to his client's desire not to reveal he is a member of a secret Society – resembling the Masons. Attendance at one of their meetings is, in fact, his client's alibi.[87] He is also involved in finding a lap dancer whose knowledge is key to his client's innocence of a murder charge.[88] He also uncovers the secret Trotskyist past of the Home Secretary[89] and the rock band history of the Head of Chambers.[90]

Another interesting aspect of the Rumpole saga is how he suggests the concerns of society in general alter over time. This changing nature of "moral panics"[91] can be seen in the way we move from the things which concerned him as a newly qualified barrister to later social problems.

> When I was a young white-wig, it was frauds on the Post Office and the stealing of stamps, then it was the trashing of telephone kiosks. Later, spraying graffiti on the walls of multi-storey car parks and high-rise flats was temporarily regarded as worse than manslaughter.[92]

A slightly more desperate tone is expressed by the mature Rumpole but with different issues.

> Every week, it seemed, brought a new list of things which were to be cracked down on: single mothers, who didn't make sure the children went into school, noisy neighbours, graffiti artists, and mobile-phone stealers would be cracked down on with particular severity.[93]

Although some novel issues are mentioned, few are featured in the stories which started out on television.[94] After the end of the television series, following Leo McKern's retirement we find that there is an exploration of novel issues like smoke free zones,[95] ASBOs[96] and CPD.[97] These are, however, generally treated by Rumpole as unwelcome incursions into his cosy world.

RUMPOLE'S LIMITED CRITICAL PALETTE

Given what John Mortimer envisaged as one important aspect of the function of his creation to insert his own views,[98] what we find in the stories focuses extensively on character and narrative rather more than the editorialising found with Henry Cecil.[99] The comments on the justice system and its operation, though, are limited. They remain steady and repetitive rather than showing any fundamental changes in the 30-odd years of Mortimer's Rumpole. They reflect the *stasis* in his own politics[100] together with the constraints on progressive politics for 18 years during the right-wing Thatcher/Major regimes from 1979 to 1997. In view of the extensive work which Mortimer undertook with plays, screenplays and non-Rumpole fiction[101] this is hardly surprising. His attention to detail in his Rumpole stories was not exemplary. The celebrated Penge Bungalow Murders are known as R v Samuel Poultney[102] and later as R v Simon Jerold.[103] He himself explained that "(a)s I write quite rapidly, I'm always forgetting exactly where (Rumpole) lives.[104]

Police Corruption

The nub of the first outing of Rumpole in the Play for Today *Rumpole of the Bailey* aired in December 1975 involved a "verbal" in which the accused signs his alleged "confession."[105] This has, of course, been made up by the police since it turns out that the accused cannot read. A more complex issue is covered in a 1981 tale[106] with a reference back in the title to the bane of George Dixon's life in *Dixon of Dock Green* – a "rotten apple" as a corrupt or "bent" policeman was known.[107] Here Rumpole's policeman client is *not* guilty of corruption and has been framed by his senior officer who is himself guilty of accepting bribes. A similar theme is found in a story from 1992 where a senior police officer is accused of seeking to procure the murder of his wife's lover.[108] The client is one who takes pleasure in castigating defence barristers and describes the presumption of innocence as "lawyers' language."[109] As a result, however, of Rumpole's own detective work, the true facts are established. There is indeed corruption but higher up the command chain.

Juries Are a Good Thing and Have a Decisive Role

Rumpole's task as a criminal defence lawyer on middle range and sometimes serious issues is to appeal to juries. Swaying them is his stock in trade. Appealing to their sense of self-importance is central. He shows them how central they are in the process.

> for once we start in the business of censorship and the banning of books, that is the ending of freedom. Our priceless liberties are in your hands today, members of the jury. There could be no safer place for them![110]

He refers to trial by jury as "our most cherished institution"[111] and reminds us of "(t)he 'Golden Thread' which runs through our justice – the immutable principle that everyone is innocent until 12 good men and women and true are certain that the only possible answer is that they must be guilty."[112] The jury have this vital power because they are the crucial deciders on the facts and no one else. Not the lawyers and certainly not the Judge.

> And what you do, members of the jury, is a matter entirely between God and your own consciences. Can you really find it in your consciences to condemn a man to ruin for a crime he didn't commit? . . . You are the only judge of the facts in this case, Members of the Jury.[113]

He is keen to pass on this approach to his pupil barrister, Fiona Allways,

> "Soon this case will be over, members of the jury" I gave her my usual peroration. "In a little while you will go back to your jobs and your families, and you will forget all about it. At most it is only a small part of your lives. But for my client it is the whole of his life! And it is that life I leave with confidence in your hands, certain there can be only one verdict in this case – 'Not guilty'. . ."[114]

He refers to the danger posed to the jury system by those who would seek their abolition in the name of efficiency

> We are being flushed out of our natural habitats in Crown Courts and before the magistrates. Batty bureaucrats are going to take away our right to juries and shift the burden of proof and leave us defenceless. Soon we'll be replaced by a couple of chartered accountants and a good computer.[115]

Later in his career, Rumpole waxes even more lyrical to the point of parodying comedian Tony Hancock's brilliant appeal to his fellow jurors in the Galton and Simpson pastiche of *12 Angry Men.*[116]

> What distresses me most about the hard times is the cheerful manner in which we seem prepared to chuck away those blessed freedoms we have fought for, bled for and got banged up in chokey for down the centuries. We went to all that trouble with King John to get trial by our peers, and now a lot of lawyers with the minds of business consultants want to abolish juries. We struggled to get the presumption of innocence, that golden thread that runs through British justice, and, no one seems to give a toss for it any more. What must we do, I wonder. Go back to Runnymede every so often to get another Magna Carta and cut off King Charles's head at regular intervals to ensure our constitutional rights? Speaking entirely for myself, and at my time of life, I really don't feel like going through all that again.[117]

Even Hilda recognises that the jury system is what drives Rumpole on rather than fame, ambition or fortune when she suggests that "Rumpole feels romantic about 'Steak and kidney pudding. The jury system, the presumption of innocence.'"[118]

Closely related to the sanctity of trial by jury comes the presumption of innocence and unknowability of guilt by anyone other than the jury.

Defending the "Guilty"

Rumpole is a stout opponent of the notion that lawyers are prepared to defend those they "know to be guilty."

> It's the one great error everyone makes about my learned profession; they think we defend people who have told us they did the deed. This legend doesn't add to the esteem in which barristers are held, I sighed a little as I exploded the myth for the thousandth time . . . if she ever admitted it to me, I'd have to make her surrender and plead "Guilty".[119]

As he points out, that ignores the presumption of innocence and the role of the jury in determining guilt.

> Guilty or innocent. What does it matter? What matters is – that he may have been convicted on faked evidence. . . . We can't decide guilt or innocence. That's not for us. That's for twelve puzzled old darlings pulled off the street.[120]

He is prepared to argue,

> It was time, I realised, to make my position clear, so I gave him half a minute of the Rumpole Creed. Listen to me, Mr Gannon. Listen. The police, the judges, the public interest, the interests of justice – they're too much for me, altogether too much. I've got a job to do Maybe it's a small job, but to me it seems important. I'm here to see that no one gets banged up for a crime they probably didn't do.[121]

He expresses this core belief in a variety of ways whenever the issue arises and explains how this operates in practice.

> My belief is suspended. It's been left hanging up in the robing room for years. It's not my job to find you innocent or guilty. That's up to the jury. All I can do is put your case as well as you would if you had, and I said in all modesty, anything approaching my ability.[122]

He patiently outlines the nature of the adversarial system. His belief in it is total although there is no discussion at any time in any of the stories of the possibilities of anything like the inquisitorial system where both sides are involved in the pursuit of what actually happened. This is something which might have been of some interest, one might have thought to anyone interested in justice.

> My job is to put my client's case as well as it could be put. The prosecutor does the same and then the jury chooses to believe one of us. It's called our judicial system. It seems to work more fairly than any other form of criminal trial, if you want my opinion.[123]

It is never made clear whether there is an empirical basis for this belief in the adversarial system.

The Right to Silence

There appears to be limited engagement with this concept. Rumpole has pragmatic reasons for wishing to retain an accused's right to say nothing and give no evidence on his own behalf

> By morning I had decided not to put . . . in the witness-box. More customers sink themselves by their own evidence than ever get scuppered by the prosecution [124]

As Mortimer explained in a BBC Radio interview, "the purpose of the defence counsel is to prevent the truth emerging."[125]

Prison Conditions

This is the other major recurrent theme which concerns Rumpole and is very much an issue with which John Mortimer in his professional life was exercised as president of the reform-focused Howard League for Penal Reform between 1991 and 2003.[126] It explains why Rumpole avoids the role of prosecutor which barristers undertook on behalf of the Crown.

> I'm not going to use my skills, such as they are, to force some poor devil into a condemned Victorian slum where he can be banged up with a couple of psychopaths and his own chamberpot. I gave my learned Head of Chambers article one of the Rumpole Creed.[127]

It is one reason, among many, why he does not care for the comfort and security of a place on the Bench as a judge.

> I should find it almost impossible to order any fellow citizen to be locked up in a Victorian slum with a couple of psychopaths and three chamberpots, and I cannot imagine a worse way of passing your life and having to actually listen to the speeches of the learned friends.[128]

The recurrence of the sanitary arrangements is notable:

> As we were leaving Brixton, where prisoners not yet convicted are now kept in conditions that are considerably worse than those enjoyed there a hundred years ago, when we were out in the free world, away from the stench of chamberpots and the jangle of warders' keys, I asked my instructing solicitor what I had come to think of as the thousand dollar question.[129]

This situation is all related to the lack of any kind of effective penal policy

> This pattern of offending and reoffending continues because nobody seems able to think of anything better to do with (his regular clients) and their like.[130]

Prison conditions have been an issue where the changes which have been made for the better stem from challenges through the European Convention on Human Rights rather than any reforms Governments in Britain have embarked upon.[131]

Women at the Bar and Other Gender Issues

Rumpole has no compunction in using the sexual history of the alleged victim in his attack on the character of this witness in a rape trial in a story set in 1968 but broadcast and published 10 years later in 1978.[132] The issue was, however, debated heatedly with his future daughter-in-law, Erica, and it is fair to say that Mortimer brought this issue under the spotlight and gave her the opportunity to advance an alternative argument.[133] It was not until the Youth Justice and Criminal Evidence Act, 1999, that the cross examination of complainants in sexual cases as to their sexual history was limited by s 41(1). This meant that leave to question the complainant on such a matter could only be granted in very limited circumstances. The move to video evidence was introduced in 2020[134] and there was funding to enable the expansion of such evidence announced in 2023.[135]

We find Rumpole associated with young women barristers throughout all his adventures.[136] The exceptions are the brief appearances of Wendy Crump, the middle-aged female pupil of fellow member of Chambers, Claude Erskine- Brown.[137] and another of Claude's female pupils, the mature Mrs Heather Whittaker.[138] We never witness any women actually pleading apart from the ignominious start of Phyllida Trant engineered by Rumpole. He misinforms her that the magistrate she is due to appear before likes lots of law and precedents to be cited and as her opponent he scores an easy victory.[139] Rumpole himself appears before the occasional female judge in his long career. These range from Mrs Justice Appleby[140] and Judge Emma McNaught[141] to Mrs Justice Templett,[142] Dame Mildred Wrightsworth.[143] and Mrs Recorder Erskine-Brown.[144] Other than Phyllida Erskine-Brown, they receive no more than "namechecks" and Rumpole's only observations are minimal. None of them reappear unlike the recurring Mr Justice Graves, Judge Bullingham[145] and Ollie Oliphant.

With the exception of his early joust with the woman who became the "Portia of our Chambers," Phyllida Trant, no women appear as direct adversaries. There are a couple of passing mentions of the Sisterhood of Radical Lawyers – to whom "harassment, discrimination and verbally aggressive male barrister conduct" is reported.[146] Rumpole does, however, note the dual aspect of attractive female advocacy which is oddly out of character for the normally sexless character of Rumpole.[147]

> Apart from her beauty, Mrs Erskine-Brown has brains. For nothing I named her Portia. When she spoke up for the defence the general opinion in the jury box was that if a nice girl like that was on his side, the villain in the dock couldn't be nearly as black as he was painted. When prosecuting, she could pot the prisoner with all the aplomb of the avenging angel on a good day.[148]

A somewhat patronising judgment is accorded to Erskine – Brown's pupil Wendy Crump

> She stood up, her cheeks flushed, her voice clear and determined. Mizz Crump might be no oil painting, but I thought I saw in her the makings of a fighter.[149]

On the other hand, sometimes out of sheer perverseness Rumpole does take pleasure in advancing the female cause as where he supports the entry of Fiona Allways into Chambers as a pupil [150] and, later, retaining Liz Probert.[151] The motives, however, for his progressive actions are to do with upsetting the settled bourgeois expectations of his colleagues rather than gender equality. [152]

Gender Role Stereotyping

Rumpole is a character from a bygone age as far as his general perception of the role of men and women is concerned.[153] As with many of his traits, his constant reference to Liz Probert as "Mizz Liz," Ballard as "Bollard" and Luci Gribble as "Luci with an 'i,'" become wearing, like his poetry and his frequent disparaging of cleaning products

> frittered away on such luxuries as income tax and sliced bread, washing powder, Brillo pads and. . . .[154]

It would be interesting to see the impact of the long-promised re-emergence of the Rumpole phenomenon with a female lead if this were to come to pass. It was reported both in 2019 and in the summer of 2021 that John Mortimer's actor daughter, Emily, was planning to revive the Rumpole series, updating it for modern times. The most novel feature was that the main character would be a female barrister with various actors such as Lily James and Keely Hawes tipped for the lead role.[155] The new version would also feature more females in significant roles to reflect changed days at the bar. In 1970, women accounted for only 8.2 per cent of those called to the Bar, but by 2020 that figure had risen to 38.2 per cent.[156]

CONCLUSIONS

Rumpole is a much-loved and endearing character. The values he holds and his unwillingness to compromise these principles noted above are admirable. That said, though, in some senses, Rumpole is the Pub Bore Supreme. Throughout his career, as outlined in his "memoirs" Rumpole makes frequent references to his "finest hour." Mortimer wants us to know that Rumpole is, indeed, no flawless character like Atticus Finch.[157] He also seems aware that, perhaps, he needs to rescue his character from appearing a mere blowhard. In his 2006 account of the infamous Penge Bungalow Murders, Mortimer notes the advice of his clerk

> My sincere advice as a clerk with some 30 years of clerking in the Temple is to play it down, Mr Rumpole. Try not to refer to it in conversation. Don't smirk about it. Do your level best not to boast.[158]

As many Rumpole stories demonstrate, for some reason, this was advice which Rumpole chose to ignore from his early days through to his final adventures

> It will be remembered that I achieved my greatest triumph, victory in the Penge bungalow murders, as a junior counsel, alone and without a leader.[159]

Even when he is involved in conversations with himself, he goes back to his great triumph

> A man who has, let us say, won that great classic, the Penge bungalow murders, may find himself dealing with some petty matter such as turning back the mileage metres of clapped-out Ford Cortinas or receiving stolen fish.[160]

The references are a recurring feature.[161] What he is remembered for though, is probably not self-repetition about juries, the presumption of innocence and the woeful conditions of prisons. Nor is his male chauvinism the principal reason why he sticks in our minds in a way no other British lawyer does but our memory of his witty ruminations. We do not mind if he claims that Phyllida Trant was his pupil[162] when in fact she served her time under Erskine-Brown.[163] Many of the narratives may not be particularly arresting but when we read the Rumpole stories we hear the rich fruity voice and delivery of Leo McKern. To borrow from the Irish Tourist Board "It's the character you remember long after you've forgotten the story.[164]

Apart from the specific social and political issues noted above Rumpole comes away with several interesting thoughts. Some are random but memorable such as "Murder is nothing more than common assault, with unfortunate consequences."[165] He is happy to suggest that law and legal principles in the practice of law are minor and that "Court cases are all about performance."[166] This reflected Mortimer's own early *ennui* with legal practice and the artifice of the legal process.

> As I grow older I find it more and more unsatisfactory, one is always saying only half the truth. In the law courts everybody is giving a performance. The judge is acting being a judge, I'm acting being an advocate. The whole thing is a very stagey outfit.[167]

By the same token, it could be suggested that Rumpole is appreciated, because, apart from his grouses about the threats to such institutions as the jury, he also recognises the defects, limitations and hypocrisy of white-collar respectable professions:

> (on being a City Trader) Nigel became the first Timson to relieve the punters of money in a way which was not only legal but considered, in the strange times in which we live, far more worthy of reward than teaching in schools or nursing the sick.[168]

He is not afraid to question such notions as private prosecutions which allow private citizens to prosecute each other for crimes with the aim of sending each other to jail, which he is not at all sure ought to be encouraged.[169] Nor, more importantly, is he happy with the role that money plays in the world of the justice system in such matters as breach of confidence cases for the protection of privacy which he described as a "luxury reserved for the rich."[170]

Throughout his career Rumpole is caustic about judges. In order to create a sense of the embattled fighter for justice we have frequent appearances of larger-than-life characters on the Bench like the irascible Judge Roger (The Mad Bull) Bullingham,[171] Mr Injustice Graves[172] and "prosecuting" judge Ollie Oliphant.[173] Their role as one – dimensional characters is to hinder the work of Horace Rumpole in his endeavours on behalf of his clients. As a result, Rumpole takes a dim view of judges and their role. Discussing the possibility of his elevation to the Bench he bemoans the downside.

> I might develop judgeitis.
>
> Of course, I asked him what that was.
>
> A ridiculous inflation of self importance, with increased intolerance; fatal tendency to suck up to juries, to interfere with the cross examinations by defending counsel; and doing your best to find all the customers in the dock guilty.[174]

There are, however, occasional judges who make Rumpole's life difficult by being fair and impartial. These include Judge Denny Densher,[175] Judge Emma McNaught,[176] Mrs Justice Templett[177] and Dame Mildred Wrightsworth.[178] They make single appearances only. Rumpole is clearly a much happier advocate when the chips are stacked against him with the judge bullying him and his witnesses enough for a reversal on appeal. As is noted below,[179] this would seem to stem from the era about which Mortimer was writing, which was rather different from the time when the Rumpole stories were published. Such is the power of the visual media that it is the memorable faces of the actors Bill Fraser, Robin Bailey and James Grout whom the reading public are likely to call to mind when thinking about British justice. This along with the crumpled features of Leo McKern are John Mortimer's gift to us from his legal comic writing. Although he stated he was "proud of having written Rumpole,"[180] he was also saddened to think Rumpole would be his legacy rather than any of his other plays or novels. He suspected correctly that his Obituary would focus on him being the creator of Rumpole. Graham Lord reports of this fear revealed in an interview with Angela Levin in the *Daily Mail*.

> Mortimer confessed, although he was now less aggressive and unpleasant than he had been in mid-age, he was still devious, manipulative, and not a good person and forecast glumly that when he died, the newspaper placards would read RUMPOLE MAN DIES, 'which means I shall be fused with him for ever and ever.'[181]

In fact, his fears were realised. The headlines included "Rumpole creator John Mortimer dies at 85,"[182] "Sir John Mortimer, creator of Rumpole of the Bailey,"[183] "John Mortimer, Barrister and Writer who Created Rumpole, Dies at 85,"[184] and most candidly "Barrister who portrayed himself as Rumpole"[185] as well as the slightly more nuanced "QC who took on liberal causes but found most fame as the creator of the fictional barrister Rumpole."[186] John Mortimer aspired to literary recognition and his output was considerable.[187] His greatest success was, however, the enduring and endearing character of Horace Rumpole, as the Obituary headlines testify. As is discussed below this legacy was not itself an unqualified success in the view of all commentators.[188]

APPENDIX

Note – all story titles start with “Rumpole” or “Rumpole and . . .” (except the misleadingly titled *Rumpole’s Last Case* [1987] and *Hilda’s Story*).

* indicates one of the ten stories selected by John Mortimer for his 1994 Folio Edition *Rumpole*

TITLE	*YEAR*	*LEGAL THEME*	*OTHER ISSUES*	*COMMENT*
Rumpole of the Bailey	1978			
1.The Younger Generation *		Theft at a butcher’s shop	Rumpole fails to become Head of Chambers Alibi defence	Set in 1965 with Rumpole 67 and an introduction to his family and Chambers
2.The Alternative Society		Possession of cannabis - changes plea and gets 3 years	Alternative use of dock as a form of protest about outdated laws and imprisonment of brother abroad	Rumpole uses *agent provocateur* defence until client admits guilt to get a platform
3.The Honourable Member		Rape by MP of his secretary	Replacement of Chief Clerk in Chambers against Rumpole’s wishes	Rumpole attacks character of alleged victim
4.The Married Lady		Divorce	Sub plot of misleading Phillida Trant into quoting lots of statute and case law to a “no nonsense” magistrate	Divorce all cooked by the scheming son, Norman who benefits from the attention – due to detective work of Rumpole about typewriters
5.The Learned Friends		Robbery	Rumpole up on disciplinary charges – dropped when client was found not guilty	Fitting up a man with form by a “bent” copper - evidence from tape recording post-trial
6.The Heavy Brigade		Murder by Kray like gang of a collector of protection money		Rumpole selected because he was expected to fail by crime gang
The Trials of Rumpole	1979			

1.The Man of God		Theft – shoplifting by a clergyman – actually his sister is guilty		Judge Bullingham acts reasonably and George Frobisher becomes a Circuit judge but does not marry a woman with an arson conviction
2.The Showfolk *		Murder and vindication of guilty actress		Link between the theatres and the courtroom
3. The Fascist Beast		Race Relations Act offence by a Britain First politico		Rumpole employs laughter but discredits his client in the eyes of his fellow racists
4.The Case of Identity		Assault	Hostile witness test	Problems with alibi defences
5.The Course of True Love		Unlawful carnal knowledge – sex with a minor – ruse by nasty couple, of students to discredit teacher	Head of Chambers with Bench ambitions prosecutes weakly in a burglary case	Circumstantial evidence Judge operating without fear or favour
Rumpole's Return	1980	Murder	Sub plot of a cult in Florida	Back from retirement in Florida . Identity and bloodstains are back
TITLE	YEAR	LEGAL THEME	OTHER ISSUES	COMMENT
Rumpole for the Defence aka Regina v Rumpole	1981			
1.The Confession of |Guilt		Attempted murder – stabbing of someone at a bus stop near Lord's cricket ground	Classic pre - Police and Criminal Evidence Act of 1984 "fit up" with a written confession by someone who was illiterate	The written version of the first outing of Rumpole on BBC TV in 1975
2 The Gentle Art of Blackmail		Blackmail – or was the money a present for a young gay lover by an old academic		Aim of the academic was to discredit his former lover by accusing him of blackmail to avoid scandal

(*Continued*)

TITLE	YEAR	LEGAL THEME	OTHER ISSUES	COMMENT
3. The Dear Departed		Will fraud	Beneficiary of 1974 will was mistress of testator – as well as earlier his brother – who stood to gain by earlier 1970 will	Spiritualism a factor One of the most unlikely of the Rumpole tales – so probably true
4.The Rotten Apple		Bribery and corruption (by a police officer)	Set up by another officer using a doctored tape	A hint of the Cecil twist in the tale
5. The Expert Witness		Murder – of a rich wife	Reliability of forensic evidence and who provides it	Rumpole duped into thinking his client has been "set up" by an ex-girlfriend who gave crucial evidence against him
6. The Spirit of Christmas		Murder – in a brawl between families	Another family feud between the Timsons and the O'Dowds	Rumpole conned into excessive drinking thinking he was softening up the prosecutor – quite the reverse
7. The Boat People		Murder – turns out nobody was killed.	Rumpole on holiday acts as detective to defend a case of murder with no body - done for the insurance	Echoes of David Nobbs' *The Return of Reginald Perrin* (1977)
Rumpole and the Golden Thread	1983			
		Art forgery - by a man who wanted his genius recognised by pretending to "pass" off his work as that of a famous deceased artist	Subsidiary focus on Guthrie Featherstone becoming a High Court judge and starting his work there	Beauty versus value in art with a Cecilesque twist in the tale
2.The Golden Thread		Murder – in Neranga with the death sentence still operative	Alibi from wife of the rival group and no jury Client murdered later by his brother	Centres around tribal rivalry between the Apu and Matatu in Neranga and revolution by the "Boys in the Bush" to prevent death sentence

3.The Old Boy Net *		Brothel-keeping and blackmail	Rumpole again fails to become Head of Chambers with a religious Q.C. pipping him	Centres on the unwritten code of public schoolboys not to "sneak"
4.The Female of the Species		Robbery of a bank – Molloys try to frame a Timson	Fiona Allways gets into Chambers with Rumpole's backing	Sexism of the client gets Rumpole the brief
5.The Sporting Life		Murder – of violent husband – accident in fact		Christie like "coincidences" provide the key along with knowledge of the number of pellets in a shotgun cartridge
6.The Last Resort		Fraudulent selling of holidays and computer booking system malfunction	Rumpole feigns a stroke/seizure in court to obtain time	Mendacious client's brother and computers and their problems to the uninitiated
Rumpole's Last Case	1987			
1.The Blind Tasting		Fraud – insurance – replacing good wine with inferior – to be stolen and claimed	Sub plot of receiving by a Timson	Entry of Liz Probert into Chambers – Ballard thinks Brother "Red" Ron is a cleric not a Marxist
2 The Old, Old Story.		Attempted murder – arranged by "victim" to allow him to sell land for a profit		Early attempt at smoking ban in Chambers
3.The Official Secret		Official Secrets Act breach about expenditure on biscuits	Technical expertise on use of typewriter by skilled/less skilled users key	Echoes of Clive Ponting case in 1984 – he leaked secrets about the sinking of the Belgrano in the Falklands War
4.The Judge's Elbow		Living on immoral earnings – from "massage" parlour	Sub plot about Guthrie Featherstone keeping out of the press as a user of – as it turns out – a different massage parlour and ousting an unpleasant new barrister	Judge innocently in massage parlour for tennis elbow and pays by credit card – changes approach when he sees he is in the clear

(Continued)

TITLE	*YEAR*	*LEGAL THEME*	*OTHER ISSUES*	*COMMENT*
5. The Bright Seraphim *		Murder of an apparently gay crossdressing Sergeant – court martial	All an elaborate Army coverup by the Regiment to cover up for his guilty abused wife	A Court martial
6.The Winter Break		Murder – opens with an unexpectedly successful defence of a likely serial wife killer	Rumpole encounters the murderous client he has just defended in disguise in Spain on his break	A slight 9-page indulgence in place of the usual 30
7.Rumpole's Last Case		Armed robbery of a bank and GBH by a pair of Timsons – reduced to theft in the end	Sub plot about a wager where the person entrusted with the bet absconds with Rumpole's "winnings"	Cutthroat defence – each accused blames the other – all down to the Molloys
TITLE	YEAR	LEGAL THEME	OTHER ISSUES	COMMENT
Rumpole and the Age of Miracles	1988			
1.The Bubble Reputation *		Defamation by a newspaper of a romantic novelist – all a fit up to obtain money	Sub plot with Erskine-Brown photographed in a strip club – visiting the *locus*	Use of Fig Newton and his evidence crucial
2. The Barrow Boy		Fraud – by insider dealing		Elaborate scheme to blacken the name of the "unsuitable" Nigel Timson stockbroker
3.The Age of Miracles		Adultery – by a cleric – "conduct unbecoming" – heard in an Ecclesiastical Court	Ballard, the Presiding Judge, affected by seeing a "ghost"	Actually giving money to his errant sister - in a hotel bedroom
4.The Tap End *		Attempted murder by a Timson of his wife – very summarily dealt with	Attempted robbery	Major part is over the ill-judged remarks of Guthrie Featherstone about gender roles
5.The Chambers Party		No actual trial – Rumpole finds a fake solicitor – and ex-client – trying to make off with petty cash	Offers of work from a smooth solicitor at the Chambers Christmas party	Short piece of six pages only

6.Portia		Terrorist activities – storing arms for Irish paramilitaries Special Branch involvement hinted at	Mini sub-plot of possession-of-drugs case of Phillida Erskine-Brown Hilda's cousin, Boxey, briefly sponges off them	Phillida turns out to be tough on the Bench as a Recorder
7.The Quality of Life		Murder by a young wife of her elderly infirm artist husband – not guilty	Rumpole's leader becomes unavailable	Euthanasia debate canvassed
Rumpole à la Carte	1990			
1.à la Carte *		Breach of Food Hygiene Regulations Concurrent divorce of restaurateur	Sub plot of Claude Erskine-Brown entertaining a lady – not Phillida – in a Michelin starred restaurant	Very long introduction
2.The Summer of Discontent		Manslaughter of coach driver ferrying scabs during an industrial dispute about coach drivers	Sub plot of judges carrying out a "work to rule" to scupper rights of audience for solicitors in the higher courts	Plants – including a Molloy - in the picket line – reminiscent of activities in the Miners' Strike 1984–5
3.The Right to Silence		Murder of a University Vice Chancellor	Alibi of a Masonic type meeting by the accused	
4.at Sea		Rumpole and Hilda on a cruise where other passengers include Mr Justice Graves	Rumpole is sceptical and it turns out he recognises the not-dead wife whom everyone suspects has been done away with by a vicar	Bit of fun on the dangers of circumstantial evidence
5.the Quacks		Misconduct by a G.P. In relation to a female patient - before the G.M.C.	Subplot about a middle-aged vamp who has taken to Rumpole	All a ruse by one of the partners to get the accused out of the practice as he won't prescribe medicines from Big Pharma
6. For the Prosecution		Private prosecution for murder undertaken by Rumpole	Subplot of "who is re-directing briefs"	True murderer seems to have escaped the law – Rumpole "changes sides" mid case

(Continued)

TITLE	*YEAR*	*LEGAL THEME*	*OTHER ISSUES*	*COMMENT*
Rumpole on Trial	1992			
1.The Children of the Devil *		Satanic abuse of children – heard by a Tribunal	Denunciation of Timsons by a Molloy	Attack on "interfering" social workers
2.The Eternal Triangle		Murder of a member of a music trio who had been blackmailing another member of the trio	Subplot of Rumpole having his head turned by a lady musician	The murderess cosied up to Rumpole so he would go soft on her in the court case against her innocent husband
3.The Miscarriage of Justice		Murder of a police officer and signed confession by a young man with learning difficulties	Overturned by the Court of Appeal and the "fitter up" charged – but not actually the corrupt one	Another example of the higher up officer being the one corrupting – as in the Rotten Apple above
4.The Family Pride *		Accidental or not death of a "bag lady" at a country house – Coroner's Court hearing	Long visit to Hilda's distant relatives	*Deus ex machina* appearance of long-lost mother Perry Mason style
5.The Soothsayer		Fraud – use of microphones etc to "speak with the dead" – but the machinery was defunct		Only 11 pages in this brief tale
6.The Reform of Joby Jonson		Theft and assault	Not really a robbery as such but harassment to sell to a developer – the charitably inclined Fagin character	Another Fagin character acting ostensibly for underprivileged youth
7. Rumpole on Trial *		Manslaughter of his wife by a boring client – or accident?	Rumpole accused of unprofessional conduct by talking to a witness during the lunch break	Rumpole's toothache the central factor in this classic mistaken overheard conversation
Rumpole and the Angel of Death	1995			
		Assault on a prison guard – before the Board of Visitors	Subplot of receiving by a Timson	Friendship and institutional dependence of prisoners Some drama put on by prisoners

2. The Way through the Woods		Murder of a hunt aficionado allegedly by a man who has an alibi he is not keen to reveal	Recurrence of desire to make a political speech from the dock and real culprit known only to Rumpole gets away with it	Mortimer a keen supporter of fox hunting in his private life
3.Hilda's Story		Murder case being conducted by Horace – not done by the son but a jealous cousin	Alibi by New Age travellers	The world of a Rumpole case as seen by She Who Must Be Obeyed
4.The Little Boy Lost		Child abduction – client lost her own son at 4 weeks – a ruse to get money for a tabloid newspaper story and revenge on an adversary from school	Sub plot of another failed Erskine-Brown dalliance in the press	Power of the press
5.The Rights of Man		Murder – ends up in Strasbourg	Strategy to get judge to show racial prejudice – but fails – but then private speech reveals his true colours	A few anti-European tropes Big arms dealer conspiracy behind it all
6.The Angel of Death		Murder of a retired judge – euthanasia by GP? Actually by his niece for financial reasons	Plea bargaining as a way of increasing profitability in Chambers	Quite Christie like in the setup of the euthanasia supporting doctor being brought in to attract suspicion
Rumpole Rests His Case	2001			
1.The Old Familiar Faces		Theft - safe cracking – culprit had an alibi – which collapsed	Blackmail by Rumpole – squeezing money for the local church out of a now respectable ex-con whom Rumpole once represented	Alibi – different actor in the Pantomime Dame costume – wife of the safe cracker
2.The Remembrance of Things Past		Murder many years ago by husband who buried her after shouting at her – died of heart attack	Ballard's past in a rock band as a weapon backfires when he embraces it	'60s hippie background versus fundamentalist Christian beliefs

(Continued)

TITLE	*YEAR*	*LEGAL THEME*	*OTHER ISSUES*	*COMMENT*
3.The Asylum Seekers		Immigration appeal case of a doctor from Afghanistan	Fear of people traffickers who substituted a fake appellant	Cultural relativism noted
4. The Camberwell Carrot		Drug possession by anti-drug MP and agent provocateur defence		Tabloid exposé Dark political forces behind the prosecution
5. Rumpole and the Actor Laddie		Theft by an actor seeking the spotlight of a ring	Denouement – the ring was not actually stolen at all	Short piece less than eight pages all about the theatricality of the courtroom
6. The Teenage Werewolf		Assault and harassment by emails by one teenager of another – actually the boy's stepfather guilty	Denouement consists of the accused stepfather sprinting from court and never being seen again	Excessive use of poetry
7. Rests His Case		Unlawful wounding, grievous bodily harm and firearms offence – defending his home or a set –up?	Collapse of Rumpole at the end of his address to the Jury	Defence of one's home Fig Newton investigates and discovers the "victim" was obsessed with the accused's girlfriend. A bit "Midsomer Murders"
Rumpole and the Primrose Path	2002			
1.The Primrose Path		Life insurance fraud		Rumpole recognises the qualities of the Director of Marketing and Administration, Luci Gribble
2.The New Year's Resolution		Theft – defence of a Timson	Fagin type worker with young, disadvantaged children	
3.The Scales of Justice		Conspiracy to Murder	A setup to discredit a senior police officer who would benefit from the death of the husband of the wife – the object of his affections	Rumpole defends a man who berates defence lawyers and their ruses

4.The Right to Privacy		Right to privacy case about an indiscreet photo of a rich businessman	All a ruse to prevent the evidence of sleaze and corruption coming out	Access of big money to Government contracts
5.The Vanished Juror		Murder	Separate reason for juror to disappear to do with fear of a violent father	
6.Redeemed		Burglary – defending a Molloy – set up by a supposedly reformed ex con	Brief allocated on the basis of a favour done	Rumpole bemoaning marketing of the Bar and prison conditions and cultural relativism
TITLE	YEAR	LEGAL THEME	OTHER ISSUES	COMMENT
Rumpole and the Penge Bungalow Murders	2004	Murder of two men by the son of one of them who turns out to be innocent		Rumpole tells the story of the fabled murders lest its details be forgot
Rumpole and the Reign of Terror	2006	Terrorism charge against a non-British relative by marriage of the Timsons – "good" friend at the bottom of it to avenge a family feud	Terrorism legislation up against notions of human rights	Interspersed with comments from Hilda Bit reductive about foreign feuds
The Anti-social Behaviour of Horace Rumpole	2007	Murder – Rumpole's client with facial birthmark frequented a brothel subplot of the A.S.B.O. served on a child playing football, which is really cover to protect the up-market brothel operation	Detective work of Fig Newton establishes that the brothel is being staffed by illegally imported foreign women. Sub plot of Hilda deciding to read for the Bar – abandons the idea in the end. Rumpole fails to become a Q.C. After ruffling feathers of Home Office Minister	

(Continued)

TITLE	*YEAR*	*LEGAL THEME*	*OTHER ISSUES*	*COMMENT*
Rumpole at Christmas	2009			
		see above	Originally published *The Strand Magazine* in 2001	Repeat of story in *Rumpole Rests His Case* (2001)
2.The Christmas Break		murder after threat in letter to academic victim by religiously motivated young student	murderer's mistress admits to collusion to implicate the threat maker rather than anything forensic	Originally published in *The Strand Magazine* in 2001
3.The Boy		blackmail which never was – "victim" folds in court	son of victim's paramour keen on the Bar and real reason for success of Rumpole	Originally published in the *Daily Mail* in 1997
4.The Millennium Bug		Successful accidental defence of Hughie Timson when actual Molloy culprits apprehended - HT had confessed to impress his girlfriend	Tale of Rumpole being conned out a Christmas delivery by a Timson but getting credit from Hilda for this act of "charity"	Originally published in the *Independent* in 1999
5The Christmas Party		no legal elements in this 3.5-page tale	Hilda appears at the Chambers Christmas party having foregone Christmas with Dodo Mackintosh who has gone vegan-ish	Originally published in the *Daily Express* in 2004
6.Father Christmas		former client of Rumpole, playing Father Christmas, steals from the Chambers but returns it all overcome by pangs of guilt	Solely located in Chambers and another Christmas Party – for various children	Originally published in the *Sunday Express* in 2005 and in *The Strand Magazine* in 2006
7.The Health Farm Murder		murder mystery in health farm and Rumpole plays detective to unmask the real murderer and prepares to defend the woman set up to take the fall	Solely located at the Health Farm	Originally published in *The Strand Magazine* in 2007 entitled *Rumpole's Slimmed Down Christmas*

NOTES

1. Mortimer (1982); Mortimer (1994 a) Mortimer (2000) and Mortimer (2007).

2. Lord (2005); Grove (2007).

3. Larsen (1997); Hanley (1989); Berlins (2002) and (2004); Carl (2012); Hewett (2014); see also collected ruminations such as Mortimer (2007).

4. Guardian 16 January 2009 Obituary (available at https://www.theguardian.com/culture/2009/jan/16/mortimer-rumpole-dies-obituary).

5. Ibid.

6. Mortimer (1950) – Antonia White regarded this as the book's "trump card" – New Statesman Review – Grove p. 95. His first two novels have no legal elements – Mortimer (1947) – based on his work for the Crown Film Unit during World War II and Mortimer (1948) – a satire of village politics.

7. To whom Mortimer dedicated his first Rumpole Collection but who fell out with him over the production of series 2 of Rumpole – see note 13 below.

8. Although the first line of the first story set in 1965 reads "I, Horace Rumpole, barrister at law, 68 next birthday," and calls into question why he was serving in the RAF at the age of 40 – Rumpole and the Younger Generation p. 1.

9. St Joseph's College (Rumpole and the Gentle Art of Blackmail p. 46); Keble College (Rumpole and the Younger Gereration) p. 11.

10. In fact quite early on his role as RAF ground staff appears (Rumpole and the Alternative Soicety p. 50) and much later on we learn that he got his "big break" in the Penge Bungalow murders because his leader CH Wystan was unable to continue with the case due to having to appear in the Court of Appeal on a planning application (Rumpole and the Penge Bungalow Murders p. 105).

11. Shubick (2000) at p. 178.

12. Mortimer (1994a) at p. 74.

13. Shubick (2000) at p. 182 – albeit with a different producer after series 1 following a falling out between Shubick and Channel 4 Head of Drama, Verity Lambert, about money – loc cit at 198. Confirmed by Grove (2007) at 311–32.

14. Grove (2007) at p. 323.

15. Robson (2007a) and (2007b).

16. Graham (2022).

17. Washington Post (1981).

18. Moran (2008) is particularly interesting on this.

19. Rumpole Clubs in San Francisco and Australia discussed in Mortimer (1994 b at ix and in Grove (2007) at 400.

20. Moran (2008), Flood (2020); Harmes, Harmes and Harmes (2022).

21. See Conclusions.

22. Mortimer (1994b) p. vii.

23. Ibid.

24. Interview with the author – 2005.

25. Rumpole and the Younger Generation p. 9.

26. Rumpole and the Learned Friends p. 137.

27. Rumpole and the Little Boy Lost p. 617 – which is of course what artistic licence is all about.

28. Grove (2007) at p. 323.

29. Ian Rankin, the creator of Edinburgh detective John Rebus admitted that it was his wife who reminded him that he had gifted his protagonist a dog in a previous adventure – Harrogate Crime Writing Festival 2018 interview.

30. Rumpole and the Bubble Reputation p. 22.

31. Rumpole and the Heavy Brigade (1978) p. 198.

32. Rumpole and the Remembrance of Things Past p. 67 & 68.

33. Rumpole and the Little Boy Lost p. 651.

34. Rumpole and the Primrose Path p. 37; Rumpole and the Angel of Death p. 697.

35. Rumpole's New Year's Resolutions p. 47.

36. Rumpole and the Scales of Justice p. 68.

37. Ibid.

38. Ibid.

39. The Anti-Social Behaviour of Horace Rumpole pp. 6 & 50; Rumpole and the Reign of Terror p. 7.

40. Rumpole and the Scales of Justice p. 68.

41. Rumpole and the Judge's Elbow p. 561

42. The Anti-Social Behaviour of Horace Rumpole p. 43.

43. Loc cit p. 159.

44. Loc cit pp. 6 & 50.

45. Rumpole and the Scales of Justice p. 69; Rumpole and the Summer of Discontent p. 272; Rumpole and the Age of Miracles p. 105; Rumpole and the Quacks p. 399.

46. Rumpole and the Angel of Death p. 720.

47. Rumpole and the Barrow boy p. 35.

48. See page 167 below.

49. Rape; divorce; race; receiving; brothel-keeping; Official Secrets; defamation; food hygiene; adultery; medical misconduct; Satanic abuse; child abduction; harassment; immigration; privacy rights.

50. For instance, Rumpole and the Boat People.

51. They include 3 stories which did not appear on TV – Rumpole's Last Case series 4 – *Rumpole and the Winter Break*; Rumpole and the Age of Miracles series 5 – *Rumpole and the Chambers Party* and Rumpole on Trial series 7 – *Rumpole and the Soothsayer.*

52. Rumpole's Return (1980).

53. Rumpole for the Defence (1980).

54. Rumpole and the Angel of Death (1995), 6 stories; Rumpole Rests His Case (2001), 7 stories; Rumpole and the Primrose Patch (2002), 6 stories.

55. Rumpole at Christmas (2009) Rumpole and the Old Familiar Faces; Rumpole and the Christmas Break; Rumpole and the Boy: Rumpole and the Millennium Bug; Rumpole and the Christmas Party; Rumpole and Father Christmas; Rumpole and the Health Farm Murder.

56. Rumpole and the Penge Bungalow Murders (2004); Rumpole and the Reign of Terror (2006) and The Anti-Social Behaviour of Horace Rumpole (2007).

57. Mortimer (1994 a) p. 78.

58. Speech to Conservative Party Conference at Blackpool, October 7 1970 (available at http://www.britishpoliticalspeech.org/speech-archive.htm?speech=117 (accessed 5 April 2022).

59. Rumpole and the Alternative Society p. 49.

60. Rumpole and the Reign of Terror.

61. Rumpole and the Primrose Path p. 1; Rumpole and the Reign of Terror p. 37; Rumpole and the Penge Bungalow Murders p. 1.

62. Rumpole and the Confession of Guilt p. 41.

63. Rumpole A la Carte p. 238.

64. Ibid.

65. Rumpole and the Camberwell Carrot p. 123.

66. Hanley (1989) p. 23.

67. See Appendix.

68. The name also of a popular sweet biscuit by Nabisco.

69. Rumpole and the Miscarriage of Justice p. 92.

70. Rumpole and the Soothsayer p. 123.

71. Rumpole for the Prosecution p. 435.

72. Loc cit p. 449.

73. Rumpole and the Asylum Seekers p. 71.

74. Rumpole and Gentle Art of Blackmail p. 62.

75. Rumpole and the Rights of Man p. 68.

76. Rumpole and the Right to Privacy p. 104.

77. Rumpole and the Age of Miracles p. 74 – degrees in U.K. universities range from the best – 1st through a 2.1, 2.2. to a 3rd class degree. Oxbridge used to also award a 4th class degree. but these are no longer encountered.

78. Rumpole and the Penge Bungalow Murders p. 4.

79. Grove (2007) p. 67.

80. Lord (2005) p. 48 citing the College magazine, The Brazen Nose.

81. Grove (2007) p. 54.

82. Mortimer (1982) p. 60.

83. Mortimer (1982) p. 57.

84. Rumpole and the Penge Bungalow Murders p. 4.

85. Loc cit p. 11.

86. Rumpole and the Reign of Terror p. 13 per Hilda – probably a reference to Peck's role as the inspirational Attorney Atticus Finch in the film To Kill a Mockingbird (1962) rather than his role in The Paradine Case (1959) as a conflicted barrister who falls for his enigmatic client.

87. Rumpole and the Right to Silence p. 343 ff.

88. Rumpole and the Vanishing Juror pp. 166–69.

89. Rumpole and the Reign of Terror p. 109.

90. Rumpole and the Remembrance of Things Past p. 36.

91. Cohen (1972).

92. Rumpole's New Year's Resolutions p. 47.

93. Rumpole Redeemed pp. 181–82.

94. *Pace* Rumpole and the Children of the Devil (1992).
95. Rumpole and the Remembrance of Things Past (2001) p. 27.
96. The Anti-Social Behaviour of Horace Rumpole (2002).
97. Rumpole and the Reign of Terror (2006).
98. Mortimer (1994 b) p. vii.
99. See Chapter 2.
100. Grove (2007).
101. Mortimer (1982; 1994 a; 2007); Lord (2005); Grove (2007).
102. Rumpole and the Expert Witness p. 131.
103. Rumpole and the Penge Bungalow Murders p. 28.
104. Mortimer (1994 a) at p. 79.
105. 1975 published as Rumpole and the Confession of Guilt (1980).
106. Rumpole and the Rotten Apple p. 125.
107. Dixon of Dock Green, Series 2 The Rotten Apple August 11 1956.
108. Rumpole and the Miscarriage of Justice.
109. Loc cit at p. 92.
110. Rumpole's Return p. 477.
111. Rumpole and the Man of God p. 223.
112. Rumpole and the Golden Thread p. 244.
113. Rumpole a la Carte p. 265.
114. Rumpole and the Female of the Species p. 327.
115. Rumpole and the Old, Old Story 1987 p. 489.
116. Twelve Angry Men (16/10/59), "Does Magna Carta mean nothing to you? Did she die in vain? Brave Hungarian peasant girl who forced King John to sign the pledge at Runnymede & closed the boozers at half past ten?"
117. Rumpole and the Right to Silence p. 310.
118. Rumpole at Sea p. 376.
119. Rumpole and the Alternative Society p. 56.
120. Rumpole and the Learned Friends p. 163.
121. Rumpole and the Miscarriage of Justice p. 109.
122. Rumpole and the Scales of Justice p. 99.
123. The Anti-social Behaviour of Horace Rumpole p. 128.
124. Rumpole and the Quality of Life p. 221.
125. John Mortimer in Conversation (available at https://www.youtube.com/watch?v=bA1WWclIp5U).
126. Grove (2007) p. 398 and 423.
127. Rumpole and the Genuine Article p. 196.
128. Rumpole and the Tap End p. 111.
129. Rumpole and the Eternal Triangle p. 63; Rumpole and the Reform of Joby Jonson p. 169 on the conditions for unconvicted people on remand.
130. Rumpole and the Reign of Terror p. 141.
131. See ECHR.coe.int on prison reform case law.
132. Rumpole and the Honourable Member pp. 92–95.
133. Loc cit 96–97.

134. https://www.gov.uk/government/news/pre-recorded-evidence-for-rape-victims-rolled-out-to-more-north-west-courts (last accessed 13//4/23).

135. https://www.gov.uk/government/news/thousands-more-victims-to-avoid-trauma-of-courtroom-cross-examination-under-plans-to-boost-barrister-fees (last accessed 13/4/23).

136. Phillida Trant; Fiona Allways; Liz Probert.

137. Rumpole and the Model Prisoner – "no oil painting, as uncle Tom, of blessed memory, would have been likely to say" p. 485.

138. Rumpole and the Quacks pp. 418 and 431.

139. Rumpole and the Married Lady p. 118.

140. Loc cit at p. 125.

141. Rumpole and the Model Prisoner p. 498.

142. Rumpole and the Reign of Terror p. 52.

143. The Anti-social Behaviour of Horace Rumpole p. 125.

144. Rumpole and Portia (1988) p. 180 ff.

145. Loc cit at p. 61 – he sports the name of Leonard when he takes an interest in Hilda in their Bridge playing encounters. He started life as Ronnie Bullingham in 1978 in Rumpole and the Learned Friends p. 145 but became Roger in 1980 in Rumpole's Return p. 406 as well in Rumpole and Old Boy Net p. 294 and Rumpole and the Winter Break p. 618; Under Scots law it is permissible to change your name without any formal legal process. No Scottish connection for him is mentioned in the Rumpole stories, however. The name and place are located in Northumbria next to the border with Scotland.

146. Rumpole and the Model Prisoner pp. 498 and 506.

147. Rumpole's preference for young men at University, like that of Mortimer, though, never features – Grove (2007) at p. 283.

148. Rumpole and the Quacks p. 307.

149. Rumpole and the Model Prisoner p. 496.

150. Rumpole and the Sporting Life p. 366.

151. Rumpole and the Blind Tasting pp. 449 and 476.

152. Rumpole and the Female of the Species passim and p. 338.

153. Rumpole and the Model Prisoner p. 498 on "gender awareness" being raised as a topic in Chambers.

154. Rumpole and the Barrow boy p. 39.

155. Irish Legal News (2021).

156. Mail on Sunday (2021).

157. Cf the challenge to the memory of Atticus in the New Yorker (December 10 2018) – available at https://www.newyorker.com/magazine/2018/12/17/the-contested-legacy-of-atticus-finch and Freedman (1992a) (1992b) and (1994).

158. Rumpole and the Penge Bungalow Murders p. 203.

159. Rumpole and the Barrow boy p. 66.

160. Rumpole and the Age of Miracles p. 73.

161. Rumpole and the Golden Thread p. 244 Rumpole and the Bright Seraphim p. 609; Rumpole and the Quality of Life p. 195; Rumpole and the Reform of Joby Jonson p. 199; Rumpole and the Way through the Woods p. 524: Rumpole and Family

Pride p. 123; Hilda's Story p. 611; Rumpole and the Teenage Werewolf p. 153; Rumpole and the Primrose Path p. 5; Rumpole and the Right to Privacy p. 119; Rumpole and the Reign of Terror pp. 1, 61, 63, 65 and 81: The Anti-Social Behaviour of Horace Rumpole pp. 6 & 50.

162. Rumpole and the Reign of Terror p. 74.

163. Rumpole and the Married Lady p. 107.

164. Per Sharon Horgan *Irish People are The Funniest* campaign in 2023–24.

165. Rumpole and the Learned Friends p. 168.

166. Rumpole and the Show Folk p. 268.

167. Interview in 1971 with Lynda Lee-Potter cited in Lord (2005) at p. 163.

168. Rumpole and the Barrow boy p. 37.

169. Rumpole for the Prosecution p. 43.

170. Rumpole and the Right to Privacy p. 112.

171. Rumpole and the Last Resort – no first name in book but in IMDB Roger https://www.imdb.com/title/tt0691372/characters/nm0292077 – known to Hilda as Leonard – The Anti-Social Behaviour of Horace Rumpole p. 61.

172. Rumpole at Sea (1991) in which even on his holidays Rumpole cannot escape this man's icy ambience.

173. Rumpole on Trial p. 209.

174. Rumpole and the Reign of Terror p. 74.

175. Loc cit p. 151.

176. Rumpole and the Model Prisoner p. 500.

177. Rumpole and the Reign of Terror p. 74.

178. The Anti-Social Behaviour of Horace Rumpole p. 125.

179. See Conclusions.

180. Lord (2005) at p. 259.

181. Lord op cit p. 268.

182. The Times 17 January 2009.

183. Guardian 16 January 2009 (available at https://www.theguardian.com/culture/2009/jan/16/mortimer-rumpole-dies-obituary (last accessed 12 January 2024). He would have been delighted, however with the Independent description as "wit, flirt, genius" – The Independent 17 January 2009 (available at https://www.independent.co.uk/news/people/profiles/wit-flirt-genius-john-mortimer-dies-aged-85-1418233.html (last accsessed 12 January 2024).

184. New York Times 17 January 2009 available at https://www.nytimes.com/2009/01/17/books/17mortimer.html (last acessed 12 January 2024).

185. Financial Times 16 January 2009.

186. Daily Telegraph 16 January 2009 available at https://www.telegraph.co.uk/news/obituaries/4269779/Sir-John-Mortimer-Writer-by-choice-lawyer-at-his-fathers-behest.html (last accessed 12 January 2024).

187. See Bibliography.

188. See Conclusions.

Chapter 5

Tim Kevan, David Osborne, and Peter Murphy

INTRODUCTION

There are three further barristers who have written light legal fiction in the 21st century. Their approaches vary. Two involve "coming of age" ingénu lawyers making the transfer from law graduate to barrister with a place in Chambers.[1] As was noted above in the context of Henry Cecil's Roger Thursby and Hastings Draper's Alan Pace there is a process which an aspiring barrister must go through to start off in the senior branch of the English legal profession. Tim Kevan in 2009 and 2011, and David Osborne in 2013 and 2014, provide us with the light-hearted and comical accounts of the struggles of two young men to secure a place in a set of Chambers from which to practice as barristers.[2] The other writer, Peter Murphy, takes readers into the unfamiliar world of the Circuit Judge with his stories of Charlie Walden and the life and times of a fictional Crown Court[3] in 2017, 2018, 2019 and 2024.[4] Before looking at the nature of their fiction it is worth providing some professional context for each of these writers, two of whom are alive at the time of writing.

THE BABYBARISTA FILES AND TIM KEVAN

Tim Kevan joined Middle Temple winning several scholarships. He practised as a barrister specialising in credit hire, personal injury, civil fraud and sports law between 1997 and 2008.[5] During his time qualifying and in practice he wrote and co-authored a number of legal practice texts on his areas of expertise.[6]

Two comic legal novels, *Law and Disorder*[7] and *Law and Peace*[8] were extensions of a BabyBarista blog. The first centres around BabyB's first year in chambers where he is fighting his fellow pupils to become permanently established in Chambers. The sequel, *Law and Peace*, continues the life and times of the young lawyer protagonist, BabyBarista, and appeared in May 2011.[9] It takes us through the next year in which he achieves recognition for signal assistance to Senior Counsel withe award of a red bag[10] as well as being cleared by the Bar Standards Board of unethical conduct.[11] In his fictional writings, Tim Kevan adopted the resolute mien of one determined to succeed in storming the ramparts of the legal profession by fair means or foul. His, protagonist, BabyBarista is the representative of Generation X – those born in the years between 1965 and 1980.[12] His watchword is scepticism if not cynicism. There is no trace of a concern with justice nor the public interest.

He expresses views on the legal system through the wise words of one of the barristers whom our protagonist regards as having integrity. Although BabyBarista himself may lack much by way of a moral compass, he does, however, recognise that hidden amongst the various schemers, sloths and backsliders whom he encounters during his time as a trainee barrister, there are a couple of people with principles. Through them we obtain a more or less authentic sounding picture of aspects of the justice system. Other more worldly wise characters provide a slightly jaundiced commentary on the justice system and its shortcomings. Within the world of BabyBarista it is not always possible to distinguish between those who are weary of the world and those who retain some faith in the system. The tendency towards this scepticism, bordering on cynicism, may stem from the precarious position of barristers which is always in the background.

> Being self-employed barristers have no guarantee of income, with no sick pay, company cars or pensions to look forward to.[13]

Related to this, is the subservient dependent position of barristers for work as recognised by our protagonist.

> For all their supposed independence, most barristers seem to live in a state of complete paranoia and spend so much time kowtowing to solicitors that their independence is worth even less than their pride.[14]

The precise form the dependent nature of the barrister takes is adverted to in advice from BabyBarista's own pupil master. Known as TheBoss and described as an "Unscrupulous, spineless coward,"[15] he explains the process

> Accident management companies chase ambulances, solicitors schmooze accident management company and barristers fawn over solicitors. Fail to do that and you'll have no practice even to lose.[16]

For instance, he also advises that costs should never be an issue in a case

> What I'd say is, "Never take on a lawyer on a no-win, no fee basis." Invest now in legal expenses insurance. Pay up front. But whatever you do, don't let the lawyers start worrying about getting paid. However much they protest otherwise, it's there in their mind. Not even at the back of their mind. It's a big fat ugly screaming beast jumping up and down on the head telling them to settle whether you want to fight it or not.[17]

The modern nature of legal practice is suggested as being mainly concerned with the extraction of the maximum amount of cash from the justice process. As one solicitor, noted as "skilled in the creative art of billing,"[18] points out to our protagonist

> It's all a distraction, BabyB. The law's not about ivory towers or wigs and gowns. It's about one thing and that's costs. Not justice. Not rights. Not defending the innocent or prosecuting the guilty. It's cold, hard, stinking cash. Your time, literally, is money. You sign over your life, but for a price of which even Faust himself would be proud.[19]

That said, the advice he receives from the respected colleague is rather less venal and suggests a different approach is possible.

> We're paid to fight cases, and never forget that. Yes, sometimes cases may settle but remember, the solicitors will already have given it a pretty good go even before it gets anywhere near court. So, unless something changes, you get yourself right in there and fight.[20]

There is, though, no formal "quality control" in the world of barristers. From Wilfred Morganhall in *Dock Brief* in the 1950's[21] through Rumpole's Uncle Tom to BabyBarista's OldWorrier, there seems to be little protection against "rogue" barristers beyond the internal standards of the Bar Council. There is a Code of Conduct, published in the Bar Standards Board Handbook. This involves a process by which barristers judge other barristers through the Bar Council Standards Board[22] to ensure compliance with the Code of Conduct.[23]

The position of solicitors is described as even worse

> solicitors don't seem to get any faffing time. They're constantly being judged by how many hours they've billed.[24]

When they seek to appear in court, however – effectively taking bread from the mouths of barristers – they are represented as offering little by way of real competition.[25]

BabyBarista's world-weariness stems from being left to hold the case with no instructions by his moneymaking boss who regularly takes on many cases and leaves juniors to cover them. The boss puts in an occasional appearance but charges the full fee.[26] We know from John Mortimer, that Rumpole is prepared to lie and dissemble in order to get involved in a case including claiming to have expertise in areas in which he has no knowledge. BabyB is happy to follow suit. For instance, he mugs up for a libel case despite being a rank beginner in the area.[27]

We also learn of a variety of practices and traditions. Some we know, from other writings,[28] to be genuine such as and the award of a red bag for excellence in supporting Senior Counsel (QC/KC)[29] and the implications of rejecting an offer of settlement without consulting the client.[30] Others are more doubtful and possibly apocryphal such as expenses claims for tax purposes.[31] a "rent a client" scam[32] playing the word game with animal names[33] as well as a series of subliminal mind games aimed at a judge including clothing and t-shirt messaging.[34] Some sound as though they came from the pen of John Mortimer, or more precisely, the mouth of Horace Rumpole as where BabyB employs "the old scales of justice being finely balanced" speech.[35]

There is another link to the worldview of Rumpole in the irritation of the Head of Chambers to a young man who mentioned that he "believed" something

> Believe? Believe? said Head of Chambers, his voice rising. Only priests believe. Barristers are not paid to have either feelings or beliefs. They are instead paid to give their esteemed and learned opinions . . . from now on, no feelings, no beliefs.[36]

On judges and the judicial process, we learn something about the quixotic nature of decision making. BabyBarista is warned by an experienced barrister "with integrity" whom he admires,

> It's not about the law . . . and it's often not even about the facts. Most of the time it boils down to one question: does the judge like your client or not? Is he for him or agin?[37]

Later in BabyB's career the same adviser suggests

> Everything's winnable, BabyB. It's all up for grabs once you have a real, living and above all fallible judge sitting in front of you.[38]

This seems to be an improvement on appearing before a judge who decides cases based on the attractiveness of the legal team.[39] Odd and eccentric judges[40] and magistrates[41] are encountered.

When asked to provide advice on how to impersonate a judge, our protagonist suggests his colleague should go for being a Deputy District Judge on the grounds that

> They're the bottom of the pile and no one ever remembers them from one minute to the next . . . Beyond that arrogance, stupidity and a complete lack of insight should just about make you the real deal.[42]

The Bar in the experience of our guide through the London justice system of the 1990s is metrocentric. Echoing Rumpole's disdain for things and people from "Oop North,"[43] BabyB and one of the female barristers in Chambers indulge in a game to see whether the barrister adopting the Northern accent can include more use of "whippet," "flat cap" and "grim" against the West Country accented barrister's use of "cider," "wurzel" and "combine harverster."[44] It is also a world where women are present but where sex discrimination is rife but brushed off in the interests of the smooth running of Chambers.[45] Class is briefly adverted to and it is clear that working class barristers are less than welcome in this world with the rejection of Waynes and Shanes and the humiliation of a Brummie[46] called Sharon.[47]

Women in general can also be trusted to be "unworldly." On learning that a man "runs a hedge fund in the City" BabyB's mother expresses herself thus

> Golly. Jolly good for you. Although I wouldn't have thought there was much call for hedges in this urban wilderness. Do you do funds for flowers and other plants as well?[48]

All in all, with the two appearances of BabyBarista the notion is dispelled that there is anything other than money or fun at stake in going to law.

THE LIFE AND TIMES OF INGÉNU BARRISTER TOBY POTTS – DAVID OSBORNE

David Osborne was called to the English Bar in 1974 and to the Irish Bar in 1986. He is a member of Gray's Inn and has written two books about his young barrister, Toby Potts.[49] In the world of Toby Potts what we have is someone who is also determined to make it in law but who seems to have some interest in the possibility of benefiting the community. The writing style is more straightforward and measured than we find in the BabyBarista files published a few years earlier with, again, only minimal citing of Shakespeare[50] or poetry.[51] There is a more modest use of nicknames for the other participants in the life of our aspiring barrister, Toby Potts. Toby is a whole lot more naïve and trusting than BabyBarista, probably reflecting the times when the author was seeking to enter the profession in the 1970s.[52] Following a surprise success quite early in his career appealing against the length of sentence given to a man who killed his wife with a single blow, Toby reflects on the approach of a money-obsessed colleague and his own view

> To him the Bar was a money machine, and if you couldn't afford him, then you couldn't have him.
>
> But there had to be more to it than that. To me, it was all about real people, with their weaknesses and hardships, their sweat and tattoos, their poverty and their sheer hopelessness. Even with the constant struggle over legal aid, inadequate payment, arguing over the pennies, if that was what it was all about, if the next case was just another meal ticket, then it wasn't worth the candle.[53]

The narrative of Toby Potts's early career commences in the same way as the film version of Henry Cecil's *Brothers in Law*[54] at the ceremony of our protagonist being called to the Bar. The style is instructive with the process leading up to this of "dining," the various Inns of Court,[55] pupillage,[56] taking silk[57] and the role of an "outdoor clerk"[58] all explained in an accessible manner.[59] We follow Potts' passive role observing his pupil master with both his own *faux pas* and hearing about the shortcomings of those already at the Bar.[60] He takes his seat in the jury box, for a start[61] and then we find out what is meant by a "leading question"[62] a "hostile witness,"[63] and, in due course, that "dock identification" is prohibited.[64]

Potts' early career is less than stellar. There is a nod to modernity absent from the world of Cecil, and only obliquely covered in Rumpole's career, as to how business is distributed in Chambers as Toby notes – "Golden rule number one, never upset the clerks."[65] Toby's first appearance in a magistrates' court involves a Roger Thursby–type case of mistaken identity when he thinks his client has been charged with leaving a taxi without paying rather than the charge of murder which is read out in court. Potts has confused the names and is in the wrong court. His own client ends up conducting his own defence and this is not a success.[66] This is followed by an ineffective defence of a man charged with killing two parrots.[67]

Various aspects of the judicial system are covered by our protagonist in a simple didactic fashion. For instance, the role of the Crown Prosecution Service is dealt with and how they reach their decisions.

> Every prosecution case has a reviewing lawyer, a senior member of the Service who, together with the investigating officer, is responsible for collating the evidence and advising on further evidence where necessary. He or she also takes into account any admissions made by the accused, and then gives his or her "learned" opinion on the likely outcome when the case reaches court.[68]

More commonly covered issues are also adverted to by Toby in his role as explainer-in-chief of the world of law. The chapters focus on an individual case with which Toby is involved including a range of criminal issues – criminal damage,[69] affray,[70] assault,[71] possession of drugs,[72] mugging,[73] pornography[74] and murder.[75]

Among the things we learn are the "clean slate" principle in criminal trials to avoid premature judgement of those who have erred in the past.

> There are strict rules forbidding the disclosure to the jury of the defendants previous convictions, on the basis that you don't give a dog a bad name and hang him.[76]

The descriptions then shift into assessments of policy whilst being presented as simple statements of fact

> The CPS briefed counsel on results not good looks or advocacy, and those who fell at the first hurdle were deemed unworthy to wield the trusty sword of justice.[77]

As Toby's career progresses, he takes a rather more judgmental approach and his pronouncements are less obviously "factual" For example, he describes the CPS policy on prosecuting as follows,

> The Crown Prosecution Service are always open to offers. If they can tick the right boxes and come in on budget, they'll play along.[78]

This process means that they are regarded by our protagonist as less than effective seekers after justice and are shown as lazy clock-punchers.[79]

We learn about the jury and that, unlike Henry Fonda's *12 Angry Men* setup, [80] there is no longer a need for a unanimous verdict and after two hours of deliberation the court may accept a 10–2 verdict.[81] In addition, where the jury is unable to reach a verdict through being hopelessly divided, there is no automatic retrial if the prosecution do not offer evidence.[82] It is also made clear that, due to the spousal privilege from the mists of time, a wife cannot be compelled to give evidence against her husband.[83] We also know too from the way the material is "researched" by Toby Potts what amounts to dangerous driving,[84] that a "warned list" consists of back up cases to be slotted in when other trials collapse[85] and that "returns" were those cases sent to busy counsel but which had to be picked up by less favoured colleagues in Chambers.[86] We see Toby progress in his career to such an extent that he is able to get a charge of attempted murder reduced to unlawful wounding due to knowledge that the discharge was not of shotgun pellets but the much less lethal birdshot.[87] There are also shades of Rumpole's Timson family when Toby gets work after attending a party thrown by a solicitor friend at which the "Big 5 South London Crime families" are present. This gets him a possession case under the Misuse of Drugs Act 1971. We learn the differences between section 4 (3) (a)[88] and section 5 (3).[89] The subtle difference is between "to supply or offer to supply a controlled drug to another" and "to have a controlled drug in his possession, whether lawfully or not, with intent to supply it to another." Toby also enjoys success reconciling an irascible Scottish restaurant owner with a sensation-seeking restaurant critic.[90]

Judges

Osborne's view of the judiciary and the process of judging receive a certain amount of coverage. It is suggested, via one of the more respectable barristers whom Toby encounters early on in his career that the "golden age" of judges has passed

> Being a good or able advocate is no longer an essential prerequisite to judicial advancement, and more's the pity. If you keep your nose clean, don't upset anybody on the way up, and toe the party line, you've got as good a chance as the next man. Not so long ago it was different. Judges were appointed on ability, and usually after a distinguished career at the Bar. They had a feel for it and the Bench was the richer for it.[91]

Despite the concept of a hierarchy of courts ending with the pinnacle being the House of Lords,[92] we are given to understand that in practice this is not so

> for most practitioners, the Court of Appeal was the highest court in the land. Yes, of course, that was the House of Lords, but few indeed . . . saw fit to jolt the old fossils out of their judicial torpor. The Court of Appeal was the business end of the law in action, where the buck stopped, and usually with a full stop.[93]

That said, even its role is, we are told, limited to that of supporting "the trial judge with a few well chosen and acerbic phrases."[94]

Class and Inequality in the Legal Profession

The world of Toby Potts and his fellow barristers is a comfortable one of public schools and their innate superiority, albeit in Toby's case "one rooted firmly in the third division."[95] In one of the cases in which Toby is involved we have a negative portrayal of comprehensive education ripped from the corruscating far right pages of the *Daily Mail*.[96] The happy resolution of the case involves a return to the fee-paying public school sector by the accused teacher. Luckily for him, he had been to one of the public schools which had a friendly rivalry with that of the judge in the case.[97] This whole process is made much easier as the Judge and the accused bizarrely share a love of Nietzsche. Toby is delighted at a later juncture to win a case defending an aristocrat tried for assault on a hunt saboteur

> what his lordship and Mr Simpkins didn't know was that Sir Archibald had sent me, in confidence, a copy of Gardner's previous convictions, together with a list of questions that might win the day. The old boy network was alive and well. Thank God Almighty friends in high places, eh?[98]

This right-wing xenophobic perspective – it may be a spoof, of course – is compounded with the lurid description of immigration process at Gatwick Airport[99] and a trial in Croydon suffused with crude racial stereotypes.[100] Borrowing the terminology of Margaret Thatcher[101] and anticipating and updating Sue-Ellen Braverman's notion of a nation being "overwhelmed,"[102] the Immigration Service is "swamped."

> Their worst nightmare is a sea of brown faces reeking of curry washed towards them jabbering and jostling in a foreign tongue and hardly a word of English among them. It didn't help that they all looked the same.[103]

Osborne, then, provides us with the clearest guide to a number of features of the English legal system. It has to be said that his indulging of a highly political perspective is the most clear of all the writers on the justice system – albeit it appears so close to a typical ill-informed *Daily Mail* rant that one might have thought it was a tongue-in-cheek tweaking of the tail of legal Bufton Tuftons.[104]

HERE COMES THE JUDGE – THE TALES OF PETER MURPHY

Peter Murphy was called to the Bar by Middle Temple in 1968. As a Circuit Judge he sat initially in London at Wood Green, Woolwich, and Blackfriars Crown Courts, but eventually gravitated out to Peterborough, where he became Resident Judge and Honorary Recorder of the city.[105] He wrote the *Walden of Bermondsey* series, a collection of humorous short stories in book form, based in part on his own experiences as a judge.

In this review of comic writers, the nearest to straight fiction rather than light comedy is found in the world of Circuit Judge, Charlie Walden in his fictional location of the Bermondsey Crown Court. This is a world of minor crimes and misdemeanours. Each book focuses on a handful of interesting cases which fall into the lap of our eponymous protagonist. The various cases described appear as free-standing chapters.[106] There is an almost total absence of poetry and classical allusions here,[107] the exception being a reference to jovial big-hearted Mr Fezziwig from Charles Dickens's *A Christmas Carol*.[108] We do, however, conclude Judge Walden's adventures with a slightly more contemporary cultural reference with a case of a much-loved serial bigamist[109] in the mould of Rex Harrison's William Egerton in *The Constant Husband*.[110] This involved a breach of section 57 of the Offences against the Person Act 1861.[111]

> Whosoever, being married, shall marry any other person during the life of the former husband or wife, whether the second marriage shall have taken place in England or Ireland or elsewhere, shall be guilty of felony.[112]

The defence, which proved to be unsuccessful, was in terms of articles 8 and 9 of the European Convention on Human Rights to the effect that a person is entitled to respect for private and family life, home and correspondence along with freedom of thought, conscience and religion,[113] as well as the notion of duress.[114]

Judges

What is of particular interest, though, is the wholly novel way in which the working environment of courts is explored – in this case the Crown Court. To this is added some indication of the relationships between the various members of the judiciary and those with whom they interact professionally. Murphy brings to life both the judges, prosecutors and, to a lesser extent, defence lawyers as more than ciphers. mouthpieces or caricatures. In what another serving judge, Nicholas Hilliard describes as "an accurate eye and an authentic ear," Murphy's Walden seems a reliable everyman.[115] He has no axe to grind against his superiors. There are occasional irritants and we gather, from the point of view of the judiciary, self-representation is seen as a nightmare[116] almost on a par with solicitor advocates.[117] Judge Walden, himself, has reached the pinnacle of his career and is content in a secure and happy home life. He is not surrounded by internal squabbles and intrigue by discontented colleagues. The only disturbance to his calm life come from those structural forces beyond his control whose malign influence he can only seek to mitigate. There are civil servants who, in the interests of saving money have as their goal "paperless courts"[118] That said, he does have a limited appreciation of the judges who sit in the High Court. They are drawn, we are led to believe, principally from those who have been involved in civil and commercial practice, and are then required to deal with criminal matters on which they have no experience.[119] Worse can occur when such judges sit in the Court of Criminal Appeal.[120] A slightly more sympathetic perspective appears in his posthumously published book when Charlie Walden spends a week sitting in the Appeal Court.[121]

Perhaps these individuals are more in need of the services of the Judicial Protection Unit than the Crown Court judge. Charlie Walden discovers this Unit exists for all members of the judiciary subject to a credible threat to the life or safety of a judge.[122] That said, he recognises that in all walks of life and the law, there are good and bad actors and that the notion of the High Court's intellectual superiority is so much smoke and mirrors,[123] although he respects his colleague who sits as a Deputy Judge in the High Court as a result of her expertise in fraud.[124]

The Politics of Judicial Decision-Making

Judge Walden sets the tone early on for his coverage of this issue unexplored in any of the other light insights into the world of law in England. We discover that there are factors other than the skill of advocacy, the evidence or the innate predispositions of the decisionmakers at play in the world of law. We also have "bean counters" and the dictates of modern management theory by the civil servant administrators, the "Grey Smoothies."[125] They are a constant irritant seeking to cut back on expenditure and make the judicial process more "efficient" and they are the people who decide whether there is a "business case" for such things as secure docks for the accused,[126] along with the rationale of closing small courts to realise valuable capital assets.[127] They it is who we learn are behind privatisation of all sorts of services relating to the courts.[128] From time to time they get their come-uppance in the trench warfare between the judges and the administrators.[129] In his final posthumously published book, Murphy has the "Grey Smoothies" pressuring him to get "old school" Judge Hugo Drake to resign. Hugo has fallen short in establishing identities in a complicated assault case involving a number of accused and is reported to be "losing it."[130] Related to this we hear of the practice of withholding prosecution evidence to save money on the legal aid bill.[131]

Our eponymous judge has a modest view of judicial omniscience bearing in mind that judges have no choice in the cases coming before the court.[132]

> There are few people more dangerous in this world than a judge who thinks he has some personal insight into the subject-matter of the case. They tend to

> ignore the evidence and substitute what they think they know. Far better to have a judge who is totally ignorant of the subject-matter, and has no choice but to rely on the evidence.[133]

He also recognises that a judge may appear to be "out of touch" by asking a question to which everyone would know the answer. Sometimes, he suggests, it may simply be to get the fact "on the record" rather than not knowing about breakdancing, who Jack Charlton is or what a "golden shower" involves.[134]

Another aspect of the judicial role we learn is that, like many jobs, it has a repetitive element to it. As Judge Walden explains,

> There are substantial parts of the summing up that hardly change from case to case, and there's always quite a bit that I could do in my sleep and that I can trot out without really having to think about it. . . . For example, the burden and standard of proof: the jury can't convict unless the prosecution prove the defendant's guilt so that they are sure; anything short of that and the defendant must be acquitted. Once you've got a form of words that conveys that idea, you can use it in every case.[135]

Although Charlie presides over a disparate group of judges including a "hard-liner"[136] we learn that there are guidelines for sentencing which constrain what a judge can do.[137] The format of the stories also permits discussions among the judges in their lunch breaks of issues such as sentence options in a fraud case involving insurance,[138] and what is involved in "exercising a right of audience."[139] This allows us into an area almost never covered in films or TV portrayals of court cases – how judges actually weigh competing ideas.[140] In addition to the cool evaluation of the competing arguments, one of Judge Walden's colleagues, Hubert Drake, suggests applying the "wanker test." In the event that a decision is appealed to the Court of Appeal and overturned what will the response be of members of one's club?

> "How could Hubert have made a decision like that? What a wanker!" or are they going to say "How could the Court of Appeal have reversed Hubert like that? What a bunch of wankers!"[141]

As far as politics is concerned Charlie is a Conservative but is not an extremist. He "does not read the *Daily Telegraph* or anything like that "but opts for *The Times*,"[142] and shops at Lidl.[143] He is also secure in the knowledge that his politics is cancelled out by his Liberal/Green clerical wife.[144] Her effect on some issues is such that Charlie is "buggered if he is going to send anyone to prison, if he can avoid it" for possession of cannabis,[145] although smuggling is a different matter.[146] He is also prepared to give a generous light sentence when he is feeling happy.[147] He does, however, draw the line at the licensing of brothels when his wife moots this.[148]

The Machinery of Justice

Charlie Walden muses instructively on the various reasons why courts do not run to a strict timetable

> The prison van breaks down . . . the court's recording equipment is not working . . . the video equipment isn't working . . . the defendant is on bail and hasn't turned up. The interpreter hasn't turned up. Counsel is stuck on a train somewhere . . . we don't have enough jurors.[149]

Walden is a phlegmatic realist and recognises that his instructions to the jury not to consult the internet or do their own research may go unheeded and never come to light.[150] While juries are a disparate bunch who only have to serve for a fortnight,[151] they are, nonetheless "one of the great protectors of our liberties."[152] That said he can find himself bemused by how juries find abstruse lines of defence convincing.[153] He also knows how important the role of local administrators like the list officer is in keeping cases moving through the system in which there can be no time limits on how long cases take. This may occur through changes of plea, long winded counsel or witnesses.[154]

He can put into practice his understanding of the psychology of the "real world" in a drug smuggling case involving a young woman duped by her boyfriend into being part of the crew involved in the enterprise.[155] It also comes into play in a case where an astrologer is charged with fraud.[156] In one of his final tales, he is successful in negotiating a dispute which includes a trans woman leading the fight to "cancel" a 18th-century East Anglian poet whose statue is proving controversial when it was discovered that his wealth came from the slave trade in St Kitts and Nevis.[157] Charlie Walden is able to negotiate his way round the tricky issue which lands up in Bermondsey due to the level of local fury on both sides of the argument

General Educational Pointers

This series, however, provides more than just "tales from the trenches." Some weighty issues are also canvassed as where Judge Walden is confronted by the suggestion that class is a "racial or religious group" and entitled to protection under Equality legislation. Given that the Equality Act 2010 limits the following characteristics as receiving protection to "age; disability; gender reassignment; marriage and civil partnership; pregnancy and maternity; race; religion or belief; sex or sexual orientation" and that religion is centred around belief rather than status[158] this gets short shrift. Somewhat bizarre is the less than obvious rule against photos in court which comes to light when a father turns out to have a sentimental album tracing his son's progress through the various levels of the justice system.[159] A couple of stories, however, do bring to mind AP Herbert.[160] In one a fraudster claims immunity from prosecution when he encamps on an island in the English Channel,[161] and in another instance treasure trove is claimed.[162] Other cases involving a defence of a cleric for stealing Parish funds that his visits to a dominatrix were for the purpose of "mortifying the flesh" might conceivably ring true to some ears.[163]

Issues are, however, normally presented in a straightforward factual sounding way from someone we have no reason to believe is not a reliable source such as the ability of a Crown Court judge to act as a magistrate to save the time and expense of remitting matters to a lower court for a decision normally taken by them.[164] We learn, in a case involving astrology, that the criteria for withdrawing a case from the jury are that either there is no evidence to support the prosecution's claim or that it has been thoroughly discredited by the defence.[165] Similarly, we are given to understand the simplicity of jury selection in the United Kingdom,[166] beyond a simple jury questionnaire.[167] We are here far from the manipulative shenanigans found in the United States we learn about from the world of John Grisham in *A Time to Kill*[168] and *The Runaway Jury.*[169] Not all counsel, however, appear to have resisted the lure of the American courtroom style with "sustained," "overruled" and approaching the bench all mentioned.[170] Nor do we have much by way of that staple of American law films and TV – the civil jury.[171] These are generally only used in Britain in issues of defamation. We learn extraneous titbits like the role of a legal adviser to magistrates when one has to give evidence where a non-qualified person appeared before magistrates claiming to be a solicitor.[172]

Trickier peripheral issues are also raised in cases such as whether the dignity of the Court is affected when a solicitor advocate sports pink hair[173] or where a hijab is worn by a woman who turns out to be a Cambridge educated law graduate who happens to be a Muslim.[174] The modern ways of making the giving of evidence in a rape case less of an ordeal are adverted to.[175] We see these issues through the eyes of the sensible middle of the road man on the Bermondsey Tube train, Charlie Walden.

We also learn some things which come as a surprise to a lay person. There is a prohibition against visiting the crime scene[176] and against questioning a suspect without the interview being taped.[177] Whilst the public will know from endless TV and film trials that "leading questions" are not allowed, nonetheless agreeing leading questions is used to save time when such facts are not in dispute.[178] Loss in blackmail cases refers only to money and other property not one's reputation.[179] What amounts to grievous bodily harm also comes from the mouth of our judge as denoting "really serious physical injury."[180] The test in civil cases is the "balance of probabilities"[181] and in such cases judges sit without wigs or elaborate robes.[182]

Other matters are less technical and seem more like simple common sense such as the use of leverage in exchange for early guilty pleas.[183] There is, though, against the use of early pleas, them being used to pressure people into giving up a defence and undermining the role of the jury.[184] By the same token we hear of the problem of the hearsay rule and alternatives to its exclusion. Here the alleged source of the information can be called to confirm or deny the claim. If they are not called, then that evidence may well be discounted by the jury.[185] There is, however, no rule against hearsay in civil cases.[186] An unwilling witness can be subjected to a court order called a subpoena and failure to attend will be contempt of court and jailable.[187] Material not used by the prosecution must be made available to the defence in case there is something there of use to them.[188]

From his background as a middle-ranking judge, Pater Murphy provided a range of interesting vignettes from the courts. He acknowledged a range of perspectives which come to bear on the judicial process. What he offers, in contrast to the other light-hearted versions of the justice system, is the existence of extraneous factors through the constraints on operations dictated by the imperatives of the hidden costs of running the enterprise. His accounts of the various cases with which he is confronted provide a very clear and disinterested version of the justice system and its operation in the 21st century. His is the only version which is not centred on the art and errors of advocacy which dominate not just his contemporaries, Kevan and Osborne but also the works of the other lawyer writers. This is a theme which is taken up, amongst others in the concluding chapter.

NOTES

1. Known as a "tenancy" – see Introduction to the English Legal System Appendix.
2. Osborne (2013) p. 11 on pupiilage.
3. Murphy (2024) also covers Judge Walden spending a week as a judge in the Court of Criminal Appeal.
4. In the hierarchy of judges Circuit Judges rank below the High Court and above District Judges – see Wilson, Rutherford, Storey, Wortley and Kotecha (2020) with full sentencing powers in criminal matters as determined by the relevant statute. – see Introduction to the English Legal System Appendix.
5. https://uk.linkedin.com/in/timkevan (accessed 20/1/22.
6. Kevan (1999); Kevan (2001a); Kevan (2001b); Kevan and Ellis (2008).
7. Kevan (2009) – originally entitled "BabyBarista and the Art of War."
8. Kevan (2011).

9. Since then, Kevan has moved into law publishing and legal education – see Conclusion.

10. Awarded to Junior Counsel when a KC/QC considers a young barrister has provided signal service – which replaces the blue bag in which they have kept their robes and wig box hitherto.

11. Kevan (2011) at pp. 299–300.

12. BBC News (1 March 2014) – available at bbc.co.uk.

13. Kevan (2011) at 38.

14. Kevan op cit at 20.

15. Kevan (2009) xv.

16. Kevan op cit at 59.

17. Kevan op cit at 14.

18. Kevan op cit at xvi.

19. Kevan op cit at 93.

20. Ibid per TheBusker.

21. Radio play May 16 1957; TV with Michael Hordern and in the theatre 1958 for a short run and finally the film version with Peter Sellers in 1962 – https://www.imdb.com/title/tt0055916/ (sub nom Trial and Error as the concept of the Dock Brief is unknown outwith England and Wales).

22. See Conclusion.

23. https://www.barstandardsboard.or.uk (accessed 7 December 2023).

24. Kevan (2011) at 131.

25. Kevan (2011) at 242.

26. Kevan (2009) at 223.

27. Kevan (2011) at 15.

28. Cecil (1958).

29. Kevan (2011) at 129.

30. Kevan (2011) at 158.

31. Kevan (2011) at 65.

32. Kevan (2011) at 142.

33. Kevan (2011) at 254.

34. Kevan (2011) at 212.

35. Kevan (2011) at 228.

36. Kevan (2011) at 84.

37. Kevan (2009) at 94.

38. Kevan (2011) at 226.

39. Kevan op cit at 210.

40. Kevan (2011) at 106, 128 and 246.

41. Kevan (2011) at 127.

42. Kevan (2011) at 236.

43. Rumpole on Trial p. 207.

44. Kevan (2011) at 251.

45. Kevan (2011) at 54.

46. Native of Birmingham in the Midlands – from the earlier name of the city as Brummagem – also Bromichan – hence West Bromwich to the west and the fabled Albion.

47. Kevan (2011) at 9.
48. Kevan (2011) at 17.
49. There is also a version on the internet of the first book entitled *Toby Potts in the Temple of Gloom and Other Adventures of Our Intrepid Hero* from 2006 which has a similar text – it is not available to buy but can be located in 11 libraries including Harvard University and the University of Wisconsin in the capital Madison.
50. Potts (2013) at 89 – the Court of Appeal likened to the witches from Macbeth.
51. Osborne (2016) at 127 – Felicia Heman's Casabianca – The boy stood on the burning deck.
52. See Conclusion.
53. Potts (2013) at 94.
54. British Lion (1957) (dir. John and Roy Boulting) – https://www.imdb.com/title/tt0050214/ (accessed 19 January 2024).
55. Potts (2013) at 13.
56. Potts loc cit at 15.
57. Potts loc cit at 34.
58. Potts loc cit at 60.
59. Potts loc cit at 35.
60. Potts loc cit at 25.
61. Potts loc cit at 24.
62. Potts loc cit at 28.
63. Potts loc cit at 29.
64. Potts loc cit at 199.
65. Osborne (2016) at 36.
66. Potts loc cit at 40–42.
67. Potts loc cit Chapter 5.
68. Potts loc cit at 64.
69. Potts loc cit at Chapter 5.
70. Potts loc cit at Chapter 7.
71. Potts loc cit at Chapters 8, 13, 14 and 16.
72. Potts loc cit at Chapter 10.
73. Potts loc cit at Chapter 11.
74. Potts loc cit at Chapter 19.
75. Potts loc cit at Chapter 12.
76. Potts loc cit at 65.
77. Potts loc cit at 72.
78. Osborne (2016) at 7.
79. Osborne loc cit at 153–54.
80. United Artists 1957 (dir Sidney Lumet).
81. Osborne (2016) at 75.
82. Osborne ibid.
83. Osborne loc cit p. 163.
84. Osborne loc cit p. 179.
85. Osborne loc cit p. 245.
86. Osborne loc cit p. 267.

87. Osborne loc cit at 173.
88. Osborne loc cit at 249.
89. Osborne loc cit at 262.
90. Potts (2013) at 21.
91. Potts loc cit at 32.
92. Unhelpfully re-named in 2009 the Supreme Court.
93. Potts (2013) at 87.
94. Osborne (2016) at 139.
95. Osborne loc cit at 119.
96. Potts (2013) 149-150; see also Osborne (2016) at 240.
97. Potts loc cit at 163.
98. Potts loc cit at 84.
99. Osborne (2016) at 140.
100. Osborne loc cit Chapter 7 passim.
101. "People are really rather afraid that this country might be rather swamped by people with a different culture" – World in Action January 27 1978 interview – available at https://www.margaretthatcher.org/document/103485 (last accessed 13/4/23).
102. 13 March 2023 House of Commons – available at https://www.itv.com/news/2023-03-13/mps-to-vote-on-controversial-migration-bill-which-sparked-lineker-row (last accessed 13/4/23).
103. Osborne (2016) at 140.
104. Private Eye *passim* – Private Eye's fictional right wing Conservative MP whose name derived from real-life Tory backbencher, Sir Tufton Beamish, who sat for Lewes 1945–1974, but the character was modelled on MPs who were well to the right politically of Beamish – see Conclusion.
105. See Introduction to English Law Appendix.
106. Murphy (2017) – 6 chapters covering arson, ABH and self defence, impersonating a solicitor, art forgery, sovereign immunity and brothelkeeping; Murphy (2018) – 5 chapters covering defamation, Weights and Measures infringment, drug possession, Treasure Trove, sado-masochism; Murphy (2019) – 5 chapters covering OAPs and pornography, restaurant hygiene, astrology, a civil land dispute and bigamy.
107. *Pace* Murphy (2019) at 15 where Shakespeare's Merchant of Venice is invoked to indicate *ennui.* He comes close to quoting either Abraham Lincoln or the monk John Lydgate on the problem of pleasing all the people all the time but thinks better of it as he is unsure of his source – Murphy (2019) at 330. Lydgate would have been the right pick as Lincoln talked about fooling some of the people etc.
108. Murphy loc cit at 20.
109. Murphy loc citat 329 ff.
110. British Lion Films (1955) (dir Sidney Gilliat) – https://m.imdb.com/title/tt0047948/?language=hi-in.
111. Murphy (2019) at 334.
112. Originally attracting a sanction of "up to 7 years penal servitude."
113. Murphy (2019) at 377.
114. Murphy loc cit at 404.

115. His books cite actual cases such as in relation to consent to violence a colleague mentions the 1994 House of Lords case of Brown – Murphy (2016) at 22 and Wilson from the Court of Appeal in 1996 – Murphy (2018) at 290. The issue arises in a later case heard by Judge Walden – Murphy (2018) at 289.

116. Murphy (2018) at 13.

117. Murphy loc cit at 23.

118. Murphy (2019) at 18 – sadly came to pass in the Tribunal Service arm of HM Courts and Tribunals service. As from January 2022 papers come in digital form to Tribunal members.

119. Murphy (2017) at 273.

120. Murphy loc cit at 274.

121. Murphy (2024) Part 1 A Week on Mount Olympus.

122. Murphy (2018) at 270.

123. Murphy loc cit at 273.

124. Murphy (2024) Part 4 The Twilight of the Gods.

125. Murphy (2017) at 11–13; Murphy (2019) at 17.

126. Murphy (2017) at 150 and 154.

127. Murphy (2018) at 341.

128. Murphy (2017) at 370.

129. Murphy loc cit at 406 where, in a neat *deus ex machina*, the chief of the Grey Smoothies is in the little black book of the brothel keeper.

130. Murphy (2024) Part 2 The Curious Incident of the Cat just after lunch.

131. Murphy (2019) at 141.

132. Murphy (2017) at 143.

133. Murphy loc cit at 23.

134. Murphy loc cit at 359.

135. Murphy (2018) at 90.

136. Murphy (2017) at 16–18.

137. Murphy loc cit at 96–97.

138. Murphy loc cit at 70.

139. Murphy loc cit at 193.

140. *Pace* Judgment at Nuremberg (1961) (dir Stanley Kramer) and First Monday in October (1981) (dir Ronald Neame) and to some extent Gordon Newman's Judge John Deed (2001–7) as well as Cecil's Mr Justice Duncannon TV series (1961) – discussed in Robson (2018).

141. Murphy (2018) at 295.

142. Murphy (2017) at 77.

143. Murphy (2019) at 73.

144. Murphy (2017) at 77.

145. Murphy loc cit at 108 and Murphy (2018) at 235.

146. Murphy (2018) at 235.

147. Murphy (2017) at 315.

148. Murphy loc cit at 414.

149. Murphy loc cit at 15.

150. Murphy loc cit at 16.

151. Murphy (2018) at 250.
152. Murphy (2017) at 201.
153. Murphy (2024) Part 2 The Curious Incident of the Cat just after Lunch where the jury "buys" the alleged intervention of a cat causing a kettle of hot water to pour over the head of a controlling husband.
154. Ibid.
155. Murphy (2019) at 224.
156. Murphy loc cit at 239.
157. Murphy (2024) Part 3 Some Mute Inglorious Milton.
158. Equality Act 2010 sections 4 and 10.
159. Murphy (2018) at 305.
160. See Chapter 1.
161. Murphy (2017) at 280ff.
162. Murphy (2018) at 232 and 236.
163. Murphy loc cit at 254.
164. Murphy loc cit at 323.
165. Murphy (2019) at 217.
166. Murphy (2017) at 99.
167. Murphy (2018) at 249; Murphy (2019) at 102.
168. Regency Enterprises (1996) (dir Joel Schumacher).
169. Regency Enterprises (2003) (dir Gary Fleder).
170. Murphy (2017) at 246.
171. Murphy (2019) at 259.
172. Murphy (2017) at 180–181.
173. Murphy (2018) at 27 – Judge Walden trusts that a "common sense" solution will emerge from his crusty colleague.
174. Murphy loc cit at 31 – Judge Walden has no problem with this and the defendant's lawyer withdraws his objection to the juror once her background is made clear – see R v D (R) [2013] EW Misc 13 (CC) on which Murphy himself ruled using Canadian authority. Since then there has been an Australian case taking a different view – Elzahed v State of New South Wales [2018] NSWCA 103.
175. Murphy (2017) at 148.
176. Murphy (2018) at 90.
177. Murphy loc cit at 102.
178. Murphy loc cit at 256.
179. Murphy loc cit at 390.
180. Murphy loc cit at 102.
181. Murphy (2019) at 259.
182. Murphy loc cit at 262.
183. Murphy (2018) at 107.
184. Murphy loc cit at 121.
185. Murphy loc cit at 131.
186. Murphy (2019) at 275.
187. Murphy loc cit at 106.
188. Murphy loc cit at 110.

Conclusions

INTRODUCTION

The foregoing comprises a roster of comic writers on the English legal system and their principal works, and this section seeks to assess the significance of their combined works. Firstly, a comment on the actual authors selected for coverage. The preceding chapters have looked in some detail at eight authors – A. P. Herbert, Henry Cecil, Hastings Draper, Julian Prescot, John Mortimer, Tim Kevan, David Osborne and Peter Murphy as well as briefly noting the work of two others – J. B. Morton and Theo Mathew. Of these, as was made clear above, the latter pair do not cover the justice system in any sustained way allowing for analysis of their contributions. Seven of the group are, at first sight, a remarkably homogeneous group. All were white. All were male. All were barristers called to the Bar in England. Six of them practiced at the Bar as advocates. Six were educated at fee paying schools including the prestigious public schools of Winchester, St Paul's, Harrow and Sedbergh.[1] Five studied law at Oxbridge colleges. They would certainly be regarded as members of those who influence what issues are up for debate and what ideas are beyond the pale.[2] The only real "outsider" is the provincial solicitor and H. M. Coroner, John Budd, writing as Julian Prescot. His background and ruminations, though, as we have seen, are remarkably consistent with those of his barrister colleagues. Their reflections on the justice system within which they operated, though, are a little more complex than a crude reductive class, ethnic and gender reading. When we look in detail at their works, we find both reflective and refractive elements. Their works provide a valuable picture of the operation of certain aspects of the English justice system as it has operated over the past century as well as a modest level of critique. To weigh up the quality and nature of this critical representation it needs to be placed in its broader context.

THE CHANGING CONTEXT

During the period in which these books were written, some aspects of the social, political and legal landscape have altered significantly. Others, however, remain in place and appear to be under no great threat. One major change affecting the rule of law in the time when A.P. Herbert commenced his legal sketches in 1924 and a century later has been the shift to "one person, one vote." Women in Britain secured the vote in stages between 1918 and 1928. Plural voting also ceased. Business votes were abolished in 1948 along with university constituencies.[3] In addition, the need for those with modest means to rely on charity in their legal affairs has been replaced in 1949 by a system of legal aid and assistance[4] and from the 1970's Law Centres.[5] The division of the legal profession between court pleaders and office-based workers has been to some extent undermined with the advent from the 1990s of solicitor advocates. There is no reason why these developments should not feature in the comic fiction under inspection. For example, some of these issues emerge in a variety of lighthearted TV series such as the struggle of women to be taken seriously at the Bar and the severe limitations of Legal Aid.[6] It is fair to say that they receive rather limited coverage in the literature under review.

Even the introduction of a "cradle to grave" welfare state and its development since the 1940s is barely touched on in these pages.[7] Looking to the wider world momentous events have taken place. Welfare and health provision from cradle to grave has not only been introduced but significantly eroded. Industrial conflict has been a feature of life including a General Strike, Miners' Strikes in the 1970s and 1980s along with major de-industrialisation and concerted attacks on workers' rights. A shifting of major public services away from the profit impulse of private ownership has occurred in relation to coal, water, electricity, gas, steel, housing and health. A number of these advances have been reversed for the moment. There have been changes in the context in which debates about how to distribute resources are conducted. In the time since A. P. Herbert started his writings, we have had the flourishing of radio, cinema, television, mobile phones, computers and the internet. Ideas have also emerged about human rights and their protection. These have included not only the women's movement but also LGBTQ+ issues. These are scarcely encountered in this literature. Again, in the same way that we might not expect to find an accurate picture of the changes and concerns of daily life for the population in the pages of P. G. Wodehouse or Agatha Christie, we are largely shielded from such matters in British comic legal fiction. This section examines whether issues closer to home relating to law and legal practice make a greater impact.

THE LEGAL PROFESSION

As noted, all of the writers of this fiction are trained lawyers and seven come from the barrister branch of the legal profession working in the field of court litigation.[8] Only one was a solicitor, albeit involved extensively in representation in the lower courts. In the past century the numbers and profile of the barrister branch of the legal profession has altered significantly. From the period when A. P. Herbert started his writings in the immediate aftermath of the Great War, the general population of England and Wales was recorded in the Census at 38 million in 1921. During the period from 1960 to 2022 the population went from 46 million to 60.2 million.[9] The number of barristers in this period rose from 1,000[10] to over 17,000.[11] The expansion in the past 50 years has been most dramatic. In 1961, their numbers were estimated at a little under 2,000.[12] There have been some peaks and troughs. The pressure of upward shifts in numbers is adverted to in the work of Draper and Prescot. Cecil also mentions in passing the greater availability of work at different times. The emphasis there was on the problem of obtaining work through solicitors for those without connections. Prescot talks of the competing issues facing solicitors in choosing between barristers.[13] The later disjunction between the numbers of those seeking to become barristers and the number of places the professions made available is the underlying feature in the lives of Tim Kevan's BabyBarista and David Osborne's Toby Potts.

The number and nature of solicitors has also altered over time and their work and status has also altered during this period.[14] For instance, in Anthony Sampson's series of examinations of the powerbrokers in Britain between 1960 and 2005 he observes how solicitors shift from being a quaint reminder of their Victorian heyday to the 5 Magic Circle firms becoming major figures in international business.[15] Their numbers swelled from 25,000 in England and Wales in 1960 to 41,000 in 1982[16] and by the third decade of the 21st century amounted to 157,000.[17] In terms of gender, the numbers of female solicitors has gone from some 2% in 1939[18] to over 55% in 2023[19] That said, in more recent attempts to answer the elusive question "who runs Britain," the legal profession does not rate a mention.[20] The work of the solicitors who feature in the work of one writer is a reminder of the traditional small scale nature of the small provincial firm. It is far away from the big changes in the City of London and commerce, and the shift that Sampson adverts to, effectively, takes place "offstage" and with little impact on our writers' accounts of legal life.

In terms of diversity the barrister side of the English legal profession has undergone significant changes. From 64 in the mid-1950s and 100 in the 1960s, by 2000, women comprised 29 per cent of the Bar.[21] The most recent statistics consulted indicate that this figure has risen to 40.6 pr cent by December 2023 at a time when women made up 50.2 per cent of the working age population.[22] The percentage of female pupils starting out at the Bar now amounts to 52.6 per cent.[23] In terms of ethnicity, the percentage of barristers from ethnic minority backgrounds is 16.9 per cent – at a time when in the working age population ethnic minorities amount to 16.7 per cent.[24] As far as the comic legal literature is concerned, however, ethnic minorities do not seem to make anything but a couple of tantalising "almost" appearances[25] in the literature examined reflecting their low visibility for much of the 20th century. The same limited level of representation emerges with only a couple of exceptions in other branches of popular culture such as lawyers seen on TV.[26] Sexuality is mentioned in only one of the texts although there are groups in various solicitors' firms encouraging discussion and "normalisation" of the issue.[27] Possibly due to its sensitivity rather than anything else we have almost no references to religion or religious beliefs in these works.[28]

THE JUDICIARY

Other changes in relation to the judiciary are also absent from the writings. Insofar as the novels are not actually exercises in civic education this is, perhaps, understandable. For instance, in place of a mysterious and arcane process whereby those who became judges "emerged" without any process of application or specified criteria at the behest of the Lord Chancellor a new system came into effect in 2006. Until then, this strange juridico-political figure had the ability to appoint judges at his discretion.[29] In England and Wales, the Lord Chancellor was a lawyer sitting both on the Bench, in the Executive and in the legislative branches of the State. This anomalous figure receives a few oblique mentions from Horace Rumpole in the person of "Keith from the Lord Chancellor's office."[30] This shadowy figure is mentioned in relation to Rumpole's occasional flirtation with securing a position as a judge. This system is ostensibly a thing of the past and appointments are more open. The Judicial Appointments Commission (JAC) was set up on 3 April 2006, under the terms of the Constitutional Reform Act 2005.[31] This independent body makes recommendations to the "appropriate bodies" In place of the unaccountable process with its potential for political and other kinds of favouritism, the process has been modernised. Although the earlier authors worked before the full operation of the JAC such developments do not appear in the literature.[32] It is in the world of Judge Charlie Walden alone that the notion of there being being any constraints on judicial behaviour is mentioned and the sanctions available to muzzle his outspoken colleague. The recalcitrant judge at Bermondsey Crown Court, Hubert Drake has had a letter published in the *Daily Telegraph* exposing the cheeseparing practices restricting the defence sight of relevant papers by the Crown Prosecution Service which he claims threatens the trial process. The consequences are less than clear but a promise not to repeat such behaviour seems the most likely outcome.[33]

For many years it has been noted that the judiciary with their pool of applicants limited to the Bar reflected a narrow social and educational elite.[34] That figure remains high at 68 per cent from barrister backgrounds.[35] The judiciary themselves in the past often found it difficult to recognise the narrowness and exclusivity of their backgrounds. Anthony Sampson pointed out over 60 years ago in fairly general terms that "Judges come from a small and conservative section of the community – their section is not growing much larger."[36] The more detailed analysis of their public school, Oxbridge and white composition by John Griffith[37] incurred the displeasure of Lord Hailsham.[38] Griffith went beyond the details of the backgrounds of the judiciary but also examined how their decisions could be said to reflect this background. They were prejudiced against Trade Unions, the poor and students [39] This notion of judicial partiality was taken up subsequently in an analysis of one of the purported champions of the people, Lord Denning, to reveal a similar particular warped perspective against, *inter alia*, the poor, women, homeless people and organised labour.[40]

Whilst readers are familiar with the notion of the American Attorney as a lone figure shifting seamlessly from office to courtroom, Britain retains the practice of an office-based solicitor branch of the profession, solicitors, and a court-based branch, known variously as barristers and advocates.[41] The division was never totally hermetic with solicitors appearing in the lower courts. There was a trend in the 1980s for solicitors to shift after a number of years to the Bar having established connections within the legal profession. This has been complemented by the introduction of a new fusion lawyer, the Solicitor Advocate. They consist of lawyers who can remain solicitors but appear in the upper courts. It was introduced by the Courts and Legal Services Act 1990 in England and Wales.[42] As noted above, so infrequent are the mentions of solicitors that the divided profession hardly makes an appearance other than as an obstacle to advancement at the Bar. There is no mention of "direct access" clients. This change from 2004 allows direct access to a barrister where a litigant is conducting their own case and is seeking assistance in drafting documents and advice on a range of matters, but where the barrister tends not to get involved in representation.[43]

In terms of diversity the judiciary has also altered its composition in terms of gender and ethnicity. At the rime of writing in 2024, nine of the

36 judges in the Court of Appeal are women and two of the 12 members of the Supreme Court. The picture at the apex of the profession, however, is still dominated by white, public school Oxbridge barristers. With 11 of the 12 Supreme Court judges and 29 of the 36 Court of Appeal judges sharing this educational background at the time of writing. The position in the High Court is a little more varied with 33 out of 108 judges being female. Ethnic minority candidates for the judiciary now account for 16 per cent of the eligible pool and 16 per cent of recommendations reflecting the proportion of the ethnic minorities in the working age population.[44] Again they receive no mentions in any of the literature examined. Sexuality is an issue that emerges in only one of the books and is still not out of the closet as far as the legal profession is concerned. It is fair to say that Prescot's coverage of the issue merely encapsulates the sterotypical image of same sex relationships in the 1950s and 1960s.[45]

ACCESS TO JUSTICE

Access to justice is a problem for those with limited financial resources. Prior to the introduction of the Legal Aid and Advice Act 1949[46] the role of the previous mechanisms to assist those in poverty involved with the legal system took several forms. The most well-known, thanks, perhaps, to its appearance in film[47] and on stage[48] is the "dock brief" with its provision of free court representation to impecunious accused persons. The Poor Prisoners' Defence Act 1903 was introduced in the wake of the 1898 reform allowing those accused to be heard. The 1903 Act empowered courts to grant legal aid to a prisoner of insufficient means where it appeared "desirable in the interest of justice" and "having regard to the defence set up" in serious cases. By way of contrast from a neighbouring system, the Poor's Roll which was instituted in Scotland in 1424 had the same goal in civil cases[49] and from 1587 for criminal matters.[50] It operated through a voluntary rota system. For example, in Glasgow there were twenty-six agents who took one week each for six months, so that each agent had two separate weeks in the year, and for a week's work each agent was paid.

All these provisions were superseded by the 1949 Legal Aid system. In addition, there were various *ad hoc* advice arrangements such as the Poor Man's Lawyers movement, in such places as Mansfield House from 1891 and Toynbee Hall from 1898.[51] As part of the work of these charitable settlements in East London, they provided *pro bono* help that stopped short of representation in court. Mortimer mentions one such in his third non-comic novel[52] and his character Rumpole adverts to providing such advice from an East End charity when he is short of work.[53]

LEGAL EDUCATION

There are limited comments in the comic literature about the role and nature of education in relation to entry into the legal profession. There are occasional references to it, but it remains something in the background. In the century covered by these books, the changes have been significant. Barristers retain their separate system of accession to the Bar. The process of joining one of the four Inns of Court, passing the Bar Exams and eating dinners at one's selected Inn is described in Cecil back in the 1950s.[54] By the time of the career of David Osborne's Toby Potts, nothing much seems to have altered.[55] In fact, the training altered in a number of ways by 2010 with the Bar Vocational Course (from 2010 the Bar Professional Training Course) providing a much more systematic introduction to practice than Roger Thursby, BabyB or Toby Potts report receiving.[56]

LEGAL QUIRKS AND ANOMALIES

Lawyers traditionally had their income protected by being the only people who can charge the public for a variety of services. These included the transfer of property and appearing in court. These remained virtually untouched until the 1970s. They became a particular focus in the 1960s with critiques of the value to the public of such limitations which benefited the solicitor branch of the legal profession. Michael Zander also pointed out that only non-salaried barristers had the right to be heard in the superior courts.[57] There was also a rule which required Senior Counsel to have a junior sitting alongside him or her receiving a separate fee of 2/3 that paid to the KC/QC.[58]

The interests of those principally concerned with the reform of the law have altered over the years depending, often, on the success of their particular projects. In the immediate post–World War period the focus included the perspectives of the Haldane Society encompassing stage censorship, the freedom or control of aliens, cruelty to animals, the law relating to prostitution and divorce law.[59] There was also a trenchant critique from an experienced Q.C., which pours cold water on the notion that the legal profession had a past to be proud of. He also pointed out the shortcomings of the common law in particular in relation to the notion that the rules are somehow a brilliant creation.[60] He drew particular attention to the distinction between invitees, licensees and trespassers which determined the liability owed to someone injured depending on these somewhat artificial categories.[61] He also cast doubt on the doctrine of common employment and the "reasonable man" concept in practice.[62] In the 1960s another group of left-leaning lawyers took broad aim at a whole range of substantive law areas from contract, tort, land law, family law and industrial law to criminal law, revenue law, commercial and company law.[63] Later in the 1960s, attention was drawn to a number of more specific defects in the justice system such as lack of consumer rights and access to cheap accessible legal advice,[64] There is no mention of any issues of reform in the stories examined.[65]

THE AUTHORS

As noted at the start of this chapter, there are a number of threads which connect the writers of comic legal fiction dealing with the English legal system.[66] The standard profile of these writers has been white, male, fee paying school, Oxbridge law graduate barristers. Their backgrounds, however, should not lead one, of course, to make some kind of simple reductive assumption. The same background could be claimed by people like the two most successful 20th-century Labour Party Prime Ministers. Clement Attlee[67] and Tony Blair[68] both had impeccable "public school – Oxford – Bar backgrounds" with legal pedigree too.[69] This and the material noted in the previous chapters shows that there are critical elements within the works of these authors to undermine a simple reading of educational background.

EDUCATION

The educational trajectory of almost all of the writers then seems remarkably consistent. It generally reads "public school – Oxbridge – Bar." It reflects the elite background of members of the Bar over the past century. It is worth though looking a little more closely at the detail. A. P. Herbert was indeed educated at the renowned public (i.e., private fee paying) school Winchester noted for its academic prowess. He was not from a wealthy background and was later supported financially as an Exhibitioner at New College,[70] Oxford. He studied Classics initially but switching to law achieving distinction with a First-class degree and graduated in 1914.[71] After his education, although he was called to the Bar and was entitled to call himself "barrister," Herbert, as we shall see, did not follow a conventional legal path.[72]

The next generation saw another public school educated barrister undertake writing as, in his case, a "second string."[73] Henry Cecil Leon (Henry Cecil) attended another major public school, St Paul's, and went on to King's College, Cambridge. He too was from a modest background and attended St Paul's on a scholarship. Initially at University he read Classics but switched to Law in his second year. He joined Gray's Inn a year after Herbert was called to the Bar, and himself passed barrister on 19 November 1923.[74] He was less distinguished academically – according to his own account – due to lack of work.[75] Another prolific author barrister who practised for some three years between 1952 and 1954 was Roderic Jeffries. The son of the well-established author, Graeme Jeffries,[76] he was born in London in 1923. His education was rather different from any of his fellow barrister authors examined. He is recorded as attending Harrow View House Preparatory School and the University of Southampton School of Navigation. He was called to the Bar in 1953.

The route of Julian Prescot into the the solicitors' branch of legal practice was rather more conventional and owed much to family connection. He went from school into the Blackpool law firm of his cousin, William Aldred, as an articled clerk. The firm in time bore his own name.

John Mortimer attended the Dragon School in Oxford where he was a contemporary of the eminent historian E. P. Thompson. He continued his education at Winston Churchill's old *alma mater*, the renowned Harrow School and then at Brasenose College, Oxford, where he studied law.

Tim Kevan was educated at Sedbergh School in Cumbria a public school founded in 1525. Thereafter he went to Magdalene College, Cambridge, between 1989 and 1995. where he studied Economics and Law. Between 1995 and 1996, he attended the Inns of Court School of Law on the Bar Vocational Course and joined Middle Temple winning a number of scholarships. David Osborne had a more unconventional path to the Bar. He attended Shrewsbury, another prestigious public school from where he studied law at the highly ranked Russell Group[77] University of Birmingham in England as well as graduating in Spanish Studies from the University of Granada, Spain and in Politics and Behavioural Sciences from McGill University, Montreal, Canada.[78] Finally Peter Murphy attended Queen Elizabeth's Grammar School in Blackburn and was a contemporary of the Supreme Court's first female President, Lady Brenda Hale at Cambridge University, graduating in 1966. [79]After taking an LL.B. in International Law in 1967, he was called to the Bar by Middle Temple in 1968.

What we see then on closer examination is a group of who largely enjoyed elite schooling and graduate studies before being called to the Bar in London. All but one of the writers, however, came from modest backgrounds and relied on financial support through scholarships when required to pay for their education. So what we have here are a group of elite educational institutions attended by young men from less than standard rich backgrounds. This may have prompted their very varied paths in life.

CAREERS

The careers, too, of the eight authors are characterised, largely by their unconventional nature. Their different career paths make for fascinating reading and suggest that, just as their educational backgrounds were not quite as homogeneous as at first blush, by the same token their life experiences were also quite diverse.

Unlike the rest of the lawyer authors, A. P. Herbert relied for his income solely on writing and as a member of the staff at the humorous weekly magazine *Punch*. In addition, whilst the other authors adopt the novel or short story form in which we find their observations on the English legal scene, Herbert uses the mock case judgment. These were written for *Punch*. Although, as we have seen, his major legal contribution was to write "faux" legal judgments, he did also continue to commentate on various legal issues of the day in the magazine Punch on an irregular basis.[80] His "faux judgments" appeared on a regular but spasmodic basis from 1924 onwards until the 1960s. Many of them were, as Herbert puts it, "promoted into books" in 1927, 1930, 1933 as well as an "omnibus edition" in 1935.[81] They are clearly humorous fiction written about the English legal system albeit initially encountered differently. Their appearance in book form recognises the links although the approach has not yet tempted later writers in the humorous vein other than J.B. Morton whose unique but limited contribution has been noted.[82]

Henry Cecil spent the inter-war years as a full-time barrister. After distinguished war service, for the reason of his wife's ill-health, he opted for a much more predictable and safer lifestyle to suit his family circumstances. This involved him working as a County Court judge between 1949 and 1967. This provided him the time to write and follow what he referred to as his "second string"[83] which produced a significant body of work including 37 books and a number of plays for theatre and radio.[84] Cecil carved out a successful career and had been appointed to the Bench without any family legal connections or wealth behind him. Although he attended both the prestigious fee-paying school St Pauls and King's College, Cambridge, as noted, he did so as a financially supported scholar.

The career path of Roderic Jeffries, like his education, was highly unusual. As mentioned, in 1943 Jeffries he joined the New Zealand Shipping Company as an apprentice and sailed to Australia and New Zealand. He later transferred to the the Union Castle Company to visit a different part of the world.[85] He returned to England in 1949 where he was called to the Bar and practiced briefly as a barrister. After a few terms with limited success, he ceased to practice and devoted himself to write full-time using a range of different pen names[86] and producing both detective novels and legal thrillers.[87] His first book, a sea story for juveniles, was published in 1950. His books have been published in many different countries and have been adapted for film, television, and radio.[88] He devoted himself, then, to writing full-time from 1954 and his first three comic legal novels were published in 1956, 1958 and 1961. Initially, he had taken over the Blackshirt (*sic*) "gentleman burglar" series which his father had written between 1925 and 1940.[89] These are a kind of Raffles[90] meets Bulldog Drummond[91] mashup. In all he wrote 196 books and died in 2017.[92] Although the thrillers and series covered police and legal personnel, he did not, however, return to his *nom de plume* of Hastings Draper and no other books featured his rookie barrister, Alan Pace or any other legal practitioner.

Much like Henry Cecil, John Mortimer initially juggled a legal career with writing plays, books and short stories. His legal work initially centred on divorce work and after he took silk in 1966, he concentrated on crime and divorce until his attention turned to civil work in the 1970s. From 1982 he focused on writing alone. The minutiae of his life are recorded in four volumes of his memoirs[93] as well as two biographies. Books, plays, screenplays, interviews and one-man shows litter the pages. Even allowing for a degree of artistic licence in the various accounts, Mortimer appears to have led an extraordinarily busy legal and authorial life combined with complicated personal relationships. Given his hectic lifestyle it seems ungenerous to cavil at any shortcomings in his comic legal fiction. This has not, however, stopped critics, as is noted below.

Tim Kevan practised as a barrister specialising in credit hire, personal injury, civil fraud and sports law between 1997 and 2008.[94] During his time qualifying and in practice he wrote and co-authored a number of legal practice texts on his areas of expertise.[95] The Chambers Directory noted he had "a fine reputation" in 2010 but also that he had taken a sabbatical. He did not remain in London, but he moved down to North Devon as a way of achieving some sort of work/life balance.[96] This involved segueing into law publishing and surfing. He became a director of Law Brief Publishing which publishes hard copy books, an online law journal and email newsletters. The aim of the content is to digest into manageable form the extensive information relevant to legal practitioners. He also started a business providing online CPD training for personal injury and employment lawyers through video seminars or webinars. This proved to be particularly popular as lawyers were able to gain their CPD hours watching and interacting with speakers without having to leave the comfort of their own desks or perhaps more importantly not having to lose a day out of the office going off to a conference or the like.[97] Kevan is the co-author, with Dr Michelle Tempest of two 2007 self-help tomes, *Why Lawyers Should Surf* and *Why Doctors Should Surf*,[98] which drew on his love of surfing[99] and in which professionals are urged "to look for inspiration outside of law and used surfing and the power of the ocean as metaphors for living the day to day."[100]

David Osborne's website notes that he "is regarded by judges and colleagues alike as an outstanding advocate."[101] In his career, he has appeared in the highest courts in the land, including the Old Bailey, the Court of Appeal and the House of Lords. He does not accept legal aid clients.[102] Prior to embarking upon his Toby Potts works, Osborne published a guide to public speaking[103] as well as a short comical guide to advocacy under the pseudonym, Ivor Bigg-Wigg.[104] It might be expected that his perspective on the system is somewhat jaundiced by his being fined for engaging in litigation on behalf of a direct access client while he was an unregistered barrister.[105] Although the Toby Potts books were published some years before, judging by his response to the Bar Standards Council he takes a sceptical view of authority.[106] In the end his desire not to engage with the Bar Standards Council resulted in him being fined £4,250 with costs of £3,300.[107]

He is also not a stranger to controversy with his views on consent in rape cases. He has twice in the past decade attracted publicity for suggesting that being drunk did not mean that a woman could not give consent. He has suggested in 2015 and again in 2024 that sex in these circumstances did not amount to rape. He did this in a Blog entitled "She was Gagging for It" which was one of the two defences he felt an accused could have for a rape allegation. The other was "it wasn't me gov." He condemned Crown Prosecution Guidelines which put the onus on men to seek explicit consent from drunken partners. He went on to claim, "Consent is consent, blind drunk or otherwise, and regret after the event cannot make it rape." His remarks have been vilified in the press.[108]

Peter Murphy's career in law was extremely varied. He left the Bar and became a teacher at the Inns of Court School of Law in 1968. He also published *A Practical Approach to Evidence*, later, as from the fifth edition, renamed *Murphy on Evidence*. In 1984, he went to work in the United States at South Texas College of Law teaching evidence and trial advocacy. He remained on the staff there for more than 20 years. He also became the first editor-in-chief of *Blackstone's Criminal Practice*. and continued as editor-in-chief of successive annual editions. From 1998 he worked on the International Tribunal for the Former Yugoslavia (ICTY) based in The Hague, the Netherlands until 2007. He taught on Leiden's LL.M. programme in international criminal law. He returned to England in 2007 on his appointment as a judge of the Crown Court. While at Blackfriars, he gave a leading judgment in the case of *R v D (R)* regarding the circumstances in which a female defendant in a criminal case is entitled to wear a face covering in the Crown Court as an expression of her religious faith. It was a subject of great public interest and one which had frightened away both politicians and more senior judges. He determined that, with protection behind a screen only being visible to the judge, counsel and the jury the defendant could not wear a face covering. At the time of his death, his judgment remained the only definitive statement of the law on this point in English law. At Middle Temple, he was elected a Bencher in 2013 and served as Reader for the Autumn term of 2018. He lived with his wife in Cambridgeshire until his death in July 2022 and was the author of three series of books.[109] He had long had an interest in writing fiction, and in 2011 his first novel, *Removal*, a political thriller about the American Presidency, was published by No Exit Press. It was swiftly followed by a sequel, *Test of Resolve*. After his retirement from the Bench in 2015, the pace of his writing increased greatly. In 2012 he also created the *Ben Schroeder* series of legal thrillers, featuring a barrister in practice in London in the 1960s to 1980s.

What, then we have is a group of writers on comic legal fiction who look very similar at first glance. Seven of the eight were, as noted, white, elite educated, male barristers. Examined more closely though, their career paths are markedly different. We have two who never entered the pathway of appearing in court on behalf of clients – Herbert and Murphy. One who quit very early on – Hastings Draper – and two who left to write – Mortimer and Kevan. Only one actually stuck at the task of standing up in court as a full-time career – Osborne – with another shifting from representing into judging in his forties – Cecil. Our solicitor representative, by contrast, remained solidly in post within his family firm until his work as Coroner took precedence. This perhaps might begin to explain how it is that their contributions are more varied than one might have expected.

THE AUTHORS AND THEIR RECEPTION

Critics have generally been kind to our comic legal authors. They have been assessed on their merits as comic legal authors and the focus has been on their humour. Nonetheless it has been noted that these varied depictions of the operation of the justice system have a degree of authenticity. They are seen as "the real deal." Just like the lawyers in film and the small screen lawyers they are one of the few things most of the public have to go on as few engage in the system. As Richard Sherwin has, perhaps over-ambitiously as a sales pitch, the screen is where we go for our civic education on law and justice.[110] These books it is argued occupy a similar place albeit reduced in our screen-obsessed lives in the 21st century.

So prolific was the output of A. P. Herbert in terms not only of his "faux judgments" but also his comic writings on politics and life in general that criticism has been limited. There has been praise from senior members of the judiciary and tributes from others who have enjoyed his "ribbing" of both the legal system and its tendency to take itself rather seriously. His legal fiction, though, is a singular taste and very much of its time. It conjures up the entertainers and playwrights, Noel Coward[111] and Alan Melville[112] and is the quintessence of arch comedy with which both these authors were famed from the 1930s through to the 1960s. One reviewer generously suggested

> A.P. Herbert is a special superior taste acquired first through top flight English courtroom novels, refined by the better English trial movies and plays, polished by a thorough reading of famous English legal cases and finished off with a personal subscription to Punch.[113]

Herbert's own view of his legal opinions was, as ever, modest – to a point. He noted that three great judges, Lord Chief Justice Hewart, Lords Buckmaster and Atkin had written introductions to the books and the cases had been quoted in the Supreme Court of the United States, the High Court and the House of Lords.[114]

His "fan base ranged far and wide. Lord Trenchard, the Commissioner of Metropolitan Police is reported as writing from Scotland Yard "I should like your brains here to help me with all my misleading cases."[115] By the time of his death in 1971, Herbert had gained a considerable following and was highly regarded in literary circles. Distinguished writers including J. M. Barrie, Hilaire Belloc, Rudyard Kipling and John Galsworthy all delighted in his work, and H. G. Wells once applauded him stating: "You are the greatest of great men. You can raise delightful laughter and that is the only sort of writing that has real power over people like me."[116] As to the question of possible impact Pound suggested, on the televising of the frivolous seeming *Misleading Cases* in the early 1970s, that the work of AP Herbert had a wider impact than many might have imagined

> Few viewers beyond the metropolitan pale, and not many within it, were aware that Misleading Cases had more than literary distinction. They had acquired prophetic significance in legal circles and, like his first election address (1935), had contributed to the formation of attitudes favourable to law revision and possible reform; for example in the Administration of Justice Bill, 1968.[117]

The judge who provided the Introduction to Herbert's *Uncommon Law* was generous in his appreciation of the writing.[118] Former Liberal M.P. and Lord Chancellor under Asquith, Lord Buckmaster is noted for providing one of the minority judgments in *Donoghue v Stevenson*.[119] He took the educative element of the "cases" seriously. He noted in 1935 that "through the mask of legal form he challenges some of our most venerated institutions." As he goes on to point out "the jest is barbed with truth." On the topic of divorce, he pointed out that "the covering of humour cannot there conceal the fierce and just indignation against a law which reason alone has never been able to vindicate." He urged Herbert to enter Parliament to deal with this "admitted evil." As we know that is precisely what happened that year.

Henry Cecil managed to charm reviewers in his day. He was regarded as an entertaining humorous writer. Comments ranged from "Extremely funny,"

Norman St John-Stevas, *News Chronicle*; "uproariously funny," *The Times;* "Mr Cecil is bent on entertainment," John Raymond *New Statesman*. Other reviews of Henry Cecil's work use phrases like "fun and frolic at the Bar, Bench and Solicitor's Office"[120] and "ingenious, sprightly and immensely amusing comedies of criminal life"[121] as well as receiving the commendations of PG Wodehouse in 1954. Wodehouse wrote about *According to the Evidence*, "I read it as a sitting of course, and my verdict is that it is the best he has done . . . even more laughs than *No Bail for the Judge*."[122] The book cover on which the remarks were found, is a light-hearted look at how gullible witnesses can be. *No Bail for the Judge* is a quite dark book about a judge charged with murdering a prostitute. It is unclear whether the quotation is an oblique criticism of Cecil or sloppy puffery/journalism. In 1956 he was more careful noting that the second Roger Thursby was described as "Cecil better than ever."[123]

In his overview of courtroom centred legal fiction, Jon Breen described him as "the PG Wodehouse of legal fiction."[124] He was also favourably compared to his predecessors – "Two of the funniest writers about the English Courts of Law are Charles Dickens and AP Herbert. They are now joined by Henry Cecil"[125] In the source that most use in the 21st century to obtain basic information, Wikipedia, his entry in 2021 emphasised the light side of his work.

> His books are works of great comic genius with unpredictable twists of plot, but are not intended to be realistic or strong on characterization. They typically feature educated and genteel fraudsters and blackmailers who lay ludicrously ingenious plots exploiting loopholes in the legal system.[126]

This was modified by 2024 to a rather more anodyne account although drawing attention to two of the most improbable characters encountered in Cecil's fiction.

> His books typically feature educated and genteel fraudsters and blackmailers who lay ludicrously ingenious plots exploiting loopholes in the legal system. There are several recurring characters, such as the drunken solicitor Mr Tewkesbury and the convoluted and exasperating witness Colonel Brain. He writes well about the judicial process, usually through the eyes of a young barrister but sometimes from the viewpoint of the judge[127]

That said, there was a sense that the quality of the later work was not what it had been. This was most keenly felt in the United States by his publishers who were always concerned with sales figures. They did not bring out editions of *The Buttercup Spell, Truth With Her Boots On* or *Cross Purposes* from the late 1960s, although they did, however publish his final novel *Hunt the Slipper*.

The world of Hastings Draper's Alan Pace was also greeted with a degree of enthusiasm by critics. The novels were sold at the time as "a light-hearted burlesque,"[128] "a humorous and pardonably irreverent side-glance at the Law"[129] and a "comedy of the law.[130] It was also suggested that the first book had "dry undertones of reality."[131] His modern-day readers are, perforce, limited.

The reception of the "cases" series of Julian Prescot was enthusiastic at the time of publication with the Sunday Times opining that "Mr Prescot gallops through it all with tremendous gusto and enthusiasm[132]. The Telegraph recognised the books as part of the "established genre of vocational comedy" and the Times suggested "Mr Prescot bids fair to become the Henry Cecil of his profession."[133] The The Law Society's Gazette waxed even more, lyrical pointing out that "Mr Prescot has been, and inevitably will continue to be, compared with Henry Cecil. Compliment though this be, it is to underestimate . . . Judgment in favour of Mr Prescot."[134]

Along with praise for the entertaining nature of the works,[135] a more serious note was struck by some. For instance, it was suggested that "many social workers and Members of Parliament would learn more, very painlessly indeed, from the book than from many more solemn volumes on the state of society in the Britain of 1959."[136] The realism of the books was a theme taken up by other reviewers. The Times Literary Supplement noted that "His characters are simply but vividly drawn; his anecdotes, which have a suspicious ring of truth, are never sensational but always entertaining."[137] The Manchester Evening News took the matter further with the view that "If you want to know what goes on in a solicitor's office . . . *Case for Trial* will give you most of the answers."[138] The perception did not alter even when he changed tack to cover matters other than the life and times of his original protagonist, Julian Prescot. "With this octet of diverting and successful case books Mr Prescot has won himself a secure niche in the established genre of vocational comedy delighting lawyer and layman alike by the raciness and verve with which he has portrayed the pageant of life passing through a provincial solicitor's office."[139] Indeed, the Guardian were most impressed by his account of the life of the more ebullient and unconventional Jack Paxton – White in *The Case Re-opened* adjudging it "one of the best of Mr Prescot's "cases."[140] Contemporary readers' opinions are limited. A review by Katie Potter of the second novel, *The Case Continued* from 1959 finds it "well written in traditional style, witty descriptions of characters with a 1950s flavour. Much more satisfying than a lot of modern novels."[141] In her review of the third novel, *Case Proceeding*, she urges the re-publication of the series and notes that "although these books are set in the 50s/60s what they tell us about human nature is timeless."[142]

John Mortimer has been the subject of much more comment than any of the other comic legal authors. On the face of its Mortimer's *Rumpole* has provided both enjoyment as well as an exposure to a number of serious social issues from racism and police corruption to judicial partiality and the state of British prisons. His reputation has fared well in some quarters and less well in others. He appears to have secured a place in the hearts of the legal professionals outwith the United Kingdom as well as being regarded as having had an impact in practical terms. As far as how his insights expressed in his plays and books are concerned his protegé and colleague Geoffrey Robertson took the view that "Rumpole of the Bailey had a particular impact on the reception by juries of police evidence." Having seen police evidence presented uncritically in Dixon of Dock Green, he noted how "Rumpole of the Bailey presented a different picture. It showed how bent or overzealous police could secure convictions by forensic trickery.[143] He also credited Rumpole with changing the culture of the Bar and the prejudice against criminal law amongst the legal establishment. Lawyers who practiced in crime were looked down on and students with an interest in human rights (then called civil liberties) were warned they might ruin their careers.

> Rumpole helped the public – and the bar – to understand that the need to protect the liberty of the subject is the main justification for the profession, and certainly for its independence.[144]

Looking at the works from a literary standpoint a rather more sceptical view of the impact of Horace Rumpole is taken by the crime writer, Michael Dibdin. He casts the character as less Wodehouse and more GK Chesterton's Father Brown. Mortimer was, he felt, "an establishment dissenter" and so

> the stories have an implicit ideological agenda. Rumpole's task as barrister-errant is to enable "the people of England, that never spoke yet" to see through the ploys and impostures which are being foisted upon them and to find their collective voice as jurors, it being taken for granted that they cannot then fail to speak the truth.[145]

In Dibdin's view, Mortimer was restricted by the narrative hook he adopted in his Rumpole work "a miniature detective story, set against one or two sub-plots featuring thematically parallel developments in Rumpole's personal and/or professional life."[146] He suggests that this structure constricts the narratives so that they become mere "consoling fictions." Their limitations are "underlined by stories tackling – and trivialising – such topics as child abuse and police corruption in terms (Stalinist social workers/one rotten apple) worthy of a tabloid leader."[147]

Writing 10 years later, the legal commentator, Marcel Berlins, was, for his part, frustrated by the impact of Mortimer's Rumpole. In Berlins's case it was the excellence of the acting of Leo McKern on screen which was the problem. Since cameras are not allowed in courtrooms, as a general rule,[148] the public form their impressions from the TV and for many millions of viewers, Horace Rumpole and his colleagues are what barristers are like, both in court and in chambers. This has "severely damaged the nation's understanding of the English trial system and the workings of the legal profession"[149] As the characters were not realistic representations of what the law and lawyers are today, and Rumpole may be what a few eccentric barristers were like 40 years ago (i.e., around 1960 when Mortimer was involved principally in divorce practice). He was quite blunt in suggesting that "it's not a good thing that the reputation of our legal system and its personnel should be based on such unreliable fiction.[150]

Berlins expressed himself even more caustically in 2004 when he noted

> marvellously entertaining though he has been for so long, Horace Rumpole has performed one great disservice. Millions of readers and television viewers all over the world believe that our lawyers, our judges and our legal system have been accurately portrayed in the Rumpole series. Alas, the reality is not as cosy or comic.[151]

The kind of figure Berlins was adverting to was the barrister, Jeremy Hutchinson, who rose to fame in the Lady Chatterley's Lover trial,[152] defended the showgirl Christine Keeler[153] and has been credited as providing the inspiration for Rumpole of the Bailey. Elements of Rumpole were possibly based on Hutchinson. There is, however, a change of register since, according to Mortimer, Hutchinson "brought to the Old Bailey the ever so slightly amused voice of Bloomsbury,"[154] which does not quite resonate with Horace Rumpole.

Tim Kevan's shift into fiction was expected to have a different outcome – "I very much wanted to sit down and write a legal thriller. But instead, what popped out was a legal comedy about a fictional young barrister doing pupillage."[155] It was written in the form of a diary and posted online as a blog.[156] It then appeared for three years in *The Times* online and for two years in *The Guardian* online.[157] Two comic legal novels, *Law and Disorder*[158] and *Law and Peace*[159] were extensions of this BabyBarista blog. Critics within the legal profession have found the BabyBarista novels of Tim Kevan full of wit and insight. The first BabyBarista novel was described by The Times as "a cross between The Talented Mr Ripley, Rumpole and Bridget Jones's

Diary."[160] Kevan himself described it as "a fictional caricature of life at the Bar"[161] There may be no searing criticism of how the market in legal services operates so it is worth pointing out that Kevan in his undergraduate days is recorded as being Chairman of the Cambridge University Conservative Association.[162] It should be noted that the prominent Red Clydesider and leader of the Independent Labour Party, James Maxton when an undergraduate at Glasgow University shared this same affiliation before he saw the light.[163]

The reception of the work of David Osborne by the public has been quite enthusiastic. In terms of comedic effect, one reader notes about the first Toby Potts novel that she "finished the book with a smile on my face" and was "looking forward to further instalments."[164] Other reviews found the book "hilarious," "brilliant" and "entertaining and funny."[165] There was more though. The book was also seen as "enlightening" and is suspected as being based on the author's working life.[166] The same response was made by a critic of his second book who said

> "It is good to read a book which is an excellent blend of accurate narrative and sound humour; David Osborne's background as a successful barrister does much to add credence to the storyline which makes it all the more relaxingly readable."[167]

Here, the notion that we can trust the writers of fiction to depict the justice system accurately, then seems not to be fanciful. This theme of authenticity is found in responses to Peter Murphy's world of Walden. It is one of the features most appreciated by those commenting on his works. The Recorder of London, Judge Nicholas Hilliard,[168] a judge at the same level as the fictional Charlie Walden, suggested in his Foreword to the first Judge Walden book that Murphy had "recorded it all with an accurate eye and authentic ear."[169] For the way in which he deals with the judges whom he must organise, Walden "deserves a place in the pantheon of fictional legal figures."[170] One critic, Paul Magrath, suggested that Judge Walden triumphs with humour over the adversities before him and with his "self-deprecating wit and indomitable stoicism" suggests one should "think of him as what Rumpole would be like if he ever became a judge."[171] This is an issue taken up by the publishers who note on the front covers of the second and third Walden books who claim" If you enjoyed Rumpole of the Bailey, you'll love Judge Walden of Bermondsey." Indeed, Lady Hale in her comments Judge Walden suggests "His Honour Judge Walden is surely the next Rumpole, a modern, sensible fair and compassionate judge, not stuck in the past."[172] This combines two intriguing notions. One is that the reading public could come to fully appreciate the literary character as they have done John Mortimers's creation. The other is that here is a chance to see a view of the judiciary a world away from the one-dimentional Mortimer's "Mad Bull" Bullingham, icy Judge Graves or Gordon Newman's lecherous John Deed.[173]

The former Lord Chief Justice of England and Wales, Igor Judge indeed refers back to the great fear of Rumpole "judgitis" and suggests Walden's self-deprecating humour cocoons him from this. He is also "acutely aware of the foibles and prejudices of his colleagues but recognises that together they form a sound judicial team."[174] A truly serious underlying goal is identified. Allied to his criticisms of the senior judiciary and the cost cutting "Grey Smoothies" the sharper tone of Peter Murphy's stories mean that they are "much more than a series of funny legal stories."[175] Murphy's contemporary at University, Baroness Hale of Richmond, first female president of the UK Supreme Court, despite some minor reservations notes the "essential truth of all these stories" She also casts some doubt on whether the Grey Smoothies are always out to undermine the independence of the judiciary[176] although it would seem that Murphy's point is that their goal of efficiency has consequences.

THE COMIC LITERATURE – AN OVERVIEW

As noted above, with their tendency towards a focus on authenticity, these stories provide a window on the justice system in England. They provide a perspective, though, on quite a limited number of aspects. Written by lawyers and centred on their litigation work, we come across courtroom interaction in both civil and criminal cases. The essence of the barrister's role as a person instructed by a solicitor means that the link between the action at issue and how, when and why people seek legal advice and assistance is missing. For a variety of reasons, solicitors appear only spasmodically in the pages of legal fiction. Those who do appear range from the seriously incompetent to the dangerously venal in the works of Cecil[177] and Draper.[178] The day-to-day work of solicitors and other advice agencies is, therefore, almost entirely absent other than Prescot's works. Given there are in England around 160,000 actively practising solicitors[179] compared with 17,000 barristers,[180] it is not unreasonable to suggest that the focus on the senior branch provides a very limited outlook. Even allowing for the shift in the numbers over time and Prescot's contribution, this is a very partial landscape to which the public has access.

In the century of fictional work this study examines, then, there have been monumental social changes. Few of these, however, can be seen in the limited shifts in the focus and nature of the portrayal of the justice system at work. Many of the stories and issues which exercised the earlier writers ring a bell today. This is partly due to the way the authors do not tie their characters or narratives very rigidly to their social milieu and, sadly, partly due to the chronic nature of the defects and issues which they identify. The material in the foregoing chapters indicates a generally benign account of the justice system. There are, however, in each of the writers examined critical elements. Most are exercised by the flaws of the judiciary. In the case of A. P. Herbert, for the most part, it is the substance of the rules and the laws from politicians which exercise him and his avatar, Albert Haddock. Both Henry Cecil and John Mortimer know a bad judge when they see them. In their legal fiction, as, hopefully, has been made clear above, they make frequent appearances, and their failings are the fulcrum of many of the narrative arcs. Despite his mauling at their hands, Hastings Draper reserves his ire for those judges put out to grass and dozing away in the upper reaches of the courts. It is not an issue which emerges in the work of Julian Prescot. The encounters with judges of the characters of Tim Kevan and David Osborne are quite restrained, which is unsurprising given their lowly status as barristers in training. It is left to Peter Murphy to show the nuanced human side of this part of the justice system and with his fellow judges highlight some of the weaknesses. As noted, the complaints over a 50-year period from Cecil and Mortimer about prison conditions is a clear message from a literary arena where smiles are the order of the day.

TRAPPED IN TIME?

There is in most of these texts a certain timelessness. The advocates, judges, solicitors and clients operate in a world insulated from the world of gender and class struggles and politics. It is not quite a "golden age," but it does seem to be quite cosy. It is not unlike the television world occupied by solicitor Peter Kingdom between 2007 and 2009. The series *Kingdom* was described in the *Radio Times* as "Sunday night TV at its cosiest."[181] Its star, Stephen Fry described this programme as "warm cocoa for a Sunday evening."[182] In all the stories by the eight writers, we know where we are geographically. The events take place almost always in London or its near environs. Occasionally the West Country is breached and less frequently the North. Although Prescot's works are set in Blackpool there are very few hints. There are, though, precious few signs in this fiction of *when* the actions are located. A reader fresh to most of the works might well struggle to place them in time.

Partly, though, this may stem from the fact that the legal world being presented is not always contemporaneous with the appearance of the stories. The authors seem to be describing how things were when they qualified or practised rather than when the books were published. The setting, for instance, of Henry Cecil is less likely to be the 1950s or 1960s and chimes much more with the 1920s and '30s when Henry Cecil's legal practice flourished. The worlds of Julian Prescot and Horace Rumpole seems to be located rather in the 1940s and 1950s when they were building up their legal practices. The world of the 1950s and its ambience is not directly encountered in Hastings Draper's accounts of the Chambers in which Alan Pace plies his trade. If it were not for the almost total male dominance of legal actors, we could be at any time and in any place, except that everyone smokes and drinks. The specific time markers are limited. There is one brief flirtation with popular culture and the argot of the streets when the young office boy advises them "You ought to hep rock 'n' roll and dig the age."[183] Other things recall some aspects of that age but not others

> The train journey, being via British railways, was uncomfortable and dirty. The Luncheon, cooked by British railways was cold, tasteless, and outrageously expensive.[184]

Rumpole, for his part is also surprisingly timeless in most of those of his stories based on the television series. The very first two stories have clear historical references to the "flower power" era of the 1960s and early 1970s. Thereafter there is nothing to tie Rumpole into any particular time in the post-war era. There is mention of the 7/7 suicide bombing attack in July 2007.[185] Although Rumpole fills in his time when short of work at a free legal advice centre in the East End of London[186] this harks back to the work of Toynbee Hall rather than the professionally run Law Centres from the modern era. The central focus of Rumpole's final outing does involve his being in the 21st century with the concept of the hated ASBO.[187] There are also events which are somewhat arcane such as the abolition of the hearsay rules [188] and the need for Continuing Professional Development to keep a practicing certificate.[189]

David Osborne, by contrast, provides a few markers such as references to specific events and objects. The problem – if at can be regarded as such – is that these appear to be situated nearer the time when Osborne himself was qualifying in the 1970s than when the books were published in the second decade of the 21st century. In *May it Please Your Lordship* published in 2013 he has his instructing solicitor boring on about his new Vauxhall Cavalier.[190] These were produced between 1975 and 1995 which appears to locate Toby Potts' pupillage sometime around then. Toby has also identified one of the jurors as a "polytechnic student."[191] Polytechnics became universities under the Further and Higher Education Act of 1992. Whilst this would seem to locate the Potts story before the 1990s the markers are a little variable. These, however, are not always entirely reliable and suggest that his real time frame was somewhat further back. In *Order in Court,* published in 2016, Ernestine Hibbard is the Lady Captain of a golf club in a case involving being assaulted by a golf ball. The injured party had been "a close friend of Emily Pankhurst."

Emmeline Pankhurst died in June 1928 a month shy of her 70th birthday. To have become a close friend would have required Ernestine to have been born around 1910 at the latest. Playing golf in her 80s is impressive and being able to hit the drive of the accused back to the tee even more so.

In fairness, this is fiction not a doctoral thesis and John Mortimer admitted that, in relation to Horace Rumpole, he "was always forgetting where he lives."[192] Toby also has some impressive knowledge of popular culture from when he was a mere infant. Someone in his mid-to-late-20s practising in the 1990s with a knowledge of figures from much earlier including Kat (*sic*) Stevens,[193] Ena Sharples[194] and Mr Teasy Weasy.[195] Toby Potts is a quiz team member worth having.

CONCLUDING REMARKS

As noted, the backgrounds of the coterie of the writers' English comic legal fiction have several clear parallels. Educated at elite establishments mostly they went on to join the senior branch of the legal profession from whom the judiciary have traditionally been drawn.[196] This continues to be the case.[197] They were also predominantly Oxbridge educated as are, at the time of writing, 11 of the 12 Supreme Court judges and 29 of the 36 Court of Appeal judges. The focus of the work is on the areas where they themselves worked during their practice. Of the eight writers examined in some depth six of them have had major careers in writing and have established reputations as writers quite distinct from their comic legal work – A. P. Herbert, Henry Cecil, Roderic Jeffries, John Mortimer, Tim Kevan and Peter Murphy. What they have given us is an insight into the world of court practice. It is the image of law which is found on both the big screen[198] and the television.[199] It is the courtroom drama. Given that 90 per cent of court disputes raised are settled before they reach the courtroom, this is a far from accurate picture of the justice system. As Stewart Macaulay has observed, however, "(m)urder makes a much better show than embezzlement or fraud."[200] Whilst the works examined never sought to provide a guide to the complexities and range of issues in the justice system, they have nonetheless consciously sought to educate as well as entertain. The issues that have been most prominent have been prison reform and the shortcomings of the judiciary. In these fields we have seen change with the civilising of the prison experience and the introduction of the Judicial Appointments Commission. Whilst it would be foolish to suggest any direct causal link between the concerns of the writers of comic legal fiction and reforms of the law, they do nonetheless provide part of the cultural context in which politics operates. In some small way they form part of the contribution to the socio-political agenda.

The politics of the eight authors ranges from one writer expounding ideas from the hard right *Daily Mail* through a couple of writers publicly aligned with the Conservative Party to the anti-authoritarian liberalism of A. P. Herbert and the liberal democratic socialism of John Mortimer. This is not a huge range. What different products might one get if campaigning barristers like Mike Mansfield[201] or Geoffrey Robertson[202] were to opt to enter the world of fiction as well as produce the works they did. Even more amazing might be what would be produced by feminist legal icons Helena Kennedy,[203] and Gareth Peirce[204] or inspirational female writer of colour, Alexandra Wilson.[205]

The writers on comic legal themes then can be said to have in some sense rejected Molière's view that "of all follies there is none greater than wanting to make the world a better place."[206] The question which this work seeks to address is whether or not it can be said that there is evidence that they adopt that author's more positive maxim that "the duty of comedy is to correct men by amusing them."[207] British lawyers writing in this vein in both the 20th and 21st centuries appear to be no less concerned than the rather less light Charles Dickens to advance a point of view, albeit, usually, rather more obliquely.[208] It seems inappropriate to look to the theorists of mass culture who usually provide the background to my ruminations on law in popular culture, Adorno and Horkheimer to provide a key to the writers of these very distinct individuals writing in this sub-genre to a niche market.[209]

Given their uniform backgrounds, it is no great surprise perhaps to find that the overall tone of these works is "reflective" rather than "refractive." There are no Marshall Hall or Atticus Finch figures in these pages. Rather what we have are snapshots of the concerns and neuroses of part of the legal profession at different times during the past century. Most of the concerns are with the relatively mundane. We move from Alan Herbert's serious concerns with the outdated divorce laws to Henry Cecil's slightly strange serial "marrier" – Douglas a man who is constantly falling in love but cannot contemplate having an affair. The desire to inform and educate, though, is constant. All this without the benefit of computers which only feature marginally in the work of Tim Kevan. Nonetheless, just as Jon Breen observed, in relation to Henry Cecil, the books all "address very serious social and legal questions and certainly all carry an educational impulse, though always with a light touch."[210] It is clear from the above, though, that some focus more on the light touch than educational impulse. Also, as one might reasonably expect from a group of lawyers, serious questions of legal practice are rather more to the forefront than other very serious social issues like race, class, gender and identity. These, though, are found in great profusion in the non-fiction works on which I am currently engaged. This seems to appeal as the sub-genre in which those concerned with injustice are most likely to enter at this juncture in the 21st century. It is to be hoped that their works are as entertaining and instructive as the comic legal authors in this monograph.

NOTES

1. Peter Murphy attended the Queen Elizabeth Grammar School, Blackburn which was founded in 1509. It was a direct grant grammar school until 1976 where the majority of the pupils paid fees to attend. It is only 12 miles from Burnley.

2. Sampson (1962) Introduction; see also Sampson (1965), (1982), (1992) and (2004); Peston (2008); and Jones (2014).

3. Representation of the People Act 1948 s 1.

4. Albeit much eviscerated over the years from 1990 onwards – Moore and Newbury (2017).

5. Their coverage has been patchy – https://www.lawcentres.org.uk/about-law-centres/how-law-centres-started-out (last accessed 5/4/23) with funding a constant problem – https://www.theguardian.com/law/2019/jul/15/legal-advice-centres-in-england-and-wales-halved-since-2013-14 (last accessed 5/4/23) and for Scotland Craig and McIntosh (2023).

6. *Law and Disorder* (1994) and *Is it legal?* (1995–98) – women as serious players in the legal firmament; *Outlaws* (2003) – legal aid and its shortcomings.

7. The introduction and subsequent limitations on the insurance base of the system receive no mentions by any of the writers – by Calder, Gass and Merrill-Glover (2012); Bartholomew (2013).

8. Albeit AP Herbert never practiced but he was active in legal reform in his political life – see Chapter 1 – unlike, for example, Robert Louis Stevenson who "passed advocate" but was never involved in matters legal.

9. United Kingdom – England and Wales Population and Housing Census 1961 and 2021.

10. Abel Smith and Stevens (1967) at p. 67.

11. https://www.barstandardsboard.org.uk/news-publications/research-and-statistics/statistics-about-the-bar/practising-barristers.html (last accessed 23/4/23).

12. Sampson (1962) p. 150; Cecil (1958) p. 15.

13. Prescot (1959) pp. 102–3.

14. Sampson loc cit) p. 149 and (1965) p. 165.

15. Sampson (2004) p. 177.

16. Sampson (1982) p. 171.

17. Statista Research Department (available at www.statista.com/statistics/611471/number-of-practicing-solicitors-england-wales).

18. Acland and Broomfield (2019) at 25.

19. Loc cit at 67.

20. Peston (2008); Jones (2014).

21. Acland and Broomfield (2019) at p. 120.

22. Bar Standards Board (2024) at p. 12.

23. Ibid.

24. Loc cit at p. 15.

25. Lutaf Ali Khan appears in Rumpole and the Fascist Beast p. 275 but decides against staying as he wishes to prosecute rather than defend; Rumpole recalls teaching an African politician, David Mazenze, the elements of criminal law in a "crammer" for the Bar exams in Rumpole and the Golden Thread p. 243 – along with "students from India, Fiji, Singapore and Godalming" – loc cit at 244.

26. *Black Silk* (1985) with Rudoph Walker as barrister Larry Scott; Chiwetel Ejiofor as solicitor Ashley Carter in *Trust* (2001); Don Warrington as Judge Ken Winyard in *New Street Law* (2006–7).

27. Vaughan (2018).

28. *Pace* one of Mortimer's least impressive outings with Rumpole – Rumpole and the Age of Miracles (1988).

29. Although not of direct concern to any of these writers, the situation in Scotland was even more bizarre. Here the senior Law Officer, the Lord Advocate, who was traditionally a member of the governing party, was a political appointment changing on the change of Westminster Government. He – it was always he – not only had the task of appointing judges but it was a standard feature to retain a vacancy on the Bench for the Lord Advocate to appoint himself as a Court of Session (High Court) judge on ceasing to hold office – Willock and White p. 67.

30. Old Keith Hopner appears in The Case of the Fascist Beast (p. 292); "Old Keith in The Curse of True Love (playing golf) (p. 342 and Sir Robert Keith in The Case of the Barrow Boy (p. 66) and Rumpole and the Tap End (pp. 127, 149 and 150) – described as the Lord Chancellor's "right hand man" – loc cit at 132; also Old Keith in Rumpole and the Reform of Joby Johnson p. 167.

31. in Scotland the Judicial Appointments Board was established in June 2002 on a non-statutory, *ad hoc*, basis by the Scottish Government, and was given statutory authority by the Judiciary and Courts (Scotland) Act 2008.

32. Murphy (2017) at p. 273 for an insider version of how the system traditionally favoured those without expertise in criminal law.

33. Murphy (2019) at pp. 141, 149–55.

34. Harvey (1958) Chapter 3; Sampson (1962) p. 154.

35. Ministry of Justice Report 2023 Diversity of the Judiciary.

36. Sampson (1962) at p. 181.

37. Griffith (1975) passim.

38. Sampson (1982) at p.181.

39. Griffith (1975) passim.

40. Robson and Watchman (eds) (1981) passim.

41. Rutherford Kotecha and Macfarlane (2024) p. 67.

42. In 1993 in Scotland and the Justice Act (Northern Ireland) 2011 in Northern Ireland.

43. https://www.barcouncil.org.uk/bar-council-services/for-the-public/direct-access-portal.html#:~:text=What%20is%20Direct%20Access%3F,instruct%20an%20authorised%20barrister%20directly. (last accessed 23/4/23).

44. Ministry of Justice Diversity of the Judiciary Report 2023.

45. See Chapter 3.

46. Legal Aid and Solicitors (Scotland) Act 1949 which did "not differ in principle from the English Legal Aid and Advice Bill" (per Lord Morrison HL Deb 07 July 1949 vol 163 cc 979–1008 at 979. See also Brooke (2017).

47. Henry Cecil's *Brothers in Law* (1957) features Roger Thursby (Ian Carmichael) being coached to success by his assigned client, serial offender Alfred Green (Terry Thomas); *The Dock Brief* (1962).

48. *The Dock Brief* (1958) – John Mortimer's bittersweet drama about a failed barrister failing – to the benefit of his client who escapes punishment due to incompetent counsel.

49. Poor's Counsel 1424 c 45; see also Stoddart (1978).

50. Administration of Justice 1587 c 57.

51. Bradley (2019) chapter 2 The Poor Man's Lawyer.

52. Mortimer (1950) at p. 84.

53. Rumpole and the Reign of Terror (2006) at p. 81.

54. Brothers in Law (1955) pp. 7–8.

55. Osborne (2013) Chapter 1.

56. From September 2020 this has been further modified and extended – https://www.barcouncil.org.uk/becoming-a-barrister/students-and-graduates.html (last accessed 23/4/23).

57. Zander (1968) at p. 157 – he also inveighed against the various statutory monopolies of solicitors in relation to conveyancing, probate and initiating court proceedings.

58. Zander loc cit at p. 146.

59. Williams (1951).

60. Harvey (1958) at p. 78.

61. Harvey ibid.

62. Harvey loc cit at p. 83 ff.

63. Gardiner and Martin (1963).

64. Abel Smith and Stevens (1968) at p. 352.

65. *Pace* the concerns of AP Herbert about divorce reform in his rather different comedic form – see Chapter 1.

66. The TV series *Sutherland's Law* (1973–1976) dealing with the Scottish legal system and focusing on the precursor of the Crown Prosecution Service, the Procurator Fiscal produced one book. This was not in the comic mode – Galloway (1974). I have not come across any writings on the third legal system in the United Kingdom covering the north of Ireland.

67. 1883–1967 – Labour Prime Minister 1945–1951 – Haileybury and University College, Oxford – during his premiership the coal, steel, gas, electricity, rail and water industries were brought into public ownership along with a system of free health services and comprehensive Welfare State – Bew (2016).

68. 1953 – Labour Prime Minister 1997–2007 Fettes and St John's College, Oxford – during his premiership there was Devolution to Scotland and Wales, the Good Friday Agreement and the Iraq War – Seldon (2004); Bower (2016).

69. Attlee's father was a wealthy London solicitor and Blair's father a legal academic and member of the Conservative Party from 1946 to 1994 – Bew (2016) and Bower (2016).

70. Herbert (1970) at 26 – which paid him £40 per year (2023 £2,000).

71. Herbert op cit at 27.

72. Pound (1976) at 35.

73. Cecil (1975) at 67.

74. Cecil loc cit at 23.

75. Cecil op cit at 18.

76. He also wrote under the pseudonym Bruce Graeme, Peter Bourne and David Graeme. Born in London in 1900 he served in the Queen's Westminster Rifles in 1918. He was also a film producer and reporter. He died in 1982 – https://www.fantasticfiction.com/g/bruce-graeme/ (last accessed 21 December 2021).

77. 24 self-declared "world class" Universities including Oxford and Cambridge as well as Nottingham and Cardiff but excluding St Andrews and Queen's University Belfast. There are a further 118 other universities in the United Kingdom.

78. https://www.amazon.co.uk/gp/product/B0094DICJU/ref=dbs_a_def_awm_bibl_vppi_i1.

79. Murphy (2019) at p. 7 per Baroness Hale of Richmond in the Foreword.

80. Mr Baldwin and the Judges Punch October 11 1933.

81. Pound op cit at 138.

82. The contributions of Theobald Mathew can hardly be seen in the same light as Herbert's "judgments" but are one of a kind inspired, presumably, by Aesop or La Fontaine.

83. Cecil op cit at 131.

84. See Chapter 2 Appendix.

85. https://www.fantasticfiction.com/j/roderic-jeffries/ (accessed 12 March 2022).

86. Peter Alding, Jeffrey Ashford, Hastings Draper, Roderic Graeme, Graham Hastings, Roderic Graeme Jeffries – see Appendix to Chapter 3 for a full list of his works.

87. He used the name Jeffrey Ashford for the legal thrillers – see Appendix to Chapter 3.

88. https://www.lumebooks.co.uk/book/field-of-fire/ (accessed 12 March 2022).

89. Ibid.

90. A. J. Raffles is a fictional gentleman thief featuring in books by E.W. Hornung from 1898 to 1909.

91. Hugh "Bulldog" Drummond is a fictional character, created by H. C. McNeile and published under his pen name "Sapper" between 1920 and McNeile's death in 1937. Further titles were published using the name of this character until 1969.

92. https://openlibrary.org/authors/OL219378A/Roderic_Jeffries (accessed 12 March 2022).

93. Mortimer (1982); (1994a); (2000) and (2007).

94. https://uk.linkedin.com/in/timkevan (accessed 20/1/22).

95. Kevan (1999); Kevan (2001a); Kevan (2001b); Kevan and Ellis (2008).

96. Ibid.

97. Ibid.

98. 2007 (with Dr Michelle Tempest).

99. https://lawcareerplus.com/career-transition-stories/tim-kevan/ (accessed 16/2/24).

100. These do not seem to be intended as spoofs.

101. https://www.david-osborne.com/ (accessed 20/1/22).

102. Ibid.

103. Osborne (2012).

104. Osborne (1992).

105. The Bar Standards Board Handbook defines a practising barrister as a barrister who is supplying legal services and holds a practising certificate. There are many barristers who do not have a practising certificate either by choice or because they do not qualify for a practising certificate. Such barristers are now called "unregistered barristers" because they are not on the public register of barristers who have practising certificates. Available at https://www.barstandardsboard.org.uk/uploads/assets/5b88103e-e5e8-4df3-bd78768f706fb69d/Unregistered-Barristers.pdf (last accessed 13/4/23) – it is open to appeal.

106. Bar Standards Council – his response was dismissive writing on 6 July 2020, David Osborne emailed the Bar Standards Board asking to 'hear no more of this' in relation to the investigation. (available at barstandardsboard.org.uk (last accessed 21/4/23).

107. Bar Standards Council Disciplinary Finding – David Thomas Osborne 29/03/2022 (available at https://www.barstandardsboard.org.uk (last accessed 18 January 2024).

108. Mail Online January 2024.

109. https://www.petermurphyauthor.co.uk/petermurphy/ (accessed 20/1/22).

110. Sherwin (2000) passim.

111. Noel Coward 1899–1973 – Castle (1972); Morley (2005).

112. Alan Melville 1910–1983 – Melville (1970).

113. https://www.kirkusreviews.com/book-reviews/a/ap-herbert-3/bardot-mp-and-other-misleading-cases/ (accessed 13/1/22).

114. Herbert (1970) p. 138.

115. Pound (1976) p. 115.

116. Author's biography notes for his Stratus edition of Look Back and Laugh in http://www.houseofstratus.com/titles/2894-9781842325902-look-back-and-laugh (accessed 26 January 2022).

117. Pound (1976) p. 291 – the 1968 Bill became the Administration of Justice Act 1969 which introduced the "leapfrogging" procedure for appeals – see Chapter 1 note xvii on Board of Inland Revenue v Haddock (Why is the House of Lords?) (Punch 9 August 1933).

118. Herbert (1935) p. xv.

119. [1932] A.C. 562.

120. Dusk jacket, Henry Cecil, Natural Causes (London: Michael Joseph, 1961). with a review quotation for *Much in Evidence* (London: Michael Joseph, 1957) from Robert Lindley of the *Spectator.*

121. Ibid., with a review quotation for *Alibi for a Judge* (Cornwall: Stratus Books, 1960) from Julian Symons of the *Sunday Times.*

122. "I read it as a sitting of course, and my verdict is that it is the best he has done . . . even more laughs than *No Bail for the Judge*." Dust jacket, Henry Cecil, *According to the Evidence* (Cornwall: Stratus Books, 1954), paperback edition, 1965. The former is a light-hearted look at how gullible witnesses can be, but the latter is a quite dark book about a judge charged with murdering a prostitute. It is unclear whether the quotation is an oblique criticism of Cecil or sloppy puffery/journalism.

123. "Cecil better than ever." Dust jacket, Henry Cecil, *Friends at Court* (London: Michael Joseph, 1956), paperback edition, 1962.

124. Breen (1999) at p. 27.

125. JP Mallalieu *Daily Express* on *The Painswick Line* (1951) – quoted on the dust jacket of *Natural Causes* (1963 Michael Joseph edition).

126. See http://en.wikipedia.org/wiki/Henry_Cecil_Leon (accessed on 16 February 2021).

127. https://en.wikipedia.org/wiki/Henry_Cecil_Leon (accessed on 24 January 2024).

128. Draper (1956) dust jacket.

129. Draper (1958) dust jacket.

130. Draper (1961) dust jacket.

131. Draper (1956) frontispiece.

132. Review of Prescot (1958) *Both Sides of the Case* dustjacket.

133. Review of Prescot (1959) *The Case Continued – Case for Hearing* dustjacket.

134. Review of Prescot (1963) *Case for Hearing – Case for Court* dustjacket.

135. "Hilarious" The Times; "entertaing diversion" Law Times; highly diverting" Yorkshire Evening Post – Prescot (1960) *Case Proceeding* dust jacket.

136. John O'London's per Prescot (1960) *Case Proceeding* dust jacket – influential weekly literary magazine 1919–1961.

137. Review of Prescot (1960) *Case Proceeding.*

138. Review of Prescot (1962) *Case for Trial.*

139. Prescot (1967) *Case Counterfeit* dustjacket.

140. Review of (1965) *The Case Re-opened – Case Counterfeit* dustjacket.

141. Per UK review from 11 June 2012 on the Amazon website.

142. Per UK review from 15 July 2012 on the Amazon website.

143. Robertson (2009).

144. Ibid.

145. Dibdin (1992).

146. Ibid.

147. Ibid.

148. There have been limited exceptions since Berlins wrote 20 years ago but for the vast majority of cases there is no equivalent of Court TV in Britain. On Court TV see https://www.courttv.com.

149. Berlins (2002).

150. Ibid.

151. Berlins (2004).

152. R v Penguin Books Limited 1960 – Rolph (1960).

153. Robson and Combe (2019) at 442–45.

154. Argus, The (2017).

155. https://lawcareerplus.com/career-transition-stories/tim-kevan/ (accessed 20/1/22).

156. http://babybarista.blogspot.com. Much of the first six months of the blog can be found in the archives on this site from October 2006 to March 2007. (accessed 24/1/22).

157. https://lawcareerplus.com/career-transition-stories/tim-kevan/ (accessed 20/1/22).

158. (2009) (London, Bloomsbury) – originally entitled "BabyBarista and the Art of War.

159. (2011) London, Bloomsbury).

160. Op cit bookcover.

161. https://lawcareerplus.com/career-transition-stories/tim-kevan/ (accessed 16/2/24).

162. Cambridge University Conservative Association – Wikipedia – See list of notable alumni.

163. Walker (2004).

164. Goodreads per Daisy McInnes 17 October 2018.

165. Goodreads loc cit.

166. Loc cit.

167. Somerset County Gazette 9th January 2017 (available at https://somersetcountygazette.co Archive for 9th January 2017).

168. Revealed in March 2024 to be a member of the all-male Garrick Club – Guardian March 21 2024 – an issue which Murphy himself addresses with a wry admission to this weakness on the part of Charlie Walden in Murphy (2024) – much to the displeasure of the Reverend Mrs Walden.

169. Murphy (2017) at p. 5 per Judge Nicholas Hilliard.

170. Ibid.

171. Per Paul Magrath Incorporated Council of Law Reporting (Head of Product Development and Online Content) 28 May 2018 (available at https://www.iclr.co.uk -reviews).

172. Murphy (2019) p. 9 per Lady Hale in the Foreword.

173. Incidentally the portrayal was much appreciated by two High Court judges who liked the new image it gave them – interview with the author and Professor Les Moran at Birkbeck College, London, May 2002.

174. Murphy (2018) p. 8 per Lord Judge in the Foreword.

175. Ibid.

176. Murphy (2019) p. 8 per Lady Hale in the Foreword.

177. Tewkesbury in The Painswick Line (1950) and Much in Evidence (1957).

178. Messrs Fitch, Fitch, Fitch and Cromby in Wiggery Pokery (1956).

179. Law Society Statistics 2023 see The Lawyer Portal (available www://thelawyerportal.com).

180. Bar Standards Board Statistics on practising barristers (2023).

181. Radio Times 21–27 April 2007 per David Butcher at p. 68.

182. Fry (2009).

183. Draper (1961) at 11 – hep means to have or show knowledge about the newest things in music, fashion, etc. – it has not been in common usage for quite a long time.

184. Draper (1961) at 93.

185. Rumpole and the Reign of Terror p. 80.

186. Loc cit p. 81.

187. The Anti-social Behaviour of Horace Rumpole p. 18.

188. Rumpole and the Reign of Terror p. 78; The Anti-social Behaviour of Horace Rumpole p. 19.

189. Rumpole and the Reign of Terror p. 64.

190. Potts (2013) at 263.

191. Loc cit at 249.

192. Mortimer (1994 a) p 79.

193. Loc cit at 182 – success between 1967 and 1977 until his conversion to Islam – known originally as "Cat" – and known as Yusaf Islam.

194. Loc cit at 183 – written out of Coronation Street in April 1980 – mainly appeared in the 1960s.

195. Loc cit at 186 – famous in the 1950s and died in 1992 at the age of 80.

196. Sampson (1962) 152.

197. The 12 strong membership of the Supreme Court boasts 12 former barristers and no former solicitors. Of the 36 judges in the Court of Appeal, 35 were former barristers and 1 a former solicitor – two of the ex-barristers briefly worked as solicitors.

198. Greenfield Osborn and Robson (2010) and (2024).

199. Robson and Silbey (2012); Robson and Schulz (2016 and 2018); Schulz (2024).

200. Macaulay (1987) at p. 197.

201. Mansfield (2009) & (2023).

202. Robertson (2009).

203. Kennedy (2004).

204. Peirce (2010).

205. Wilson (2020) but see Wilson (2023) albeit far from light in tone.

206. Molière (1666) T*he Misanthrope, or the Cantankerous Lover.*

207. Molière (1665) *Tartuffe or The Imposter.*

208. We are familiar with Dickens and his technique of characters' names which resonated with their moral culpability or role. Lawyers like Mr Tulkinghorn and Vholes (*Bleak House*) Sampson Brass (*The Old Curiosity Shop*) and Dodson and Fogg (*The Pickwick Papers*) are bywords for venality and morally reprehensible behaviour. – Neely (1936).

209. Adorno and Horkheimer (1960).

210. Breen (1991) at Introduction – unnumbered page 4.

Appendix

The English Legal System: A Brief Guide

For those unfamiliar with the justice system which operates in England and Wales here is a very brief guide to the principal features at the time of writing.[1] For accounts of the system as it operated in earlier time the guides of Henry Cecil are a good starting point.[2] Wales has had an element of devolution since coming into force of the Government of Wales Act 1998. Wales has its own Welsh Assembly [Senedd Cymru] which produces its own legislation in certain areas in terms of the Government of Wales Act 2006. There are also quite distinct court structures and legislative processes which apply to Scotland and Northern Ireland. Since, however, the works discussed in this study concern only England, their particular features are not detailed here. They can be found in the relevant specialist texts.[3]

THE LEGAL PROFESSION

There have been traditionally two branches in the English legal profession, barristers and solicitors.[4] Barristers are engaged in court work at all levels although they have sole representation rights in the High Court, Court of Appeal and Supreme Court [formerly known as the House of Lords].[5] They also provide legal opinions and draft the written pleadings on which the cases are proceed. They operate in Chambers sharing clerical staff and are technically independent. Traditionally their work was secured by their clerks from solicitors. They did not interact directly with the public. Entry to the Bar is through the Inns of Court and elaborate system of eating dinners and joining one of the Inns of Court. This is a graduate profession with a required vocational Bar Training course and work-based training – the "pupillage" – following on. They undertake this pupillage under the supervision of a qualified barrister. Qualification as a barrister covers all of England and Wales. They have traditionally been the source of judges and, as such, have enjoyed status as the senior branch of the profession. The upper levels of the judiciary are still staffed principally by former barristers.

The office-based solicitors' branch is engaged in drawing up documents such as conveyances for the sale of land and houses and wills and contracts as well as litigation. The firms range from single person practices to multi-partner global enterprises with over 1,000 partners and associates. The latter are likely to focus their attention on corporate clients and commercial matters whilst individual and family issues are more often dealt with by smaller firms. Solicitors are the traditional "gateway" to employing a barrister for court work. They would be the first port of call for someone with a legal problem. In addition to office-based practice, some solicitors appear in the lower courts on behalf of clients – tribunals, coroner's courts, magistrates and county courts. Entry into the profession is through satisfying the entry requirements of the Law Society. They set examinations but exemption from these can be obtained through a law degree including certain relevant core subjects. There is a postgraduate Professional Skills Course also required focusing even further on practice. Qualification also covers all of England and Wales.

Although the occasionally mooted amalgamation of the two branches has not come to pass and both have separate entry procedures, since 1990 it has been possible for solicitors to have rights of audience and appear in the higher courts. These individuals are called "solicitor advocates" and they must be a qualified solicitor as well as obtain the relevant Higher Rights Advocacy Qualification. There is also provision for barristers to be consulted direct by members of the public in certain circumstances. This allows direct access to a barrister where a litigant is conducting their own case and is seeking assistance in drafting documents and advice on a range of matters, but where the barrister tends not to get involved in representation.[6]

THE COURTS

The Criminal Courts

Where citizens or companies break the law, they may be dealt with by the criminal justice system. Both the criminal and civil systems are hierarchical in that there may be appeal from the lower court decisions to higher courts. In addition, the legal principles laid down by the higher courts must be followed by the lower courts. Generally, however, higher courts will not interfere with the findings of fact on which the lower court based their decision unless they are manifestly perverse.

Court of Criminal Appeal (Criminal Division)

Appeals from the Crown Court lower in the hierarchy are heard by this court. These can cover such matters as where a judge has given misleading instructions to a jury or where the law has been applied incorrectly. Such matters as credibility of witnesses, however, are normally not appealable.

High Court

High Court judges hear the most serious cases in the Crown Court.

Crown Court

These courts hear the more serious crimes and are heard by a legally qualified full-time judge known as a Circuit Judge. They may also be hearings before part-time judges known as Recorders. They sit with a jury of 12 in the most serious cases. They may hear cases from the magistrates' court where the accused has opted for trial by jury or where the magistrates decide they do not have sufficient sentencing power.

In the past before the introduction of the Crown Court by the Courts Act of 1971 judges used to travel round the country hearing cases locally in what were called the Assizes. These were periodic courts held around England and Wales. The assizes heard the most serious cases, most notably those subject to capital punishment or, later, life imprisonment. Other serious cases were dealt with by the quarter sessions (local county courts held four times per year), while the more minor offences were dealt with summarily by justices of the peace in petty sessions (also known as magistrates' courts). Quarter sessions generally sat in the seat of each county and county borough, and in numerous non-county boroughs which were entitled to hold their own quarter sessions. In 1972, all quarter sessions were abolished in England and Wales with the commencement of the Courts Act of 1971, which replaced them and the assizes with the single permanent Crown Court. The judges "on circuit" used to stay in Judge's Lodgings maintained specifically for the visiting judges.[7] These courts – the Assizes and Quarter Sessions and their procedures are mentioned in many of the stories in this literature.

Magistrates' Court

The lowest level of courts in England and Wales are presided over by three lay magistrates of a District Judge. Magistrates are local members of the community who volunteer and are unpaid. The lay magistrates are advised on legal matters by a legally qualified Clerk. These courts hear 95 per cent of criminal cases brought before the courts. They have powers of sentencing, but cases may be remitted to the Crown Court where appropriate. Where cases are serious, they have the filtering task to determine whether there is a case to answer. If so satisfied, these are remitted to the Crown Court. Where a person comes before the magistrates and are found guilty there may be a fine or community order such as a number of hours of community service. The maximum prison sentence is 6 months for a single offence or 12 months for multiple offences.

J.P. and Police Courts

These lower courts have been superseded by magistrates' courts and are encountered in some of the older literature. They exist in the separate Scottish legal system.

The Civil Courts

The modern system is based on the reforms enacted by the Judicature Acts between 1873 and 1899. The Courts discussed in this book derive from courts created by that legislation. They deal with civil disputes between private citizens or between citizens and the State. Typically, a landlord seeking to evict someone or a person owed money or injured through the fault of another might use these courts to secure a remedy.

The Supreme Court [formerly the House of Lords]

This court is also the final appeal court for England and Wales and was established by the Constitutional Reform Act of 2005. It replaced the House of Lords (Judicial Branch). Since a 1966 practice direction the final appeal body is no longer bound by its own previous decisions. It hears appeals with leave from the Court of Appeal. There is also a "leapfrogging" procedure which allows appeals to proceed from the High Court missing out the Court of Appeal. This rarely occurs. For this to happen the High Court judge must be satisfied that certain conditions are met. These are that the case involves a point of law of general public or national importance on some statutory matter which has been fully argued and considered in the judgment being appealed. Only those appointed as Lords of Appeal in Ordinary sit in the highest chamber. The number of these Law Lords [judges in the House of Lords now Supreme Court] is currently 12. They sit with a quorum of three and where issues are thought to be of major importance may sit as a bench of five.

The Court of Appeal

The Court of Appeal hears appeals from other courts and tribunals – all three divisions of the High Court of Justice and their specialist courts including the

Administrative Court, the County Court and the Family Court. They also hear appeals from the Competition Appeal Tribunal, Employment Appeal Tribunal and various Upper Tribunals dealing with a range of matters.[8]

The Court consists of the Lord/Lady Chief Justice, the Master of the Rolls, the President of the King's Bench Division, the President of the Family Division, the Chancellor of the High Court and Lord and Lady Justices. There are currently 39 Lords and Lady Justices of Appeal.

The High Court of Justice

The High Court is divided into three divisions – the King's Bench Division [a varied jurisdiction including personal injury, negligence, breach of contract, breach of statutory duty, breach of the Human Rights Act of 1998, libel, slander and other civil wrongs known as torts and non-payment of debts and enforcement orders] the Family Division [disputes relating to family matters] and the Chancery Division [disputes relating to business, property or land, intellectual property issues, insolvency, bankruptcy, tax and the validity of wills]. Civil trials involving juries are only found in actions of slander, libel, false imprisonment, malicious prosecution, seduction/breach of promise.

County Court

The civil work of the County Court includes businesses trying to recover money owed, individuals seeking compensation for injuries suffered and landowners seeking orders to prevent trespass. The vast majority of civil cases take place in the County Court and cover contract and civil wrong cases. Where the issues are complex or where large sums of money are involved, these will be raised in the High Court. They are presided over by District Judges for cases up to a certain value[9] and above that by a Circuit Judge.[10] There are also fee-paid judges who sit occasionally in the County Court. There is provision for small claims to be dealt with in the County Court where a simplified procedure is adopted.

Magistrates Court

The lowest level of court can hear some civil matters but are principally concerned with criminal matters as was noted above.

THE LAW

There are a number of sources of law in England and Wales.

The law is an amalgam of legislation from Parliament, the common law and custom. Legislation from Parliament comes in the form of statutes such as specific crimes or civil matters. Increasingly statutes dominate. For example, the crime of theft is now contained in the Theft Act of 1968 which states that "a person is guilty of theft if he dishonestly appropriates property belonging to another with the intention of permanently deprive the other of it" (section 1). The statute contains some 35 other sections and 3 Schedules.

The decisions of judges in previous cases, known as the common law, covers those areas where there is no statute covering an issue. For instance, the crime of assault and what it involves is located in the common law. In theory, if there is no statute or common law on an issue then an answer may be found in custom, although this is most rare.

NOTES

1. For fuller accounts, see Rutherford, Kotecha and Macfarlane (2024); Gillespie (2021); Slapper and Kelly (2020); Dua (2019); Martin (2016).

2. Cecil (1965) and (1974).

3. White, Willock and McQueen (2013) for Scotland; Dickson (2005) for Northern Ireland.

4. There were also other distinct groupings in earlier times such as Serjeants-at-Law or simply Serjeants who had exclusive rights of audience in the Court of Common Pleas. They ceased to be appointed with the passing of the Judicature Act of 1873 – see Baker (1984). Matthew Shardlake is a Serjeant-at-Law in CJ Sansom's classy whodunnit novels set during the reign of Henry VIII (1491–1547) from *Tombland* to *Dissolution*. In *The Pickwick Papers*, Mr Pickwick is defended by Mr Serjeant Snubbin – Nathan (2023) at 517.

5. There is a distinction between the House of Lords legislative body – the Upper Chamber in the British bi-cameral system and the final court of appeal for UK civil matters and criminal matters for England, Wales and Northern Ireland. This was until 30 September 2009, also, confusingly, known as the House of Lords until its name and location changed.

6. https://www.barcouncil.org.uk/bar-council-services/for-the-public/direct-access-portal.html#:~:text=What%20is%20Direct%20Access%3F,instruct%20an%20authorised%20barrister%20directly. (last accessed 23/4/23).

7. It is possible to visit various former Judges' Lodging. The one in Presteigne Powys is a museum and preserves the lodgings as they were in the 1870s. – https://judgeslodging.org.uk – and has an excellent tea room.

8. Administrative Chamber; Immigration and Asylum Chamber; Lands Chamber, Tax and Chancery Chamber.

9. At the time of writing up to £25,000 – but higher than that with permission of a Designated Civil Judge.

10. Who will also hear cases between £10,000 and £25,000.

Postscript

American Comic Fiction

INTRODUCTION

John L Breen suggested back in 1991 that this was an area in which authors from the United States have seldom ventured. In his opinion it stemmed from several factors. This included the wigs and gowns of the English system and the contrast with the seriousness of the issues in the United States with the death penalty amongst other differences

> The corruption of public officials that has long been an element in American crime fiction and real life is less often seen in British fiction or fact. The kind of racial tension seen in American cities has developed more recently and less severely in Britain, and the violence of American urban life is still foreign to most Britons.[1]

The non-fused profession made for less personal involvement for barristers, which allied to a clubby legal world and judges not facing re-election all provide a very different atmosphere in which comic legal humour could thrive. Breen contrasts American seriousness about themselves and their work with the British tendency to self-deprecation.[2]

He did, however, note two authors who have provided comic material on the American legal set-up – Winston Schoonover and later Arthur Train.[3] California Criminal defence attorney Charles M Sevilla adopted the pen name Winston Schoonover, to provide the public with three books on the outrageous New York lawyer John Wilkes.[4] These are pseudo-biographical accounts of the antics of Schoonover's "law partner" John Wilkes. Starting in the 1970s, these consist of the highlights of the 20-plus years of Wilkes' career at the New York Bar. These are high farce and with as much connection with realism as A. P. Herbert's more whimsical litigation with Albert Haddock. Larger than life characters and improbable incidents inhabit these pages. Knockabout fun in the style of the later TV judge Maximum Bob Gibbs.[5] Author Rex Hurst records that "among Wilkes's picaresque misadventures is a stay in prison, where, disguised as an Arab, he leads the inmates in a riot." In addition to writing as Winston Schoonover, Sevilla has also produced a number of works of reportage under his own name on comic legal incidents in the courts – *Disorder in the court: Great fractured moments in court history* (1999) as well as *Law and Disorder: Absolutely funny moments from the courts* (2014).

Rather more tantalising is the mock legal life of Ephraim Tutt from Arthur Train.[6] These consist of a series of spoofs of an American lawyer based in New York. None of these works provide a sustained account or critique the justice system and are of limited assistance in the project being undertaken in this study. They are fascinating in their own right, and the work of Train has been the subject of academic discussion.[7]

Amongst all the courtroom and detective lawyers[8] who have followed in the footsteps of Scott Turow and John Grisham, only one could be said to be bracketed with the comic legal literature subgenre. William Bernhardt's hero, Ben Kincaid, provides an element of comic relief. He is a klutz with low self-esteem rather than a square jawed fighter for justice. He gets into comic scrapes in trying to right wrongs.[9] The books though are essentially thriller dramas with an occasional light touch. The later works retain the same mix of deadly serious themes and slightly comic characters.[10] Whether or not one regards Bernhardt's work as comic legal literature or not is, however, not of great significance since his writings do not seem to involve discussions on the weaknesses and strengths of the legal system in which his protagonist, Ben Kincaid is embroiled. There is also extensive "real life" material from the American courts, including *Disorder in the American courts: actual quotes, word for word, from real court proceedings* (2016).

NOTES

1. Cecil (1991) Introduction by Jon L. Breen at first unnumbered page.
2. Ibid et seq.
3. Cecil (1991) loc cit at third unnumbered page.
4. Schoonover (1990).
5. *Maximum Bob* (1998) ABC – 1 season – based on Elmore Leonard's novel Maximum Bob.
6. Train, Arthur (1919 a); (1919 b); (1920); (1930); (1943).

7. Manning (2012).
8. *Inter alia* Judith Van Giesen's Neil Hamel; Evan Hunter's Matthew Hope.
9. Bernhardt (1992) Primary Justice; (1992) Blind Justice; (1993) Deadly Justice; (1994).
10. Bernhardt (1996 et seq).

Bibliography

Abel, Richard (1998) *The Making of the English Legal Profession* (Frederick, Maryland, Beard Books)

Abel-Smith, Brian (1992) *The Beveridge Report: Its origins and outcomes (International Social Security Review* 45 # 1–2

Abel-Smith, Brian and Stevens, Robert (1967) *Lawyers and the Courts: A sociological study of the English legal system, 1750–1965* (London, Heinemann)

-----. (1968) *In Search of Justice: Society and the Legal System* (London, Penguin)

Acland, L and Broomfield, K (2019) *First 100 Years of Women in Law* (London, Scala Arts & Heritage Publishers Ltd.)

Adamson, Dominic, Kevan, Tim and Casey, Ben (2007) *Prosecuting and Defending Health and Safety Cases* (St Albans, Tarquin)

Afzal, Nazir (2020) *The Prosecutor* (London, Penguin)

Age, The (2002) *A toast to old Rumpole* (July 25 2002) (available at https://www.theage.com.au/national/a-toast-to-old-rumpole-20020725-gdufee.html)

Albon E and Dua S (2019) (eds) *Elliott and Quinn's English Legal System* (21st ed) (London, Pearson)

Almog, Shulamit (2022) *The Origins of Law in Homer* (Berlin, De Gruyter)

American Bar Association (1939) *A Study of portrayals of lawyers, judges and court room scenes in Motion Pictures* (American Bar Association Journal Vol. 25, No. 3, March 1939), pp. 191–94

Amis, Kingsley (1954) *Lucky Jim* (London, Victor Gollancz)

Argus, The (2017)(16 November) *Tributes to Q.C. who inspired TVs Rumpole of the Bailey* (available at https://www.theargus.co.uk/news/15662944.tributes-to-qc-who-inspired-tvs-rumpole-of-the-bailey/)

Arnold, Steve (2005) *British Comedy Guide* (available at www.comedy.co.uk)

Ashton, AJ (1924) *As I Went on My Way* (London, Nisbet & Co)

Asimow, Michael (2000) *Bad Lawyers in the Movies* (Nova Law Review Vol 13, Issue 2), 533

-----. (2009) (ed) *Lawyers in Your Living Room: Law on Television* (Chicago, American Bar Association)

Asimow, Michael, Brown Kathryn and Papke David Ray (2014) *Law and Popular Culture: International Perspectives* (Newcastle-upon-Tyne, Cambridge Scholars Publishing)

Asimow, Michael, Greenfield S, Guillermo J, Machura S, Osborn G, Robson P, Sharp C and Sockloskie R (2005) *Perceptions of Lawyers: A Transnational Study of Student Views on the Image of Law and Lawyers* International Journal of the Legal Profession 12: 407

Bainbridge, Jason (2009) *"Sexy Men in Wigs": North Square and the Representation of Law on British Television* (Journal of British Cinema and Television, Volume 6 Issue 1, Page 83–102, ISSN 1743-4521 (available online at https://www.euppublishing.com/doi/abs/10.3366/E1743452109000703)

Bannon C (2019) *Free Like Sheep: Law, Humor and Roman Political (Cicero, De Oratore 2.284)* Law and Literature 31.3 p 469

Bar Standards Board (2022) *Diversity at the Bar* (available at https://www.barstandardsboard.com)

Bar Standards Board (2023) *Statistics On practising barristers* (available at https://www.barstandardsboard.com)

Barberis Peter, McHugh John and Tyldesley Mike (2005) *Encyclopedia of British and Irish Political Organizations* (London, Continuum International Publishing Group)

Barker, Camilla (2013) *Shackles in Shakespeare: On the falsity of personal liberty in Renaissance England* Liverpool Law Review 35(1) 25

Barrister, The Secret (2019) *The Secret Barrister: Stories of the Law and How It's Broken* (London, Pan Macmillan)

-----. (2021) *Fake Justice: The Truth about Law in an Age of Lies* (London, Pan Macmillan)

-----. (2023) *Nothing But the Truth* (London, Pan Macmillan)

Bartholomew, James (2013) *The Welfare State We're In* (Hull, Biteback Publishing)

Ben, Casey, Adamson Dominic and Kevan Tim (2007) *Prosecuting and Defending Health and Safety Cases* (St Albans, Tarquin Publishing)

Bell, Gary (2015) *Animal, Q.C.: My Preposterous Life* (Cheltenham, Monday Books)

Belfiore, Eleanora and Bennett, Oliver (2008) *The Social Impact of the Arts: An intellectual history* (London, Palgrave Macmillan)

Bergman, Paul (2009) *Rumpole and the Bowl of Comfort Food* (in Asimow [ed])

-----. (2012) *Rumpole's Ethics* (*Berkeley Journal of Entertainment and Sports Law*) Vol 1: 2 117

Berlins, Marcel (2002) *A case of misdirection: Why do most people associate English barristers with wine and cigars? Rumpole, of course* (The Guardian, 30 July 2002) (available at https://www.theguardian.com/world/2002/jul/30/law.theguardian)

-----. (2004) *The case of the missing writers* (Guardian 5 October) (available at https://www.theguardian.com/books/2004/oct/05/law.world)

Bernhardt, William (1992) *Primary Justice* (New York, Ballantine)

-----. (1992) *Blind Justice* (New York, Ballantine)

-----. (1993) *Deadly Justice* (New York, Ballantine)

-----. (1994) *Perfect Justice* (New York, Ballantine)
-----. (1995) *Cruel Justice* (New York, Ballantine)
-----. (1997) *Naked Justice* (New York, Ballantine)
-----. (1998) *Extreme Justice* (New York, Ballantine)
-----. (1999) *Dark Justice* (New York, Ballantine)
-----. (2000) *Silent Justice* (New York, Ballantine)
-----. (2001) *Murder One* (New York, Ballantine)
-----. (2002) *Criminal Intent* (New York, Ballantine)
-----. (2003) *Death Row* (New York, Ballantine)
-----. (2004) *Hate Crime* (New York, Ballantine)
-----. (2006) *Capitol Murder* (New York, Ballantine)
-----. (2007) *Capitol Threat* (New York, Ballantine)
-----. (2008) *Capitol Conspiracy* (New York, Ballantine)
-----. (2009) *Capitol Offense* (New York, Ballantine)
-----. (2010) *Capitol Betrayal* (New York, Ballantine)
-----. (2012) *After Hours* (New York, Ballantine)
-----. (2013) *Yuletide Justice* (New York, Ballantine)
-----. (2014) *What we're here for* (New York, Ballantine)
-----. (2014) *Rough Justice* (New York, Ballantine)
-----. (2017) *Justice Returns* (New York, Ballantine)
Bew, John (2016) *Citizen Clem* (London, Quercus)
Bird, Kai (2021) *The Outlier: The Unfinished Presidency of Jimmy Carter* (New York, Crown)
Black, David (1999) *Law in Film: Resonance and Representation* (Urbana and Chicago, University of Illinois Press)
Blom Cooper, Louis, and Drewry, Gavin (1972) *Final Appeal: A Study of the House of Lords in Its Judicial Capacity* (Oxford, Oxford University Press)
Boal, Graham (2021) *A Drink at the Bar: A memoir of crime, justice and overcoming personal demons* (Stroud, Quiller)
Boren, Marcelle and Schug, Sonny (2016) Disorder in the American Courts: Actual quotes, word for word, from real court proceedings! (CourtComics)
Bower, Tom (2016) *Broken Vows, Tony Blair, The Tragedy of Power* (London, Faber)
Bradley, Kate (2019) *Lawyers for the Poor* (Manchester, Manchester University Press)
Branco, Patricia (2017) *Exploring Justice through Eowyu amd Niobe: on gender and race and the legal in Lord of the Rings and The Matrix* Liverpool Law Review 38 (1) 63
Braithwaite, E R (1959) *To Sir with Love* (London, Bodley Head)
Brand, David William (1996) *An Advocate's Tale: The Memoirs of Lord Brand* (Newbattle, Scottish Cultural Press)
Breen, Jon L (1984)) *Novel Verdicts: A guide to courtroom fiction* (Metuchen, N.J, and London, The Scarecrow Press)
-----. Cecil (1991) [Introduction to *Daughters in Law*] – in Appendix to Chapter 3
-----. (1999) (2nd ed) *Novel Verdicts: A guide to courtroom fiction* (Lanham, Maryland NJ, and Folkestone, The Scarecrow Press)

Bresler, Fenton, (1977) *Lord Goddard: A Biography of Rayner Goddard, Lord Chief Justice of England* (London, Harrap & Co)

Brooke, Henry (2017) *The History of Legal Aid 1945–2010 – Bach Commission on Access to Justice* (London, Fabian Society)

Bryant, John (1989) *Situation comedy of the sixties: The evolution of a popular genre* Studies in American Humor, New Series 2 (7) 118

Buckhaven, Charlotte (1986) *Barrister By and Large* (London, Pan)

Calder, G, Gass, J and Merrill-Glover K (2012) *Changing Directions of the British Welfare State* (Cardiff, University of Wales Press)

Canning, Victor (1934) *Mr Finchley Discovers His England* (London, Hodder and Stoughton)

-----. (1938) *Mr Finchley Goes to Paris* (London, Hodder and Stoughton)

-----. (1940) *Mr Finchley Takes the Road* (London, Hodder and Stoughton)

Carl, Lillian Stewart (2012) *He Who Must Be Obeyed: John Mortimer and the Rumpole Stories* (available at https://kingsriverlife.com/12/29/he-who-must-be-obeyed-john-mortimer-and-the-rumpole-stories/)

Carpi, Daniela and Ost, François (eds) (2018) *As You Law It – Negotiating Shakespeare* (Berlin, De Gruyter)

Castle, Charles (1972) *Noel* (London, WH Allen)

Caudwell, Sarah (1981) *Thus Was Adonis Murdered* (London, Robinson)

-----. (1984) *The Shortest Way to Hades* (London, Constable)

-----. (1986) *The Sirens Sang of Murder* (London, Penguin)

-----. (2000) *The Sybil in her Grave* (London, Delacorte Press – Penguin Random House)

Cavallero, Roseanna (2007) *Chester Himes's Cotton Comes to Harlem: A Reparations Parable* Law and Literature Vol 19 (1) 103

Cecil, Henry – see *Chapter 5 Appendix 1* for fictional output

-----. (1958) *Brief to Counsel* (London, Michael Joseph)

-----. (1961) *Not Such An Ass* (London, Hutchinson)

-----. (1965) *A Matter of Speculation* (London, Hutchinson)

-----. (1965) *Know About English Law* (London and Glasgow, Blackie)

-----. (1970) *The English Judge* (London, Stevens)

-----. (1972) *Brief to Counsel* (London, Michael Joseph) (2nd ed)

-----. (1974) *Learn About English Law* (London, William Luscombe)

-----. (1975a) *The Trial of Walter Rowland* (Newton Abbot, David and Charles

-----. (1975b) *Just Within the Law* (London, Hutchinson)

-----. (1982) *Brief to Counsel* (London, Michael Joseph) (3rd ed) – sold as Henry Cecil's Brief to Counsel [revised and edited by Judge Edgar Dennis Smith] – Brief to Counsel and Henry Cecil on the spine.

Charnick, David (2018) *The Real Jack Pommeroy* (available at https://footprintsoflondon.com/live/2018/01/real-jack-pommeroy/)

Chase, Anthony (1986) "*Towards a Legal Theory of Popular Culture*" Wisconsin Law Review 527

-----. (2002) *Movies on Trial: The Legal System on the Silver Screen* (New York, The New Press)

Clegg, William (2019) *Under the Wig: A Lawyer's Stories of Murder, Guilt and Innocence* (London, Quercus)

Cockburn, Henry (1856) *Memorials of His Time* (Edinburgh, Robert Grant & Sons Ltd) [1946 reprint]

Cohen, Stanley (1972) *Folk Devils and Moral Panics* (London, MacGibbon and Kee)

Comyn, James (1993) *Watching Brief: Further Memoirs of an Irishman at Law in England* (Dublin, Round Hall Press)

Cordingley, David (2007) *Cochrane: The Real Master and Commander* (London, Bloomsbury)

Craig, Sarah and McIntosh, Angus (2023) *Law Centres in Scotland* (in Keane and Robson) (eds)

Crouch, Marcus (1975) *The Home Counties* (London, Robert Hale)

Dale, Richard (2006) *Napoleon is Dead: Lord Cochrane and the Great Stock Exchange Scandal* (Stroud, Sutton Publishing)

Davis, William (2002) *Thomas Hardy and the Law: Legal Presences in Hardy's Life and Fiction* (Newark, University of Delaware Press)

de Beauvoir, Simone (1949) *Le Deuxième Sexe* (Paris, Gallimard) (English Edition published as *The Second Sex* (1953) (New York, Random House)

Dibdin, Michael (1992) *Barrister-errant to the rescue: Rumpole on Trial* (review) (available at https://www.independent.co.uk/arts-entertainment/book-review-barristererrant-to-the-rescue-rumpole-on-trial-john-mortimer-viking-pounds-16-99-1535754.html)

Dickens, C (1838) *Oliver Twist* (London, Richard Bentley)

Dickson, Brice (2005) *The Legal System of Northern Ireland* (Belfast, SLS Legal Publications)

Dolin, Kieran, (2007) *A Critical Introduction to Law and Literature* (Cambridge, Cambridge University Press)

-----. (2009) *Fiction and the Law: Legal Discourse in Victorian and Modernist Literature* (Cambridge, Cambridge University Press)

Dolin, Kieran (ed) (2018) *Law and Literature* (Cambridge, Cambridge University Press)

Draper, Hastings (1956) *Wiggery Pokery* (London, WH Allen)

-----. (1958) *Wigged and Gowned* (London, WH Allen)

-----. (1961) *Brief Help* (London, WH Allen)

Dyson, John (2019) *A Judge's Journey* (Oxford, Hart)

Elkins, James (2004) *Reading/Teaching Lawyer Films* Vermont Law Review 28; 797

Ellis, Aidan and Kevan, Tim (2016) (5th ed) *Ellis and Kevan on Credit Hire* (Minehead, Law Brief Publishing) plus earlier 4th edition 2013

Elliott and Quinn's *English Legal System* (see Albon and Dua)

Evans, Judith (1995) *Feminist Theory Today: An Introduction to Second Wave Feminism* (London, Sage)

Fendem, David (2022) *Dirty Briefs: The hilarious struggles and shocking tales of a bare-knuckle criminal barrister* (London, Mardle)

Flood, John A (1983) *Barristers' Clerks: The Law's Middlemen* (Manchester, Manchester University Press)

-----. (2020) *Rake and Rumpole: Mavericks for Justice – Purity and Impurity in Legal Professionalism* (in Weinart, Crawley and Tranter (2020)
Foote, John A (1911) *"Pie-Powder"; being dust from the law courts* (London, J Murray)
Frank, Jerome (1930) *Law and the Modern Mind* (New Brunswick and London, Transaction Publishers)
-----. (1949) *Courts on Trial: Myth and Reality in American Justice* (Princeton NJ, Princeton University Press)
Fraser, Caro. *Caper Court novels*
-----. (1994) *The Pupil*
-----. (1995) *Judicial Whispers*
-----. (1998) *An Immoral Code*
-----. (1999) *A Hallowed Place*
-----. (2002*) A Perfect Obsession*
-----. 2004) *Calculating Heart*
-----. (2007) *Breath of Corruption*
-----. (2013) *Errors of Judgment*
-----. (2020) *A Touch of Silk*
Fraser, Caro. *Standalone Novels*
-----. (1995) *The Trustees*
-----. (1997) *An Inheritance*
-----. (1998) *Beyond Forgiveness*
-----. (2001) *A Little Learning* [no legal core issue]
-----. (2003) *Familiar Rooms in Darkness* [no legal core issue]
-----. (2007) *World Apart* [no legal core issue]
-----. (2017) *The Summer House Party* [no legal core issue]
-----. (2018) *Summer of Love* [no legal core issue]
Fraser, J Cameron (2017) *Learning from Lord Mackay: Life and Work in Two Kingdoms* (Lethbridge Alberta, SoS Books)
Freeman, M (ed) (2005) *Law and Popular Culture* (Oxford, OUP)
Fried, Margaret and Frolik, Lawrence (995) *The Limits of Law: Litigation, Lawyers and the Search for Justice in Russell Banks' "The Sweet Hereafter" Cardozo Studies in Law and Literature* 7 (1) 1
Friedman, Lawrence (1988) *Law, lawyers and popular culture* Yale Law Journal Vol 98: 1579
Fry, Steven (2008) *Reflections on Kingdom* (Internet comments on the introduction of the 2nd series – since deleted and reference unavailable)
Galanter, Marc (1998) *The faces of mistrust: the image of lawyers in public opinion, jokes and political discourse University of Cincinnati Law Review* 66: 805
-----. (2005) *Lowering the Bar: Lawyer Jokes and Legal Culture* (Madison, University of Wisconsin Press)
Galloway, Lindsay (1974) *Sutherland's Law* (London, Pan)
Galsworthy, John (1906) *The Man of Property* (Wordsworth Classics edition 1994)
-----. (1920) *In Chancery* (Wordsworth Classics edition 1994)
-----. (1921) *To Let* (Wordsworth Classics edition 1994)
Gardiner, G and Martin, A (eds) (1963) *Law Reform Now* (Gollancz, London)

Gest, J M "*The Law and Lawyers of Charles Dickens*," The American Law Register, 53:7 (1905): 401–26.

-----. (1913) *The Lawyer in Literature* (London, Sweet and Maxwell)

Gillespie, Alisdair and Weare, Siobhan (2023) (9th ed) *The English Legal System* (Oxford, Oxford University Press)

Golden, John (1995) *The Form of Flaubert's "Hérodias" Cardozo Studies in Law and Literature* 7 (2) 229

Graham, Wendy (2022) *England's Finest: Rumpole and His Real Life Role Models* (available at https://cap-press.com/sites/pj/rumpole.htm)

Grant, Thomas (2016) *Jeremy Hutchinson's Case Histories: From Lady Chatterly to Howard Marks* (London, John Murray)

Graycar, Regina (1996) *Telling Tales: Legal Stories about Violence against Women* Cardozo Studies in Law and Literature 8 (2) 297

Greenfield, Steve, Osborn Guy and Robson, Peter (2001) *Film and the Law* (London, Cavendish)

-----. (2007) Genre, Iconography and British Legal Film University of Baltimore Law Review Vol 36 No. 3

-----. (2010) *Film and the Law: The Cinema of Justice* (Oxford, Hart)

-----. (2024) *Film and the Law* (in Newman and Sandberg [eds])

Grisham (1993) *The Client* (London, Penguin Random House)

Grove, Valerie (2007) *A Voyage Round John Mortimer: The Biography* (London, Penguin)

Gunn, David (ed) (1993) *The Lawyers and Popular Culture: Proceedings of a Conference* (Littleton, Fred B Rothman)

Hanley, Robert F (1989) *A Conversation with John Mortimer* (Litigation Vol. 15, No. 2, MISTAKES (Winter 1989), pp. 21–25

Hanratty, James (2016) and (2020) (revised edition) *The Making of an Immigration Lawyer* (London, Quartet)

Harmes, MK, Harmes MA and Harmes B (2022) *The Age of Rumpole is Past? Legal History on British Television* (in McKibbin, Patrick and Harmes)

Hart, Robert (2007) *Rumpole and Morality* (available at http://anglicancontinuum.blogspot.com/2007/08/rumpole-and-morality.html)

Harvey, C P (1958) *The Advocate's Devil* (London, Stevens)

Healy, Maurice (1939) *The Old Munster Circuit* (London, Michael Joseph) [reprinted 2015 by Wildy, Simmonds and Hill of London]

Heath James, Kevan Tim and Ward Damian (2006) *Fraudulent and Exaggerated Claims in Personal Injury* (St Albans, Xpl Law)

Heilbron, Hilary (2013) *Women at the Bar: An historical perspective* (Counsel) 31 May 2013 (available at https://www.counselmagazine.co.uk – last accessed 6 December 2023)

Henriques, Richard (2021) *From Crime to Crime* (London, Hodder and Stoughton)

Herbert, A P (1919) *The Secret Battle* (London, Methuen)

-----. (1927) *Misleading Cases in the Common Law* (London, Methuen)

-----. (1934) *Holy Deadlock* (London, Methuen)

-----. (1935) *Misleading Cases* (London, Methuen)

-----. (1937) *The Ayes Have It: The Story of the Marriage Bill* (London, Methuen)
-----. (1939) *General Cargo* (London, Methuen)
-----. (1950) *Independent Member* (London, Methuen)
-----. (1951) *Number Nine* (London, House of Stratus 2001 edition)
-----. (1966) *Wigs At Work* (London, Penguin).
-----. (1970) *A.P.H.: His life and times* (London, Heinemann)
-----. (1982) *More Uncommon Law*

Hewett, Richard (2014) *Regarding Rumpole: Presenting the Case for "Old" TV* (available at https://cstonline.net/regarding-rumpole-presenting-the-case-for-old-tv-by-richard-hewett/)

Holden, Wendy (1998) *Kavanagh Q.C.: The Ties that Bind* (London, Coronet)

Hostettler J and Braby R (2010) *Sir William Garrow: His Life, Times and Fight for Justice* (Hook, Waterside Press)

Hyde, H Montgomery (1964) *Norman Birkett: The Life of Lord Birkett of Ulverston* (London, Hamish Hamilton)

Ingrams, R (ed) (1974) *Beachcomber: The Works of J.B. Morton* (Colchester, TBS The Book Service Ltd.)

-----. (1991) *The Bumper Beachcomber* (London, Bloomsbury)

Irish Legal News (2021) *Rumpole rebooted – iconic series to return with a female lead* (available at https://www.irishlegal.com/articles/rumpole-rebooted-iconic-series-to-return-with-female-lead)

Jacobson, Howard (1983) *Coming from Behind* (London, Chatto and Windus)

Jackson, Robert (1959) *The Chief: The Biography of Gordon Hewart, Lord Chief Justice of England 1922–40* (London, Harrap)

Jackson, RM (1960) (3rd ed) *The Machinery of Justice in England* (Cambridge, Cambridge University Press) [1st edition 1940]

-----. (1965) (4th ed) *The Machinery of Justice in England* (Cambridge, Cambridge University Press)

Jarvis R and Joseph P (eds) (1998) *Prime Time Law: Fictional Television as Legal Narrative* (Durham NC; Carolina Academic Press)

Johnson, Alan (2015) *Please, Mister Postman* (London, Corgi)

Jones, Owen (2014) *The Establishment: And how they get away with it* (London, Allen Lane)

Kamir, Orit (2000a) *X-Raying Adam's Rib: Multiple Readings of a (Feminist?) Law-Film* Studies in Law, Politics and Society 22:103

-----. (2000b) *Feminist Law and Film: Imagining Judges and Justice* Chicago-Kent Law Review 75: 899

-----. (2005a) *Framed: Women in Law and Film* (Durham, NC: Duke University Press)

-----. (2005) *Why "Law-and-Film" and What Does it Actually Mean? A Perspective* (Journal of Media & Cultural Studies Vol 19, p 255 (available at https://www.tandfonline.com/doi/abs/10.1080/10304310500084558)

Kaufman, Bel (1964) *Up the Down Staircase* (Hoboken, New Jersey, Prentice-Hall)

Keane, E and Robson, P (2023) *The Ian Willock Collection on Law and Justice in the 21st Century* (Teaneck, New Jersey, Fairleigh Dickinson UP)

Kennedy, Helena (2004) *Just Law: The Changing Face of Justice and What It Means to Us All* (London, Chatto and Windus)
Kennedy, Ludovic (1961) *Ten Rillington Place* (London, Gollancz)
Kevan, Tim (1999) *A Guide to Credit Hire and Repair: Law and Practice* (Welwyn Garden City, CLT Professional Publishing)
-----. (2001a) *Kevan on Credit Hire* (2nd ed) (Welwyn Garden City, EMIS Professional Publishing)
-----. (2001b) *E-mail, Internet and the Law: Essential Knowledge to Safer Surfing* (Welwyn Garden City, EMIS Professional Publishing)
-----. (2005) *Psychological Injury* (St Albans, Xpl Law)
-----. (2006) *Personal Injury: Brief Update Law Journal* (St Albans, Xpl Publishing)
-----. (2009) *Baby Barista and the Art of War* (London, Bloomsbury)
-----. (2010) *Law and Disorder: Confessions of a Pupil Barrister* (London, Bloomsbury) (republished version of Baby Barista and the Art of War)
-----. (2011) *Law and Peace* (London, Bloomsbury)
Kevan, Tim, Adamson Dominic and Cottrell Stephen (2002) *Sports Personal Injury: Law and Practice* (London, Sweet and Maxwell)
Kevan, Tim and Ellis Aidan (2008) *Kevan and Ellis on Credit Hire* (3rd ed) (St Albans, Xpl Law)
Kevan, Tim, Ellis Aidan and Wright Gary (2014) *Pi Brief Update Law Journal* (Minehead, Law Brief Publishing) (January–December 2013) (2 volumes)
Kevan, Tim and Kwaitkowska Maria (2005a) *Fatal Accident Claims* (St Albans, Xpl Law)
-----. (2005b) *Periodical Payments in Fatal Accident Claims* (St Albans, Xpl Law)
Kevan, Tim and McGrath Paul (2001) *E-mail, the Internet and the Law: Essential Knowledge for Safer Surfing* (Welwyn Garden City, Emis Professional Publishing)
Kevan, Tim and Tempest, Michelle (2007a) *Why Doctors Should Surf: Inspiration for Doctors at Work and Play* (St Albans, Xpl Law)
-----. (2007b) *Why Lawyers Should Surf: Inspiration for Lawyers at Work and Play* (St Albans, Xpl Law)
Kevan, Tim, Ward Damian and Heath James (2006) *Exaggerated and Fraudulent Claims in Personal Injury* (St Albans, Xpl Law Publishing)
Koch, Hugh and Kevan Tim (2005) *Psychological Injury* (St Albans, Tarquin)
Kynaston, David (2007) *A World to Build: Austerity Britain 1945–48* (London, Bloomsbury)
Larsen, Elaine (1997) *Rumpole is their bailiwick* (available at https://www.sfgate.com/bayarea/article/Rumpole-is-their-bailiwick-3118664.php)
Langford, Sarah (2018) *In Your Defence: True Stories of Life and Law* (London, Penguin)
Laski, Harold (1925) *A Grammar of Politics* (London, Routledge)
Lawson, Mark (2012) *The Guardian* October 27, p. 10
Legal Services Consumer Panel (2024) *Satisfaction level and trust in lawyers continue to rise* (17 July)
Leith, Sam (2013) *Introduction to the Collected Stories of Rumpole* (available at https://www.prospectmagazine.co.uk/arts-and-books/rumpole-john-mortimer-sam-leith)

Lincoln, Geoffrey (1957) *No Moaning of the Bar* (London, Bles) [pseudonym of John Mortimer]

Little, Laura (2019) *Guilty Pleasures: Comedy and Law in America* (New York, Oxford University Press America)

Llewellyn, Karl (1931) *Some Realism about Realism: Responding to Dean Pound* Harvard Law Review 44 (8) 1222

-----. (1960) *The Common Law Tradition – Deciding Appeals* (New York, Little Brown and Co)

Lodge, David (1975) *Changing Places* (London, Secker and Warburg)

-----. (1984) *Small World* (London, Secker and Warburg)

-----. (1988) *Nice Work* (London, Secker and Warburg)

Loony Literature (2012) *Review of Rumpole and the Man of God* (available at https://theconsultingdetectivesblog.com/2012/03/02/rumpole-and-the-man-of-god-review/)

Lord, Graham (2005) *John Mortimer: The Devil's Advocate: The Unauthorised Biography* (London, Orion)

Lothian, Andrew (1991) *Lawful Occasions* (Edinburgh, T & T Clark)

Lowe, Shirley (1997) *Kavanagh Q.C.: Blood Money* (London, Coronet)

Lucia, Cynthia (2005) *Framing Female Lawyers: Women on Trial in Film* (Austin, University of Texas Press)

Macaulay, Stewart (1987) *"Images of Law in Everyday Life: The Lessons of School, Entertainment and Spectator Sports"* Law and Society Review 21: 185

Machura, Stefan (2016) *Law and Cinema Movement* (in Picart, Jacobsen and Greek)

Machura, Stefan and Litvinova, Olga (2021) *Reflections of Legal Culture in Television Comedy: Social Critique and Schadenfreude in the US Series "Frasier"* International Journal for the Semiotics of Law Vol 34 89

Machura, Stefan and Robson, Peter (eds) (2001) *Law and Film* (Oxford, Blackwell)

Mail on Sunday (24 July 2021) *Rumpole's back – and has SHE got news for you! Sir John Mortimer's legendary lawyer is given a sex change by daughter Emily with rumours Lily James will be approached for the part* (available at https://www.dailymail.co.uk/tvshowbiz/article-9822067/Sir-John-Mortimers-legendary-lawyer-Rumpole-given-sex-change-daughter-Emily-Mortimer.html)

Majeske, Andrew (2009) *Equity's Absence: The Extremity of Claudio's Prosecution and Barnardine's Pardon in Shakespeare's Measure for Measure* Law and Literature Vol 21 (2) 169

Manning, Molly Guphill (2012) *The Myth of Ephraim Tutt: Arthur Train and His Great Literary Hoax* (Tuscaloosa, University of Alabama Press)

Mansfield, Michael (2009) *Memoirs of a Radical Lawyer* (London, Bloomsbury)

-----. (2023) *The Power in the People: Not the People in Power* (London, Octopus)

Margulies, Peter (1996) *The Violence of Law and Violence against Women* Cardozo Studies in Law and Literature 8 (1) 179

Martin, Jacqueline (2016) (8th ed) *The English Legal System* (London, Hodder Education)

Masson, Antoine and O'Connor, Kevin (eds) (2007) *Representations of Justice* (Brussels, Peter Lang)

Mathew, Theobald (1926,1928 and 1929) *Forensic Fables* (London, Wildy & Sons Ltd) [see also O] [1999 reprint]
-----. (1937) *For Lawyers and Others* (London, Edinburgh and Glasgow, William Hodge & Co Ltd)
-----. (1959) *Forensic Fables* (London, Wildy)
Mavis, Paul (2011) *Rumpole of the Bailey: The Complete Series* (available at https://www.dvdtalk.com/reviews/47552/rumpole-of-bailey-the-complete-series/)
McBride, Alex (2009) *Defending the Guilty: Truth and Lies in the Criminal Courtroom* (London, Penguin)
McCall, Douglas (1991) *Monty Python: A Chronological Listing of the Troupe's Creative Output and Articles and Reviews About Them, 1969–89* (Jefferson, N.C., McFarland)
McConville, M and Marsh, L (2020) *The Myth of Judicial Independence* (Oxford OUP)
McGregor, Tom (1995) *Kavanagh Q.C.* (London, BCA)
-----. (1996) *Kavanagh Q.C. II* (London, Pan)
McInness, Colin (1957) *City of Spades* (London, MacGibbon and Kee)
-----. (1959) *Absolute Beginners* (London, MacGibbon and Kee)
-----. (1960) *Love and Justice* (London, MacGibbon and Kee)
McIntyre, William (2012a) *Relatively Guilty* (Falkirk, Best Defence Ltd.)
-----. (2012b) *Duty Man* (Falkirk, Best Defence Ltd.)
-----. (2013a) *Sharp Practice* (Falkirk, Best Defence Ltd.)
-----. (2013b) *Killer Contract* (Falkirk, Best Defence Ltd.)
-----. (2014) *Crime Fiction* (Falkirk, Best Defence Ltd.)
-----. (2015) *Last Will* (Falkirk, Best Defence Ltd.)
-----. (2016) *Present Tense* (Falkirk, Best Defence Ltd.)
-----. (2017) *Good News, Bad News* (Falkirk, Best Defence Ltd.)
-----. (2018) *Stitch Up* (Sheffield, Sandstone Press)
-----. (2019) *Fixed Odds* (Sheffield, Sandstone Press)
-----. (2020) *Bad Debt* (Sheffield, Sandstone Press)
-----. (2022) *Best Defence* (Twickenham, Amazon Press)
-----. (2023) *How Come* (Twickenham, Amazon Press)
-----. (2024) *No Problem* (Twickenham, Amazon Press)
McKibbin S, Patrick, J and Harmes MK (eds) (2022) *The Impact of Law's History: What's Past is Prologue*. (Swizerland, Springer)
McNeil, William (2017) *His dark legalities: Intellectual properties Pscychmachia in Philip Pullman's "His Dark Materials" trilogy Liverpool Law Review* 38 (1) 11
Megarry, RE (1955) *Miscellany-at-Law: A diversion for lawyers and others* (London, Stevens)
Melville, Alan (1970) *Merely Melville* (London, Hodder and Stoughton)
Milner, Henry (2020) *No Lawyers in Heaven: a Life Defending Serious Crime* (Hull, Biteback Publishing)
-----. (2021) *Murder at the Bailey* (Hull, Biteback Publishing)
Ministry of Justice (2023) *Diversity of the Judiciary: Legal professions, new appointments and current post-holders – 2023 Statistics* (8 September 2023)

Moore, Sarah and Newbury, Alex (2017) *Legal Aid in Crisis: Assessing the Impact of Reform* (Bristol, Bristol University Press)
Moran, Leslie (1998) *Heroes and Brothers in Love: The Male Homosexual as Lawyer in Popular Culture* (*Studies in Law, Politics and Society*) 18
-----. (2008) *Cause lawyering 'English style': reading Rumpole of the Bailey* (in Sarat, A. and Schiengold, S. (eds.) pp. 297-330
Moran, L, Sandon, E, Loizidou, E and Christie, I (eds)(2005) *Law's Moving Image* (London, Glasshouse)
Morison, John and Bell, Christine (1996) *Tall Stories? Reading Law and Literature* (Aldershot, Ashgate)
Morley, Sheridan (2005) *Noel Coward* (London Haus)
Mortimer, John (1948) *Charade* (London, Bodley Head)
-----. (1948) *Rumming Park* (London, Bodley Head)
-----. (1950) *Answer Yes or No* (London, Bodley Head)
-----. (1954) *Like Men Betrayed* (London, Bodley Head)
-----. (1967) *The Judge* (London, Methguen)
-----. (1982) *Clinging to the Wreckage: A Part of Life* (London, Penguin)
-----. (1994a) *Murderers and other Friends: Another Part of Life* (London, Penguin)
-----. (1994b) *Rumpole* (London, The Folio Society) [10 stories selected by and with an Introduction by Mortimer]
-----. (2000) *The Summer of a Dormouse: A Year of Growing Old Disgracefully* (London, Penguin)
-----. (2007) *Where There's a Will* (London, Penguin)
Moss, Bob (2019) *Jack Temple Guilty* (Independently Published) see https://www.amazon.co.uk/Jack-Temple-Guilty-Bob-Moss-ebook/dp/B081ZDZK89/ref=tmm_kin_swatch_0?_encoding=UTF8&qid=&sr= (accessed 13 October 2021)
-----. *Jack Temple Not Guilty* (Independently Published)
-----. *Jack the Lad* (Independently Published)
Murphy, Peter. *Judge Walden series*
-----. (2017) *Walden of Bermondsey* (Harpenden, No Exit Press)
-----. (2018) *Judge Walden: Back in Session* (Harpenden, No Exit Press)
-----. (2019) *Judge Walden: Call the Next Case* (Harpenden, No Exit Press)
-----. (2024) *A Week on Mount Olympus and other tales from the bench* (Harpenden, No Exit)
Murphy, Peter. *American Series*
-----. (2012a) *Removal* (Harpenden, No Exit Press)
-----. (2013) *Test of Resolve* (Harpenden, No Exit Press)
-----. (2018a) *A Statue for Jacob* (Harpenden, No Exit Press)
Murphy, Peter. *Ben Schroeder Series*
-----. (2012b) *A Higher Duty* [early 1960s] (Harpenden, No Exit Press)
-----. (2014a) *A Matter for the Jury* [1964] (Harpenden, No Exit Press)
-----. (2014b) *And is there honey still for tea?* [1965] (Harpenden, No Exit Press)
-----. (2016) *The Heirs of Owain Glyndŵr* [1969] (Harpenden, No Exit Press)
-----. (2017) *Calling Down the Storm* [1971] (Harpenden, No Exit Press)
-----. (2018b) *One Law for the Rest of Us* [1970s]; (Harpenden, No Exit Press)

-----. (2020) *Verbal* (Harpenden, No Exit Press)

-----. (2022) *To Become an Outlaw* (Harpenden, No Exit Press)

Nathan, Barrie (2023) *Dickens and the Law* Amicus Curiae Vol 4 No 2 515

Neely, Robert D (1936) *The Lawyers of Dickens and their clerks* (republished by Union NJ, Lawbook Exchange, 2001) (originally published Boston, Christopher Pub. House)

New York Times (1984) (October 11) *Rumpole Returns to the Old Bailey* (available at https://www.nytimes.com/1984/10/11/arts/rumpole-returns-to-the-old-bailey.html)

New Zealand Law Society (2019) *Rumpole of the Bailey: Where defiance is a virtue* (available at https://www.lawsociety.org.nz/news/lawtalk/issue-932/rumpole-of-the-bailey-where-defiance-is-a-virtue/)

Newman, Daniel and Sandberg, Russell (eds) (2024) *Law and Humanities* (London, Anthem Press)

Northern Echo (2004) *Interview with John Mortimer* (available at https://www.the-northernecho.co.uk/news/6975373.real-rumpole-love-child/)

Nostalgia Central (nd) *Rumpole of the Bailey* (available at https://nostalgiacentral.com/television/tv-by-decade/tv-shows-1970s/rumpole-bailey/)

O (1926, 1928 and 1929) *Forensic Fables* (London, Wildy and Sons) [see also Mathew, Theobald] (1999 reprint)

Ődmark, Sara (2020) *Moral Transgressors vs. Moral Entrepreneurs: The Curious Case of Comedy Accountability in an Era of Social Platform Dependence* Journal of Media Ethics Vol 26 Issue 4 (available at https://doi.org.10.1080/23736992.2021)

Osborn, Guy (2001) *Borders and Boundaries: Locating the Law in Film* (in Law and Film, Machura and Robson [eds])

Osborne, David (1992) *No Holds Barred: An idiot's Guide to the Art of Advocacy* [writing as Ivor Bigg-Wigg] (St Albans, Stag Publications)

-----. (2012) *A Guide to Public Speaking* (South Carolina, CreateSpace Independent Publishing Platform) now Kindle Direct Publishing

-----. (2013) *May it Please Your Lordship* [writing as Toby Potts] (Cheltenham; Monday Books)

-----. (2016) *Order in Court* (CreateSpace Independent Publishing Platform)

Pannick, David (1987) *Judges* (Oxford, Oxford University Press)

-----. (1992) *Advocates* (Oxford, Oxford University Press)

Papke, David Ray (2001) *Lawyer Fiction in the Saturday Evening Post: Ephraim Tutt, Perry Mason and Middle-Class Expectations* Cardozo Studies in Law and Literature 13 (2) 207

Peirce, Gareth (2010) *Dispatches from the Dark Side: On Torture and the Death of Justice* (London, Verson)

Peston, Robert (2008) *Who Runs Britain? How the Super-Rich are Changing Our Lives* (London, Hodder and Stoughton)

Picart, Caroline, Jacobsen, Michael and Greek, Cecil (eds) (2016) *Framing Law and Crime: An Interdisciplinary Anthology* (Madison, Teaneck, Farleigh Dickinson University Press)

Podlas, Kimberlianne (2009) *Impact of Television on Cross-Examination and Juror "Truth"* Widener Law Review 14: 479

-----. (2012) *Testing Television: Studying and Understanding the Impact of Television's Depiction of Law and Justice* (in Robson and Silbey)
-----. (2016) The CSI Effect (in Oxford Encyclopedia of Criminology (Oxford, OUP)
Potts, Toby (2013) – see Osborne, David q.v.
-----. (2016) – see Osborne, David q.v.
Pound, Reginald (1976) *APH* (London, Michael Joseph)
Prescot, Julian (1958) *Both Sides of the Case* (London, Arthur Barker)
-----. (1959) *The Case Continued* (London, Arthur Barker)
-----. (1960) *Case Proceeds* (London, Arthur Barker)
-----. (1961) *Case for the Accused* (London, Arthur Barker)
-----. (1962) *Case for Trial* (London, Arthur Barker)
-----. (1963) *Case for Hearing* (London, Arthur Barker)
-----. (1964) *Case for Court* (London, Arthur Barker)
-----. (1965) *The Case Re-Opened* (London, Arthur Barker)
-----. (1966) *The Krakatoa Colt* (London, Arthur Barker)
-----. (1967) *Case Counterfeit* (London, Arthur Barker)
Pritt, Denis (1966) *The Defence Accuses* (London, Lawrence and Wishart)
Quabeck Franziska (2013) *Just and Unjust Wars in Shakespeare* (Berlin, De Gruyter)
-----. (2021) *The Lawyer in Dickens* (Berlin, De Gruyter)
Rafter, Nicky (2001) *American Criminal Trial Films: An Overview of their Development 1930–2000* (in Machura and Robson)
-----. (2006) *Shots in the Mirror* (Oxford, Oxford University Press)
Rapping, Elayne (2003) *Law and Justice as Seen On TV* (New York, New York University Press)
Rasmusson Report (2022) *Can You Trust a Lawyer?* (full report available on subscription)
Richards, I A (1924) *Principles of Literary Criticism* (London, Routledge and Kegan Paul)
-----. (1929) *Practical Criticism: A Study of Literary Judgment* (London, Routledge and Kegan Paul)
Robertson, Geoffrey (2009) *How Rumpole helped John Mortimer change the world* (available at https://www.theguardian.com/books/booksblog/2009/jan/16/john-mortimer-rumpole-tribute
-----. (2018) *Rather His Own Man: In Court with Tyrants, Tarts and Troublemakers* (Hull, Biteback)
Robins, Jon (2018) *Guilty until Proven Innocent: The crisis in our justice system* (Hull, Biteback)
Robson, Peter (1994) *Watching the Detectives: Images of Law in Popular Culture* (Strathclyde University Inaugural Lecture)
-----. (1996) *Images of Law in the Fiction of John Grisham* (in Morison and Bell) 201
-----. (2002) *Fade to grey: Portraying the ethnic minority experience in British film* 3 *International Journal of Sociology of Law* 2002 p 235
-----. (2007a) *Lawyers and the Legal System on TV: The British Experience International Journal of Law in Context* 333

-----. (2007b) *Developments in Law and Culture: The Case of the TV Lawyer* (in Masson and O'Connor eds)
-----. (2014) *The Law Through the Eyes of Courtroom Comedy* (in Asimow, Brown and Papke)
-----. (2015). *Women Lawyers on TV – the British Experience.* (*Nordic Journal of Law and Social Research*, (5), 101–16. https://doi.org/10.7146/nnjlsr.v0i5.111083
-----. (2018) *Future Directions in Law and Popular Culture: A British Perspective* (in Visconti (ed)
-----. (2022) *Vigilantes, the Law and Popular Culture: The British Experience* (in Robson and Spina)
-----. (2023) *The Future of Law and Popular Culture* (paper presented to the Oñati Seminar on Law and Popular Culture in the Digital Age, June 2023) – in press
-----. (2024) *Lex Caledonia – Scots Law in Popular Culture* (paper presented to the Research Committee on Sociology of Law, Oñati, June 2024)
Robson, Peter and Combe, Malcolm (2019) (4th ed) *Residential Tenancies* (Edinburgh, Green)
Robson, Peter and Schulz, Jennifer (eds) (2016) *A Transnational Study of Law and Justice on TV* (Oxford, Hart)
-----. (2018) *Ethnicity, Gender and Diversity: Law and Justice on TV* (Lanham, Lexington, New York, London: Lexington Books)
Robson, Peter and Silbey, Jessica (eds) (2012) *Law and Justice on the Small Screen* (Oxford, Hart)
Robson, Peter and Spina, Ferdinando (eds) (2022) *Vigilante Justice in Society and Popular Culture* (Lanham, Md, Fairleigh University Press)
Robson, Peter and Watchman, Paul (eds) (1981) *Justice, Lord Denning and the Constitution* (Aldershot, Gower)
Rolph, CH (1960) *The Trial of Lady Chatterley: R v Penguin Books Ltd* (London, Penguin)
Rossi, Giuseppe and Carbone, Paula (2023) *The Law and Comedy* (Berlin, De Gruyter)
Rutherford, Helen, Kotecha, Birju and Macfarlane, Angela (2024) (6th ed) *English Legal System* (Oxford, Oxford University Press)
Salzmann V and Dunwoody P (2005) *Do Portrayals of Lawyers Influence How People Think About the Legal Profession? Southern Methodist University Law Review* 58: 411
Sampson, A (1962) *Anatomy of Britain* (London, Hodder and Stoughton)
-----. (1965) *Anatomy of Britain Today* (London, Hodder and Stoughton)
-----. (1982) *The Changing Anatomy of Britain* (London, Hodder and Stoughton)
-----. (1992) *The Essential Anatomy of Britain* (London, Hodder and Stoughton)
-----. (2004) *Who Runs This Place? The Anatomy of Britain in the 21st Century* (London, Hodder and Stoughton)
Sansom, CJ (2003) *Dissolution* (London, Viking)
-----. (2018) *Tombland* (London, Viking)
Sarat, A, Douglas, L and Umphrey, M (2005) *Law and the Screen* (Stanford, Stanford UP)

Sarat, A and Schiengold, S (eds.) (2008) *The Cultural Life of Cause Lawyers.* Cambridge, UK: Cambridge University Press

Schoonover, Winston (1990) *Wilkes: His life and crimes* (New York, Ballantine)

-----. (1990) *Wilkes for the Defense* (New York, Ballantine)

-----. (1993) *Wilkes on Trial* (New York, Random House)

Seccombe, Wally (1986) *Patriarchy Stabilised: The Construction of the Male Breadwinner Wage Norm in Nineteenth-Century Britain Social History* (11)(1) 53–76

Seldon, Anthony (2004) *Blair* (New York, Free Press)

Sevilla, Charles M (1999) *Disorder in the court: Great fractured moments in court history* (Washington, D.C.; National Geographic Books)

-----. (2014) *Law and Disorder: Absolutely funny moments from the courts* (New York, WW Norton & Co.)

Sherwin, Richard (2000) *The Law Goes Pop: The Vanishing Line Between Law and Popular Culture* (Chicago, University of Chicago Press)

Shubick, Irene (2000) *Play for Today: The evolution of television drama* (Manchester, Manchester University Press)

Silbey, Jessica (2007) *Truth Tales and Trial Films* 40 Loy L.A. Rev 551

Simonsen, Karen-Margrethe (2013) *Law and Justice Literature, Film and Theater: Nordic Perspectives* (Belin, De Gruyter)

Slapper, Gary and Kelly, David (2020) (19th ed) *Slapper and Kelly's The English Legal System* (Abingdon, Routledge)

Smith, Stephen D (1996) *Boozers, Ballcocks and Bail* (Barnsley, Neville-Douglas Publishing Ltd)

-----. (1997) *Plonkers Plaintiffs & Pleas: A Further Solicitor's Tale* (Barnsley, Neville-Douglas Publishing Ltd)

-----. (1998) *Junkies, Judges and Jail* (Barnsley, Neville-Douglas Publishing Ltd)

-----. (2003) *Muggers, Mobsters and Me* (Barnsley, Neville-Douglas Publishing Ltd)

Solicitors' Regulation Authority (2023) *Diversity in Law Firms' Workforce* (https://www.sra.org.uk)

Somerville, E and Ross, M (1899) *Some Experiences of an Irish RM* (London, Longman's Green & Co) (later 1945 London, Faber and Faber)

-----. (1908) *Further Experiences of an Irish RM* (London, Longman's Green & Co)

-----. (1915) *In Mr Knox's Country* (London, Longman's Green & Co)

Stern, Daniel (1998) *The Fellowship of Men That Die: The Legacy of Albert Camus* Cardozo Studies in Law and Literature 10 (2) 183

Stoddart, C (1978) *Law and practice of legal aid in Scotland* (Edinburgh, Green)

Stringfellow, Frank (1995) *Kafka's "Trial": Between "The Republic" and Psychoanalysis* Cardozo Studies in Law and Literature 7 (2) 173

Sweeney, Joseph C (2000) Rumpelheimer v. Haddock: Port to Port *Journal of Maritime Law and Commerce*, Vol. 31, No. 4, October, 2000, 551–557.

Symposium: *Picturing Justice: Images of Law and Lawyers in the Visual Media* (1996) *University of San Francisco Law Review* 30: 891

Taylor, Alan (2020) *How Robert Tressell's novel The Ragged Trousered Philanthropists became a sacred text for aspiring socialists* (available at https://www

.newstatesman.com/international-politics/2020/10/how-robert-tressell-s-novel-ragged-trousered-philanthropists-became-sacred (accessed January 22 2024)

Taylor AJP (1965) *English History 1914–1945* (Oxford, OUP); (1970) London Penguin)

Terrell, Roger (2012) *"An Uusual Brief": The Life and Times of a High Street Lawyer* (Peterborough, FastPrint Publishing)

Thomas, James (2023) *Script Analysis for Actors, Directors, and Designers* (Waltham, Mass, Focal Press)

Tiefenbrun, Susan (1999) *On Civil Disobedience, Jurisprudence, Feminism and the Law in the Antigones of Sophocles and Anouilh Cardozo Studies in Law and Literature* Vol 11 (1) 35

Times, The (26 July 2021) *Rumpole and the curious case of a return to the Old Bailey as a woman* (available at https://www.thetimes.co.uk/article/rumpole-and-the-curious-case-of-a-return-to-the-old-bailey-as-a-woman-wbj7h8pvr)

Tomeo, Vincenzo (1973) *Il Giudice Sullo Schermo* (Bari, Laterza)

-----. (2025) *The Judge on the Screen* (translation of Tomeo's *Il Giudice Sullo Schermo*) (Teaneck, New Jersey, Fairleigh Dickinson)

Train, Arthur (1919a) *Tutt and Mr. Tut* (Alan Rodgers Books) (reissued 2005)

-----. (1919b) *By Advice of Counsel* (2nd. Mr. Tutt novel) (The Curtis Publishing Co.)

-----. (1920) *The Hermit of Turkey Hollow*. (3rd. Mr. Tutt novel) The Curtis Publishing Co.

-----. (1930) *The Adventures of Ephraim Tutt, Attorney and Counsellor-at-Law.* New York: Charles Scribner's Sons.

-----. (1943) *Yankee Lawyer: The autobiography of Ephraim Tutt* (Pleasantville, NY, Akadine Press)

Turnbull, Sue (2014) *The TV Crime Drama* (Edinburgh, Edinburgh University Press)

Underwood, Michael (1954) *Murder on Trial* (London, Hammond)

-----. (1991) *The Seeds of Murder* (London, Macmillan)

-----. (+29 more detective novels with courtroom action and barrister as detective – see https://www.google.com/search?q=Michael+Underwood+books&rlz=1C1GCEA_enGB989GB989&oq=Michael+Underwood+books&aqs=chrome..69i57.19288j0j7&sourceid=chrome&ie=UTF-8 – accessed 25/1/22)

Vaughan F (1955) *Dickens and his lawyers: A literary mystery that remains unsolved* ABA Journal Vol 41 No 7 595

Vaughan, Steven (2018) *LGBTQ+ in professional firms* (paper presented to the Legal Profession sub-group of the Research Committee on Sociology of Law, Andorra, July 2018)

Villez (2005) *Séries Télé; visions de la justice (*Paris, Presses Universitaire de France)

-----. (2010) *Television and the Legal System* (Abingdon, Routledge)

Visconti, Jacqueline (2018) *Handbook of Communication in the Legal Sphere* (Berlin, De Gruyter)

Walker, James (2004) *James Maxton (Jimmy) (1885–1946)* Oxford Dictionary of National Biography

Ward, Ian (1999) *Shakespeare and the Legal Imagination* (Cambridge, CUP)

Ward, Stephen and Parsliffe, Frank (2020) *Tales of a Barristers' Clerk* (Gloucester, The Choir Press)

Washington Post (1981) *Combat and Bombast and the Old Bailey* (available at https://www.washingtonpost.com/archive/lifestyle/1981/02/17/combat-and-bombast-at-old-bailey/f33b4e60-4e9d-4ad6-ab45-0b2f100d787c/)

Weinart, K, Crawley, K and Tranter K (eds) (2020) *Law, lawyers and justice through Australian lenses* (London, Routledge)

Wheatley, Lord (1986) *One Man's Judgement: An autobiography* (Edinburgh, Butterworths)

White R, Willock, I and McQueen, H (2013) *The Scottish Legal System* (London, Bloomsbury)

Williams, Glanville (ed) (1951) *The Reform of the Law* (London, Gollancz)

Williams Melanie (2006). Only Connect: 'Howards End' and Theories of Justice, *Law and Literature, Vol 18* (No. 2), 253

-----. (2013). "Hardy and the Law" in (ed) *Thomas Hardy in Context*, (Cambridge, Cambridge University Press) 306

Wilson, Alexandra (2020) *In Black and White: A young barrister's stories of race and class in a broken justice system* (London, Octopus Publishing)

-----. (2023) *The Witness* (Boston, Mass, Little Brown)

Wilson, S, Rutherford, H, Storey, T, Wortley, N and Kotecha, B (2020) (4th ed) *English Legal System* (Oxford, OUP)

Wodehouse, PG (1915) *Extricating Young Gussie* (Saturday Evening Post 18 September)

-----. (1922) *The Clicking of Cuthbert* (London, Herbert Jenkins)

-----. (1926) *The Heart of a Goof* (Harmondsworth, Penguin [1982 edition])

-----. (1937) *Lord Emsworth and Others* (New York, Viking [1975 edition])

-----. (1950) *Nothing Serious* (Bury St Edmunds, Arena)

-----. (1959) *A Few Quick Ones* ((Harmondsworth, Penguin)

-----. (1974) *Aunts Aren't Gentlemen* (London, Barrie and Jenkins)

Yallop, David (1969) *Let Him Have It* (Gollancz, London)

Zander, Michael (1968) *Lawyers and the Public Interest : A study in restrictive practices* (London, Weidenfeld and Nicolson)

PRIMARY SOURCES

Cecil, Henry *Archive 1915–1978 – McMaster University*, Hamilton, Ontario, Canada (Ref Fonds RC0047 – 78 boxes of manuscripts, student works, published work, audio recordings, dinner lectures and correspondence – broad index [Finding Aid] available online at https://www.library.mcmaster.ca) – the material itself is not available digitally.

Index

About the Author

Professor Peter Robson has an LL.B. from St Andrews University and a PhD from Strathclyde University. He is a solicitor and sits as a judge in Her Majesty's Courts and Tribunal Service dealing with disability issues. He was appointed Professor of Social Welfare Law in the University of Strathclyde in 1992. He works and advises on housing law and is the author of Homelessness and the Law (3rd ed; 1996), Housing Law in Scotland (2010) and Residential Tenancies (3rd ed; 2012) and was Chair of Shelter (Scotland) from 1984 to 2005, Chair of Shelter from 1999 to 2005 and Chair of a Registered Social Landlord company in West Lothian, Weslo Housing from 2005 to 2018. Works on law, film and television in journals and edited collections include co-editing *Law and Film* (with Stefan Machura) in 2001. His most recent film work (with Steve Greenfield and Guy Osborn) *Film and the Law: The Cinema of Justice* was published in 2010 and updated the influential 1st edition. He is co-editor with Jessica Silbey of *Law and Justice on the Small Screen* (2012). and author of essays on British Lawyers on television and co-editor with Jennifer Schulz and contributor to a global TV lawyers project – *A Transnational Study of Law and Justice on TV* (2016). Essays include *Law and Theatre, Law in Modern Popular Fiction and Women in Lawyers on TV in 2014*. His later work was on the development of Scottish Court architecture, and he has undertaken research into this funded by the Royal Society of Edinburgh. The book based on this research, with Johnny Rodger, is entitled *The Spaces of Justice: The Architecture of the Scottish Court* (Fairleigh Dickinson, 2018) He has published the annotations on the Private Housing (Tenancies) (Scotland) Act of 2016 and has co-authored a 4th edition of Residential Tenancies published in April 2019. A second volume of international essays on *Ethnicity, Gender and Diversity: Law and Justice on TV* was published in December 2018. *Future Directions in Law* *and Popular Culture* was published in the *Handbook of Communication in the Legal Sphere* (November 2018). His judgement contribution to the *Scottish Feminist Judgments* project was published in 2019. His essay on *Women Academics in Scotland* appeared in 2020. His most recent work on Vigilantes and Rape Revenge films appeared in a Special Issue of the *International Journal for the Semiotics of Law* in 2021, he is joint editor and contributor to *Vigilante Justice in Society and Popular Culture* (2022), *The Ian Willock Collection on Law and Justice in the 21st Century* (2023), and the translator and editor of *The Judge on the Screen* (2025).

www.ingramcontent.com/pod-product-compliance
Ingram Content Group UK Ltd.
Pitfield, Milton Keynes, MK11 3LW, UK
UKHW041451071026
15587UKWH00010B/759

9 781683 934141